Living with
Koryak
Traditions

Living with Koryak Traditions

Playing with Culture in Siberia

ALEXANDER D. KING

University of Nebraska Press | Lincoln & London

Portions of the introduction and conclusion originally appeared as the author's "Without Deer There Is No Culture, Nothing," reprinted from *Anthropology and Humanism* 27, no. 2 (2002): 133–64, with the permission of the American Anthropological Association, Arlington, Virginia. Copyright American Anthropological Association 2002.

Portions of the introduction, chapters 2 and 3, and the conclusion originally appeared as the author's "Dancing in the House of Koryak Culture" in "Generation P in the Tundra: Young People in Siberia," special issue, *Folklore: Electronic Journal of Folklore* 41 (2009): 7–26. Reproduced by permission.

Portions of the introduction, chapter 3, and the conclusion originally appeared as the author's "Authenticity and Real Cultural Properties in the Russian Far East," in *Properties of Culture—Culture as Property: Pathways to Reform in Post-Soviet Siberia*, ed. Erich Kasten, 51–65 (Berlin: Dietrich Reimer Verlag, 2004). Reproduced by permission.

Library of Congress Cataloging-in-Publication Data

King, Alexander David.
Living with Koryak traditions: playing with culture in Siberia / Alexander D. King.
p. cm.
Includes bibliographical references and index.
ISBN 978-0-8032-3509-0 (pbk.: alk. paper)
1. Koryaks—Russia (Federation)—Kamchatka Peninsula —History. 2. Koryaks—Russia (Federation—Kamchatka Peninsula—Ethnic identity. 3. Koryaks—Cultural assimilation—Russia (Federation)—Kamchatka Peninsula. 4. Culture and globalization—Russia (Federation)—Kamchatka Peninsula 5. Kamchatka Peninsula (Russia—Ethnic relations. 6. Kamchatka Peninsula (Russia)—Social life and customs. I. Title.
DK759.K6K56 2011
305.89'46—dc22   2010040522

Set in Sabon.

For Christina Kincaid

Contents

Illustrations

Preface

This book participates in an intellectual tradition embedded in Boasian anthropology, which started with a focus on Native Americans but quickly became curious about connections between the cultures and peoples of North America and North Asia from a perspective where Asia lies to the west across the Pacific and America lies in the east. I attempt to make some comparisons of the cultures and histories of Native Americans with those of Koryaks, continuing a line of inquiry first developed by Franz Boas, Waldemar Bogoras, and Waldemar Jochelson. Bogoras and Jochelson referred to Chukotka and Kamchatka as parts of Siberia, and I continue that tradition. Following Stalin's reorganization of the Russian empire, what had been referred to as eastern Siberia was designated the Soviet Far East. In most contemporary Russian language descriptions of Kamchatka it is referred to as being part of the Russian Far East, and Siberia is often thought of as ending somewhere far from the coast, although I should note the title of an excellent book co-authored by Russian and American anthropologists: *Russian Old-residents of Siberia* is based in Chukotka (Vakhtin et al. 2004). While Kamchatkans often make a distinction between the Russian Far East and Siberia, they also often talk of similarities, especially in sociopolitical terms, with other Siberian indigenous peoples. I do not think anything is gained by maintaining a rigorous distinction between Siberia and the Russian Far East, so I often talk of Kamchatka and Siberia, assuming that the Russian Far East is part of Siberia.

This book emerged out of the work of my PhD dissertation, written under the supervision of Richard Handler and Dell Hymes, with Peter Metcalf, Roy Wagner, and Robert Geraci also serving on my committee at the University of Virginia. I want to thank especially Richard and Dell for reading not only several drafts of that dissertation but also this book manuscript. Many teachers and fellow students in Charlottesville helped me along the way, and I would like to thank Michael Uzendoski and Amanda French, in particular, for personal and intellectual support. Edith Turner and Virginia Hymes have been important teachers and intellectual models throughout my career. Marjorie Mandelstam Balzer and Igor Krupnik have long been helpful teachers and colleagues, generous with their time. My colleagues at the Max Planck Institute for Social Anthropology taught me a lot about other parts of Siberia and what makes Kamchatka interesting in comparison and contrast. Chris Hann, Patty Gray, John Ziker, Erich Kasten, Aimar Ventsel, Florian Stammler, Deema Kaneff, Otto Habeck, and Brian Donahoe all commented on previous iterations of the material presented in this book. I want to thank David Anderson for suggesting that I come to Aberdeen, and he read the entire manuscript. Tim Ingold also read the entire manuscript and provided very helpful advice as well as wonderful collegial support. Many colleagues and students at the University of Aberdeen have taught me much about the circumpolar north and how Kamchatka fits into that broader frame, especially Nancy Wachowich, Rob Wishart, Hiroko Ikuta, and Donatas Brandisauskas. Much of my skill at writing English prose was developed under the tutelage of my mother, Lillis King. I thank her and my father David for their support, especially with trip logistics and many rides to the Seattle airport. My wife's parents, Bob and Joan Kincaid, also have provided help and inspiration, and Joan adeptly handled my power of attorney while I was living in Kamchatka for nearly a year and a half. Without her help managing grant income and bill expenditures I would not have remained solvent.

David Koester has been most generous with his time and advice from my first e-mail full of ignorant questions about Kamchatka. He generously gave me the name of his friend and colleague in Kamchatka, Viktoria Petrasheva, and told me to simply call her up. Vika, as she is known to her friends, is boundless with her generosity, hospitality, and good advice. Many, many people in Kamchatka have helped me learn about the place and their lives. I am most indebted to the friendship and collegiality of Valentina Dedyk and the deep friendship of her family, especially Igor, her husband. Sergei Kutinkavav, Andrei Kosygin, Nikolai Bondarenko, and Alexsandra Urkachan have all been generous with their hospitality, knowledge, and warm friendship. The families of Tatiana and Vladimir Yatylkut and Anna and Dima Kechigilan in Middle Pakhachi provided a lot of help, as did Nina Nikolaevna and Vasili Borisovich Milgichil in Manily. Albina Yailgina in Tilichiki provided hospitality and support, sometimes at considerable inconvenience. The families of Anna and Zinaida Popova and the family of Natalia and Valeria Murashkin in Ossora provided generous hospitality and orientation during my first trip in 1995. Valentina Nikishina and her family helped me in Ossora and Tymlat when I returned in 1997. Vladimir and Nadezhda Lvov and their family in Paren' showed amazing hospitality to a complete stranger. There are too many others to mention, and I am thankful for their help and understanding.

Funding for field research related to the dissertation was provided by a Graduate Training Fellowship of the Social Science Research Council (SSRC) Joint Committee on the Soviet Union and Its Successor States, by a Boren Fellowship of the National Security Education Program, by a Dissertation Research Grant of the Wenner-Gren Foundation, and by an Individual Advanced Research Opportunities in Eurasia Fellowship of the International Research and Exchange Board (IREX). Postdoctoral research fieldwork was supported by a Summer Scholars Fellowship of the California State University, Chico, and by a Summer Stipend of the National Endowment for the Humanities. Writing the PhD dissertation was supported by a Dissertation Fellowship of the Graduate School of Arts and Sciences of the University of Virginia. Additional support for writing was provided by a Max Planck postdoctoral fellowship at the Institute for Social Anthropology in Halle an der Saale, Germany. I also benefited from a research sabbatical provided by the Department of Anthropology at the University of Aberdeen and a Great Lakes Colleges Association Scotland Faculty Exchange, where I spent six weeks in residence at the College of Wooster, Ohio. I thank Pamela Frese and David McConnell at the College of Wooster for their collegial hospitality and interest in my project. The costs of producing some of the illustrations in this book were met by a research grant from the University of Aberdeen, College of Arts and Social Sciences.

This book is dedicated to my wife, Christina Kincaid. Her love, support, and understanding go beyond anything normal. I thank my family for putting up with all the tribulations associated with the writing of this book.

In writing names of Siberian places and peoples in English, I follow the model set by the Arctic Studies Center of the Smithsonian Institution. Names are spelled following the

United States National Image and Mapping Agency (formerly the U.S. Geographic Service). All transliterations of Russian words (marked in italics) and names of authors publishing in Russian are transliterated following a simplified version of the Library of Congress system, which facilitates digital searching for sources. Russian nouns and adjectives are marked for gender, number, and case, and this affects word endings. For example, *mestnaia kul'tura*, "local culture," is singular, feminine nominative case, but *mestnye liudi*, "local people," is plural nominative case.

Koryak words are not transliterated through their common Russian spellings but written in a simplified version of the International Phonetic Alphabet. Please note that Koryak has no voiced stops, *q* is pronounced farther back in the throat than *k* and contrasts with that sound, *g* is a back velar fricative (similar to a French *r*), and *h* is used to represent a sound that alternates between glottal stop and pharyngeal fricative, depending on the variant being spoken (which village).

I have been in a lot of places and talked to a lot of people in Kamchatka. People in Kamchatka were eager to help and often insistent that I acknowledge my sources of information, and so people are most often referred to by real names. It became clear to me that the standard anthropological practice of mass anonymity is unethical for my project. Whenever I refer to an event or statement that might be embarrassing or get someone into trouble, I have used a pseudonym. Thus readers inside and outside Kamchatka will know where I got my statements and who told me what, unless the statement is potentially controversial or troublesome, in which case only the source will know for sure.

Map 1. Kamchatka in the circumpolar north
Kamchatka has closer ties with Pacific cultures and economies than
with Moscow despite its long-standing political ties to the Russian
center.

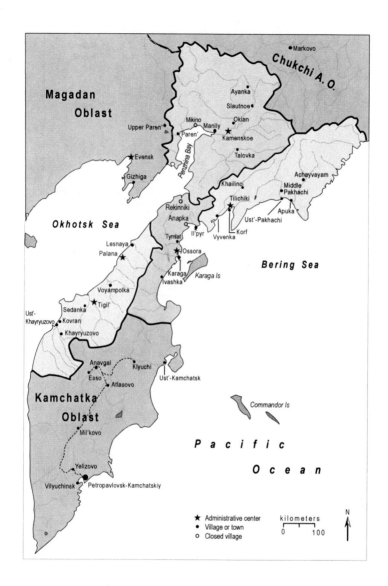

Map 2. Rayons and settlements of the Koryak Autonomous Okrug
All official settlements and some important closed villages are
shown in the KAO, while only a few important towns in the oblast
are shown. The four KAO rayons (districts), clockwise from top, are
Penzhinskiy, Olyutorskiy, Karaginskiy, and Tigil'skiy.

Introduction

A Semiotics of Koryak Culture

This book, if it can be summarized in a phrase, is an ethnography of speaking about indigenous culture in Kamchatka, Russia, specifically Koryak culture. People in Kamchatka are very aware of having a culture (*kul'tura*) that entails distinctive customs (*obychi*) or traditions (*traditsii*). Unlike most anthropologists visiting other parts of the globe, I had the usual Siberian experience of local people knowing exactly what an anthropologist (ethnographer) is and does— he studies local customs, documents traditions, and tries to learn "our culture" from the wisest elders. They were surprised (usually pleasantly), however, that I wanted to do more than quiz elders on the details of past practices, that I wanted to participate in people's daily lives, and that I was just as interested in the knowledge of traditions carried by younger people as in what the elders had to teach me.

Indigenous Kamchatkans are also well aware of how global trends in discourse about indigenous peoples make different assumptions about what cultures are and how cultures define people and groups of people. Once while traveling by dogsled from a reindeer herd in the tundra back to the village, I stopped for a rest with my close acquaintance, Dima, near an abandoned village. We had tea outside a house used by hay makers in the summer. Dima had rabbit fur and a little fat for the fire, called *enelwit* in Koryak and best translated as "spirit offering" or "spirit food." He added a pinch of the *enelwit* to the growing flames and commented, "Earlier I thought only we did that, offering to the fire. Then I learned that it is common all over the world, Indians, in Africa, South America, in short, every nation of the world practices it, honoring the fire." His initial experience of cultural difference was vis-à-vis Russian culture and European civilization during the Soviet era. Watching TV programs and reading magazines that proliferated after glasnost, however, gave Dima a sense that perhaps European culture was not the standard by which all others should be compared. In the chapters that follow, I discuss the different models of culture implicit in my conversations with all kinds of people in Kamchatka and their understandings of themselves and their culture in a world of many cultures.

People and Cultures in Kamchatka

My first introduction to Kamchatka was through a telephone call with Dr. Viktoria Petrasheva, an Itelmen who had been working on the ethnography of her people for decades. It is not quite accurate to call her a gatekeeper, since she works so hard to keep the gates to Kamchatka open wide. In 1995 I was planning a five-month trip to survey the area and narrow in on a PhD dissertation topic. As I was still enrolled in third-year language courses and lacking confidence in Russian, my wife, Christina, then more fluent in the language, made that call. After Christina introduced herself and explained why she was calling, Petrasheva's first question was: "So you need an invitation for a visa?" In early July we landed in Petropavlovsk-Kamchatskiy, or "the city," as it is known locally, on the second ever flight to the Russian Far East operated by Alaska Airlines from Seattle (see map 1, fig. 1). Vika, as her friends call her, met us at the airport and took us to her small flat in the city, where we shared floor space with David Koester (who had given me Vika's name and number) and one or two of his graduate students. They had arrived on the first flight from Seattle two weeks earlier and were working on a large Itelmen ethnography project that Koester and Petrasheva were leading. Petropavlovsk is a sprawling city of about two hundred thousand people, mostly Russians, and was in the midst of falling apart in the mid-1990s. It took a couple of weeks to get the necessary travel permissions, and then Christina and I flew to Ossora in the Koryak Autonomous Okrug (KAO; see map 2).

About the size of Arizona and with a population in 2002 of about twenty-five thousand people, the KAO was established in 1930 along with several others as a territorial manifestation of the Communist Party's dedication to minority groups' "rights" to their distinct cultures (Slezkine 1994a).[1] Abolished through a 2005 referendum and merged with Kamchatka Oblast in 2007 to form the new administrative territory Kamchatka Krai, the territory of the Koryak Autonomous Okrug included four officially recognized indigenous ethnic groups: Koryaks, Chukchi, Itelmen, and Eveny (see *oblast* and *okrug* in glossary). As is typical across Siberia, the indigenous population is mostly rural, while immigrant Russophones dominate the larger settlements of Palana, Ossora, Tilichiki, and Korf. Kamchatka's population dropped precipitously in the 1990s, due to immigrants returning to their homes "on the mainland." Birth and mortality rates among native groups tend to result in low population growth, so while the number of Koryaks and other native peoples in the KAO had not grown substantially, they became a much greater proportion of the total population in the late 1990s.

Petropavlovsk-Kamchatskiy was founded by Vitus Bering

Fig. 1. Petropavlovsk-Kamchatskiy is Kamchatka's largest city. Photo by the author.

during his ill-fated second expedition and has been the focus of Russian settlement in Kamchatka for three centuries, although few local Russians over forty years old in the KAO were born in Kamchatka. Archeological evidence indicates continuous habitation of Itelmen people in central and southern Kamchatka for a very long time.[2] Itelmen were also the most numerous indigenous people at the time of contact with Europeans, but disease, oppression, and changing identity categories have reduced their official numbers to only about fifteen hundred people. Descendants of Russian-Itelmen marriages now refer to themselves as "Kamchadal" and have petitioned with mixed results for status as an officially recognized indigenous Northern minority (Hancock 2002). Some ten thousand Kamchadals live in the oblast town of Mil'kovo and nearby villages on the Kamchatka River.[3] People calling themselves Itelmen, and so recognized by the administration, are concentrated in southern Tigil'skiy Rayon. Near the village of Kovran (see map 2) are the closed villages of Sopochnoe and Moroshechnoe. Ust'-Khayryu-zovo (*ust'e*—river mouth or confluence) is a Soviet-developed commercial fishing town, populated mostly by Russians but also home to the Itelmen-owned Iyan Kutkh—a successful and powerful fishing company owned by the brothers of one-time KAO governor (1996–2001) Valentina Bronevich.

Being native in Kamchatka often includes coming from a village that does not exist any more. At the turn of the twentieth century there were scores, if not hundreds, of native villages and reindeer herder camps spread across Kamchatka, each within a one- or two-day walk of another. Soviet collectivization in the 1930s included closing the majority of small and remote villages and consolidating the population in larger towns in locations of administrative convenience (not necessarily optimal locations for traditional subsistence production). This trend of closing villages and consolidating populations increased after World War II up to 1984, when Rekinniki (on the Okhotsk coast of Karaginskiy Rayon, see map 2) was closed. This was part of a directed policy of industrializing agriculture and urbanizing rural areas (Grant 1995:124–30; Melvin 2003). Later I discovered that now closed villages like Rekinniki and Anapka (due west of Il'pyr on a nice bay) continue to be important in social networks and identities.[4] Anapka was closed in 1974 ("One day the authorities showed up with a barge and told us, 'Pack your stuff. You are leaving.' We had three days.") Residents were resettled in Il'pyr, Tymlat, and Ossora based on the economic status of the household head: fishermen and hunters to Il'pyr, reindeer herders to Tymlat, and pensioners, teachers, and other office workers to Ossora. Thus extended families were scattered, but Anapka people continued to maintain social connections over long distances. When Rekinniki was closed ten years later and most residents relocated to Tymlat, that village grew to just over one thousand people but remained divided into three social clusters of families—*Tymlatsi*, *Rekinnikitsi*, and *Anapkintsi* (to use the Russian plurals). Likewise, the closed villages of Mikino, Itkana, and others on Penzhina Bay must be recognized if one is to understand the cultural and linguistic diversity of people commonly called "Koryak."

While using Ossora as a base for two months in the summer of 1995, I visited the village of Karaga and spent time with families at different fishing camps. The salmon were running well that summer, and people were busy fishing, drying, and canning salmon for winter. Like Itelmens, maritime Koryaks (often called "Nymylan" from the Koryak word for village) traditionally harvested salmon in the summer months and hunted various terrestrial and marine animals, much like Indians on the northwest coast of America. Summers were busy in fishing camps preserving salmon; winters were spent in permanent villages near the coast, and this pattern has continued, although the houses themselves look much different. Hunting, fishing, and collecting wild plants (especially berries) have continued to be popular and spiritually important activities for native people in Kamchatka, but they increased in economic and nutritional importance with the enduring economic crisis of the 1990s. Nymylan villages include Lesnaya, Karaga, and Tymlat in the south; Vyvenka and Apuka in Olyutorskiy Rayon to the northeast; and Paren' on Penzhina Bay (map 2). Manily on the same bay has only a few Nymylans; most Koryaks there come from a reindeer-herding tradition and have only recently learned how to fish salmon.

In September 1995 we flew from Ossora to Palana (fig. 2), the administrative center of the Koryak Okrug, because I wanted to talk to people working on Koryak language teaching in the Palana Teachers' College as well as to people working in the KAO Regional Museum. I went to the museum and introduced myself as a graduate student (*aspirant*) from America interested in Koryak language and culture. The museum had a total of two staff at the time—Alyona Yefimenko and Ulyana

Korotkova—and they showed every kindness, even allowing us to stay in Ulyana's new and not-quite-furnished flat for two months. The next day I went to the Teachers' College to meet the director. Vika Petrasheva had given me her name, Raisa Nikolaevna Avak.[5] Raisa Nikolaevna received me warmly and asked about my interests. When I explained my desire to learn Koryak, she fetched the Koryak language teacher. Valentina Romanovna Dedyk entered Avak's small office smartly dressed in a skirt and jacket, with her long black hair pulled into a tight bun. Valentina Romanovna was cautious in her initial conversation with my wife and me. We went to her classroom to discuss learning Koryak, and she started by explaining that she did not want our money. She had recently started graduate studies in linguistics at Herzen University and was tasked with reading a thick book by Edward Nelson, *The Eskimo about Bering Strait* (1983 [1899]). Dedyk suggested a trade. She would teach us Koryak, and we would help her read and translate the book and explain principles of English grammar to her. This was the beginning of a deep friendship between our families.

Palana is the most diverse settlement due to its status as the former okrug capital. At the turn of the twentieth century there were two or three Nymylan villages along the Palana River. The one marked on maps included several Kamchadal (creoles) and Russian households, and it had a Russian Orthodox priest and church. During the intense collectivization of the 1930s, reindeer herders were forcibly settled in the area now occupied by the Palana state farm (*sovkhoz*).[6] Palana Nymylan Koryaks have many friends and family in nearby Lesnaya to the north, while reindeer-herding Koryaks—have more connections with the reindeer-herding village of Voyampolka to the south. The Palana state farm is separated from the rest of the town by a small stream running into the Palana River,

Fig. 2. Palana is a Soviet town amalgamating three Koryak villages along the Palana River and settling nomadic reindeer herders who had occupied nearby tundra lands. Photo by the author.

and it has several barns for cattle, pigs, and chickens; a diesel-powered electricity plant; and a heliport for cargo deliveries flown in from Esso. The state farm also constitutes a kind of native ghetto of substandard housing, often without indoor plumbing. Attracting native people from all over the KAO to Palana are white-collar jobs in the okrug administration, the Teachers' College, a vocational school for drivers and mechanics, and the professional dance troupe, Mengo. Every village in the okrug, from Paren' in the northwest and Ayanka in the north to Achayvayam in the east and Kovran in the south, is thus represented among the population of Palana. Another important aspect of native geography in Palana, not on any map, is Starikovskaya (Elders' Place), which is an hour's walk upriver from town. During the warmer months of May to October elders preferred living at the fishing camp instead of in the dominant Russian urban spaces. I found similar patterns of seasonal residential mobility in nearly all villages, where children and adults also moved between a fishing camp and a village apartment. The village of Middle Pakhachi in Olyutorskiy Rayon seems unique in that a mini-village of a dozen or so traditional *yayaŋo* (singular, *yayaŋa*) are set up in the spring about a five-minute walk from the edge of the village. These dome-shaped reindeer-skin tents are a place where elders can live away from wooden houses, children can play with grandma, and women of all ages can process hides into clothing (mostly for winter). Russian newcomers sometimes refer to a yayaŋa with the words *yurt* or *chum*, which come from other indigenous Siberian groups. Koryak people find such terms annoying, to say the least.

After a few weeks of learning and teaching Koryak and English, Christina and I became friends with Valentina Dedyk, her husband, Igor, and their children, Kostya and Yana. During this time in Palana we also got to know Valeri and Liza Yetneut, who had formed a successful dance troupe called Weyem with several students from the Teachers' College and a few other local people. The friendships between my family and these two families came to shape my research. We returned to Virginia in January, and in the summer of 1996 Valentina was able to fly to America after her summer examinations at Herzen in St. Petersburg and stay with us for the two hottest months of the year. We continued working on Koryak and English and occasionally took breaks from the heat by sitting in the ice rink downtown simply to enjoy the cold. We made a trip to New York to inspect together the extensive Bogoras and Jochelson collections of Koryak, Chukchi, and Eveny items in the American Museum of Natural History, aided by a small grant from the museum. We toured the museum and looked into all the relevant storage drawers. Valya wanted to photograph some things, particularly objects she had not seen before or could not identify. She showed the photographs to elders in Kamchatka and learned that many were craft tools, children's toys, and even some pieces used in games played by adults.[7]

Christina and I returned to Kamchatka in April 1997. This time we traveled quickly from the city to Palana and Igor Dedyk met us at the airport. He had organized an apartment in the center of Palana through a friend, and I quickly got to work learning Koryak at the Teachers' College, getting to know the new staff at the Okrug Regional Museum and attending dance rehearsals by the group Weyem. That summer Valya took us to her home village, Middle Pakhachi, to meet her sister Tanya's family and her brother Vladimir (called Volokha), who worked at the herd of privately owned deer. Most people in that village are proud, reindeer-herding Chukchi, but the state reindeer farm had fallen on hard times and everyone was struggling to get by. Most people were fishing for salmon in the summers, and I spent a lot of time helping with that, visiting Volokha at the reindeer herd with Tanya's husband, Volodya, only for a short time. That stay of just a few days with the reindeer herders proved important for helping me understand local ideas of culture as experience. I had noticed that native people living in the regional capital Palana frequently talked at length about reindeer and the problems confronting herders. It seemed to be a much bigger issue than demography or economics would warrant. Valya's brother-in-law Volodya was eager to take me out to spend time at the herd. He missed his deer and wanted to check up on them. They could not be far, as soon they would be crossing the river for the summer slaughter near the village. Everyone was pining for meat, tired of fish every day. One morning Volodya and I motored downriver in his outboard boat for a couple of hours before turning up a tributary. After poling the boat along the shallow stream for a couple more hours, we encountered a man standing on the riverbank with a rifle over one shoulder and a lasso over the other. He was one of the reindeer herders.

"Hello. Where are you going?" he asked.

"To you!" we exclaimed in unison. We had expected to hike for a day and a half, lugging a tent across the swampy tundra and spending the night alone without a rifle in bear country (all of Kamchatka is bear country). Volodya introduced me to Slava, who took us to the campsite he and another herder, Viktor, were setting up in advance of the herd.

Volodya and I went to find the herd, farther up the valley. I had to work hard to keep up with him over the rough terrain. Kamchatka tundra is bog punctuated with rugged hills thick with pine bushes (farther south they grow as proper trees). Volodya walked with an unhurried, steady pace that covered ground quickly. As soon as we left the herders' camp I heard him making noises I had never heard before. They were a breathy song of whistles and heavy breathing. I was puzzled, and my only guess was that breathing like that helped his measured walk; I tried to imitate his rhythm. After a half hour Volodya spied deer on the ridge to our left, making their way along higher ground. As we got closer I heard a cacophony of grunts, snorts, and snapping tendons.[8] Although the herd was small, less than fifteen hundred head, it was never quiet. Even while resting, the deer were talking to one another and rustling about, though it was a calm, unhurried kind of rustling. The men constantly whistle as they walk, loudly and softly, as a sort of conversation with the deer, which as a herd are also constantly making noises, answering the men and talking among themselves. This strange conversation was my first inkling of a host of complex relationships among people and deer.

From the first hour when we had met some weeks earlier, Volodya had begun explaining things to me in great detail with clear language and answering all my questions. Whereas many people expected me to work from a schedule and waited for my questions, Volodya volunteered whatever he thought was interesting or important. When we got to the reindeer herd, he did something he had never done before: he began giving me Koryak vocabulary. "In Chukchi . . . , in our own [language]," he explained, "we call the deer in front '*yanothoy*.'" We walked across the front of the herd and up the hill. Volodya's whistles were now intermixed with calls and other kinds of grunts. He was talking to the deer, reassuring them, telling them where he was and where they should be going. As we went toward the back of the herd, Volodya continued his vocabulary lesson: "The deer that are always in the back, coming up last, are called '*yavalahoy*.'" Behind those deer was the herder, Volokha, Tanya and Valya's younger brother. He was making noises similar to Volodya's, talking to the deer. In his mid-thirties, tall, and with a thick, black mustache, he cut an imposing figure on the hillside above us.

We made tea up on the hill overlooking the deer. Volodya and I got wood as Volokha rounded up some final stragglers into the herd and fetched water. I started breaking twigs near a previous campfire, and Volodya told me we had to move to where we could see the whole herd, and the herd could see us. Volokha asked, "Would you like some Korean noodles? 'Ready in three minutes,' it says." Such packages of instant ramen noodles in styrofoam bowls from South Korea had become ubiquitous since the mid-1990s. He broke up the noodles into small pieces and added only enough water to the styrofoam bowl to soften them up to eat them on bread.

After we moved on again, another herder came to relieve Volokha, and we headed back to the tent. On the way Volodya pointed to a pretty area of willows and alders near the stream and said, "Tanya and I had tea here two years ago when we

Fig. 3. The author finishing tea with Volokha Ivkavav at Pakhachi private herd. Photo by V. Yatylkut (author's collection).

were collecting cloud berries." I was amazed at how he could identify and remember every bend in every little stream. To me it was wilderness. To him it was where he lived.

As we ate a dinner of cold fish soup I asked Slava about the operation of the herd of privately owned deer. "Who pays you?"

"We work without pay," he answered. I asked him if it was fun work.

"Yeah, it's fun work," he answered sarcastically. Then he continued seriously, "These last deer are everything. Without deer we are not people. Without deer there is no culture, nothing." Slava's word choice is interesting. He said "*liudi*" (people), not "*narod*" (a people, folk). Reindeer are not some token of heritage for Slava and others in his community, as one would think if listening only to activists and politicians in Palana. Rather, deer are an important part of what makes people persons, and indeed are persons themselves and bound up with people in complex social relationships. Reindeer are more than "good to eat" or "good to think"; they are part and parcel of people's very *being*. The use of deer as a root metaphor in Koryak/Chukchi herders' lives is more than an index of their subsistence activities. Nonherding natives in Kamchatka do not have a similar metaphor in salmon or bears or whales. Hunters have diverse rituals of thanks, welcoming, and communion with spirits of hunted animals, but these animals are not part of the social order. Deer are socialized into the human world like no other nonhuman entity.[9] As I learned later, every individual deer has an individual owner, and deer are gathered into herds in a manner parallel to human social organization—networks of extended families and other co-residents. I had to leave Middle Pakhachi the following week but made plans with Tanya and Volodya to return in the spring for some months. At the time things were far from clear, of course, but I had a sense that Koryaks and Chukchi living in small villages thought and talked about culture and tradition in a manner very different from that of the educated teachers, politicians, and artists in Palana.

In August I had to return to the United States to renew my visa and finalize arrangements for a grant from the International Research and Exchanges Board (IREX). Upon returning to Kamchatka in September, I met up in Petropavlovsk with Valeri Yetneut and several dancers from Mengo, the professional dance troupe in Palana, and watched their performances that were part of the celebrations of "300 years of Russian and Kamchatkan unity." The night before we went to the airport to fly to Palana, many of us were celebrating and drinking at Vika's apartment, but Valeri was angry about how the festival organizers had sidelined his dance group Weyem. I was not able to get on the plane with the others the next day (seats on flights are sometimes tricky to get), so I had to stay behind, and the next day Christina called and told me that Valeri was dead. He had apparently killed himself with a knife after a long night of drinking; I was crushed.

I arrived back in Palana the afternoon after Valeri's funeral and cremation on a traditional pyre. His death deeply affected me, but life and work went on. I got to know Sergei Kutinkavav and other people dancing in Mengo and made friends with Andrei Kosygin and Alexandra Urkachan, working at the Okrug House of Culture (Okruzhnoi Dom Kul'turi) in Palana (see chapter 3). During the course of the following twelve months I divided my time roughly in half between investigating the ideas and practices connected to "local culture" (*mestnaia kul'tura*) in Palana and in small villages around the KAO, including Lesnaya, Ossora, and Tymlat. Koryaks living in Ossora and Tymlat (and in villages I have not visited, like Vyvenka and Il'pyr) are also called Alutors. Alutor Koryaks are famous for their combination of small reindeer herds (usually no more than three hundred animals) with maritime hunting and fishing. Many now live in Tymlat, where they still hold Nymylan hunting rituals (Hololo) and rituals associated with reindeer herders.

I returned to Middle Pakhachi in the spring of 1998 for almost three months. Reindeer herders were nomadic, ranging within known territories, and I learned that they have never been the homogeneous group portrayed in most ethnographic descriptions, both academic and popular. Reindeer-herding Koryaks were also known in Russian as Chavchuven (from *chauwchu*, the Koryak word for "rich person/rich in reindeer"), and that is the name currently used for their variant of spoken Koryak. Koryak reindeer herds of Penzhinskiy Rayon (and what is now eastern Magadan Oblast) were huge; some individuals owned as many as ten thousand deer. A single herd, in any case, would rarely exceed five thousand head, beyond which it became difficult to manage. Reindeer herds in Penzhinskiy and Olyutorskiy rayons peaked in the 1980s, but by the mid-1990s any kind of lifestyle focused on reindeer herding was meager and becoming impossible to continue with the lack of markets and infrastructure.[10] The people of Middle Pakhachi and Achayvayam are famous for being Chukchi, but they speak a variant of Chavchuven Koryak. Chukchi and Koryak reindeer herders warred with one another for centuries over pasturage and deer, and by all accounts the northern Chukchi were more successful in their aggression. They pushed south into northern Kamchatka around the turn of the twentieth century and had occupied pastures along the Pakhachi and Apuka rivers by the 1920s, after which "Pax Sovietica" eliminated raiding. The 2002 census counted about fourteen hundred Chukchi in total living in the KAO.[11]

The villages of Khailino in Olyutorskiy Rayon and Ayanka, Slautnoe, and Oklan in Penzhinskiy have a significant Even population, many of whom speak Koryak. In the KAO Evens numbered about 750 people. Another community of Even reindeer herders lives to the south in the Kamchatka Oblast villages of Esso and neighboring Anavgai (map 2). Evens are also found in greater concentration in Magadan Oblast and are scattered about Siberia. Along with Evenk people, they speak Tungusic languages.[12] Their traditional dress is distinctively un-Kamchatkan, with a long, open coat, apron, and very elaborate beadwork. They also stand out from Koryak and Chukchi reindeer herders by riding astride deer, which Koryaks and Chukchi consider a sin. This practice is common in southern Siberia among Tuvans, Buryats, Evenks, and other cultures where deer herding is primarily for transport while hunting for food in a forest or mixed forest-tundra ecology. Many Penzhina Evens have been moving to Palana, where there are better job prospects and habitable apartments. Penzhinskiy Rayon has great difficulty supplying reliable electricity and other infrastructure. Severe flooding in the spring of 1998 damaged several of the northernmost villages, and extensive repairs were not possible.

In the late summer and autumn of 1998 I spent about two months in Manily, Paren', and Upper Paren' (see map 2).[13] The Nymylan village of Paren' on Penzhina Bay is famous for its blacksmiths. The term *Paren' knife* (*paren'skii nozh*) now refers to any homemade Bowie-style knife, essential for native life. These large, strong knives are used to skin and dress animals, to prepare and repair various materials, to cut food (a knife, bowl, and cup constitute a full "place setting" in traditional life), and even to chop wood—trees do not grow large north of Tilichiki. Paren' men were apparently cold-working iron before the arrival of the Russians, and they learned hot-forge techniques from the Europeans.[14]

Koryak and Chukchi traditional social organization was based on residence; often two or more brothers and their families made up a household. However, one could and still can find residence groups based on sisters. Koryak kinship was (and continues to be) bilateral, and individuals were mobile, moving from one group to another (see Antropova 1971; Vdovin 1973). An important institution in traditional social organization was the trading friendship or partnership, which is found all over Siberia. Typically, a Nymylan man had a reindeer-herding partner. As one Koryak Nymylan explained it to me, when one's trading partner showed up, he would leave with a full sled come hell or high water (*krov' iz nosa,* literally "blood out of [your] nose"). These exchange networks provided Nymylans with reindeer skins and meat and provided Chavchuvens with seal skins, dried fish, and other marine products. Deer fur is the most effective material for winter clothing, but sealskin is stronger and is needed for boot soles and ropes. When coated with seal oil, a pair of sealskin boots is waterproof, which is important during the spring melt when slushy snow is still very cold. Sealskin straps and cords are also essential for lashing sleds, snowshoes, and deer and dog harnesses. These exchange networks likewise moved European commodities around. So iron, tobacco, tea, and sugar were common all over northeast Asia long before Russians were a common feature of the local landscape. Such partnerships are still important in people's lives, and I saw them exemplified most clearly between maritime people living in Paren' and reindeer herders living upriver, across the okrug border in the Magadan Oblast village of Upper Paren'. I have found no convincing evidence of any clan structures. As Jochelson's (1908:431ff.) discussion of clans suggests, the Russian grouping of Koryak people into *rody* (clans) was an accounting fiction for the purposes of *yasak* tribute collection by the tsar.

 This overview of places and people in northern Kamchatka hints at the diversity and hybridity of indigenous Siberian cultures as lived in villages, towns, summer fishing camps, and with reindeer herds and on the roads, trails, and air corridors among these places. It also reflects the standard accounts of culture groups found in the scholarly literature in English and in Russian (e.g., Antropova 1971; Levin and Potapov 1964; Rethmann 2001). Much if not most anthropology of Siberia foregrounds ethnicity and identity as a central aspect of people's lives and as a key problem to analyze. People in Kamchatka, however, seemed to be much more interested in talking about "culture" and "traditions" than about personal and collective identities. As I explain throughout this book, people in Kamchatka often talked about culture in ways that replicated a reified model of a culture as a bounded social group speaking a single variant of a unique language and holding to a stable set of "traditions" and "customs." This is a model easily learned from Russian-language anthropology, which is widely read and discussed in Kamchatka, as well as from official government policies on cultural minorities. Nonetheless, I also found that people often talked about culture, tradition, and language in a quite different way, one implicitly akin to current theoretical approaches that understand culture as separate from groups, not having clear boundaries, and being more of a process than an object.

Boasian Semiotics of Culture

I want to emphasize that Koryak culture, as well as all the other cultures (including Russian) that I have touched upon, do not necessarily correspond to specific groups of people. Indeed, in the 2002 Russian Federation census, over half of the people in the Koryak Okrug responding to the question of ethnic (cultural) identity indicated two or more categories.[15] This matches my own impressions of people in Kamchatka generally thinking of themselves as coming from and participating in various cultures simultaneously. Eveny and Chukchi speak Koryak; Russians participate in and produce Koryak things (hats, carvings, etc.); Koryaks enjoy Russian songs and poetry. Cultures can blur into one another and still be distinctive in their differences. If we follow the Boasian model of portraying what is prototypical and divergent in a culture (e.g., Benedict 1934; Mead 1935), we get a sense of the stylistic center of that culture without needing to worry about the boundaries or exactly where Koryak culture ends and Chukchi culture begins, for example (see Bashkow 2004).

Franz Boas and his students (particularly Edward Sapir, Ruth Benedict, Margaret Mead, and sometime fellow traveler B. L. Whorf) provide a subtle and sophisticated model of culture in their writing.[16] Indeed, the old saw that Boas never formulated a tidy or coherent set of theories presents an immediate rebuttal to the postmodern critiques of anthropology from the 1980s and points to his enduring relevance today. Boasian anthropology understands culture as open-ended, without distinct borders, shifting through time, and the work of people yet not beholden to any one person. Culture is a shorthand reference for a specific pattern of actions and meanings, which are diverse and even self-contradictory at times but do seem to "fit together" somehow. The most important patterns are largely unconscious, but these patterns can be made conscious. Therefore culture is not a prison from which there is no escape. No matter how heavy the shackles of tradition, they can be loosened and discarded.

Nonetheless, culture, having a culture, or "culturing" (if I may be permitted the awkward attempt to express the processual nature of "cultural life" learned from reading Boasians) is an essential part of being human. This means that any understanding of culture is itself cultural—all meaning and action is relational, by which I mean that our activities are carried out in relation to other people, in relation to other meanings, in relation to other activities. This "relationality" is also an essential part of being human. Knowledge and understanding are constituted through intersubjective negotiations of interconnected beings in an environment. In simpler words, a person is not a brain in a vat being deceived by a demon, as hypothesized (and rejected) by Rousseau. Culture is the product of persons (human and nonhuman) talking to one another, acting and reacting to one another in specific contexts that always include memories of precedents. Greg Urban sums up this interactive approach as one that understands "that culture is localized in concrete, publicly accessible signs, the most important of which are actually occurring instances of discourse" (2000:1).

Reflecting upon my experience in Kamchatka has convinced me that Boasian relativism, positing cultures and meanings as plural, is a valuable tool for understanding the diversity of possible perspectives. Acknowledging this possibility, I argue, does not cast one into the abyss of moral relativism or necessitate plotting "culture traits" on diffusionist maps. Even a superficial acquaintance with Boas's biography shows that he was a man deeply committed to social justice and personal liberty. I also take as unproblematic the fact that things and concepts (from arrowheads to tea to myths and even phonemes) can move through communication networks far beyond the travels of individual people. Thus locating culture in the specific interactions of people does not deny the power of large-scale institutions of social and economic organization (Silverstein 2004:623, 638ff.) Problems arise only when one tries to package meaning into discrete bits and to trace their movements back to "original sources" (Boasian history is the story of antecedents, not origins), as exemplified by the misguided work of Driver and Massey (1957) or the even more misguided scientistic calculus of "memetics" (Dawkins 1976). While it is useful to think about how Chukchi culture has a certain style and emphasis different from Alutor or Siberian Eskimo cultures (see, e.g., Kerttula 2000), I believe that it is fruitless to attempt a systematic typology of Kamchatkan cultures or to assign various traits (hat designs, vocabulary items, legends, etc.) to their proper culture. Separating Koryak culture systematically from Chukchi culture can only be achieved in the same manner that Alexander severed the Gordian Knot. There is no lowest common denominator of essential traits distinguishing one from the other or, indeed, from any culture. As I show in the following chapter, plenty of anthropologists have already hacked about in the ethnographic record, and it only makes a mess of trying to understand people's lives.

I spent a lot of time in Kamchatka sitting in on school lessons at primary schools and at the Palana Teachers' College. School and public meetings of a political bent were the best places to hear about culture as a set of codified traditions. A culture group was understood in these contexts to comprise the conjunction of a specific population practicing one set of customs and speaking a single language. This is a model of culture that Boas (1911) took apart long ago, but it still remains common and is, for better or for worse, effective in politics. This was not the only model of culture current in Kamchatka, however, as I learned from conversing with people like Valeri Yetneut and Valentina Dedyk about local culture(s) and language(s). For them, and for people less concerned with ethnography learned from books and more concerned about traditions embodied in elders' habits and stories, culture was a process, a way of life rather than a thing. Talk about dance groups, especially small family dance groups based in villages, was grounded in a (largely implicit) theory of culture that I find very interesting. Whether analogous to styles or personalities, the cultures of which these people speak are ideal types, not bounded (either geographically or conceptually) sets of traits.[17] Following Max Weber, it is important to recognize that ideal types are heuristic devices, places from which to start discussion and analysis of what people are like and what they are up to. I believe most of the problems presented by discussing cultures (in the plural) result from presenting ideal types as the conclusions of analysis when they are at best well-informed hypotheses preceding it.

Peircean semiotics provides the necessary foundation to anchor Boasian culture firmly to an epistemological ground. I am not building castles in the air. A recent edition of Charles Peirce (1998:4–22, 267–300) provides the most succinct state-

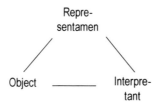

Fig. 4. The equal parts of a sign.

ment of his semiotics, although it has been widely available in other editions of his writings. Peirce's discussions of the sign (semiotics narrowly understood) is actually only a subset of his larger project, which is a theory of meaning and reasoning. Meaning resides neither inside the heads of particular individuals, nor in the objects-in-themselves, but in our relationships with every constituent of the world we inhabit, whether it be a blade of grass, one's mother, or some person encountered during foreign travels.

The key unit of analysis in Peirce's pragmatic epistemology is the "sign." Its significance results from the tripartite relationship among a *representamen* (sometimes also called "sign" by Peirce), an *object* (that which is referred to), and an *interpretant*, the concept generated in a mind (see fig. 4). This triadic scheme can be contrasted with Saussure's dualistic notion of the sign as the unity of the signifier and signified. Peircean semiotics does not admit dualities, and the meaning of the sign (or process of signification, if you will) is not equivalent to object plus interpretant but is generated through a triadic relationship of something standing for something else in a context, as one point of an equilateral triangle is related to the other two (Hanks 1996). The critical thing for me is that Peircean semiotics allows for a direct engagement of people in the world. Peirce's epistemology is grounded in experience, as is anthropology. Using Peirce as a foundation for a theory of culture and interpretive apparatus for what people in Kamchatka are doing with their dance groups and language revitalization efforts and other things presents us with an understanding that is necessarily partial, perspectival, incomplete, constituted in history, and hybrid. In other words, Peircean semiotics and Boasian anthropology together provide us with a theory of meaning and culture that is grounded in everyday realities: people live in a world of relations to one another and the world around them. As Edward Sapir succinctly put it, "The true locus of culture is in the interactions of specific individuals," and the stuff of culture—whether that be language, making things, or knowledge—consists of products of such interactions (1949 [1932]:515). Uses of semiotics in anthropology have been dominated by contributions from linguistic anthropologists (see Silverstein 2004 for a review). Many other anthropologists also have used aspects of Peirce's semiotics to good effect (e.g., Gell 1998; Harris 1996; Keane 1997; Parmentier 1994). This semiotics puts the ethnographer (the interpretant) in view, and so I am in the frame and voiced as the first person. Just the same, I try not to fill the picture and rather focus on the signs, which is to say the interactions I shared with people in Kamchatka form the substance of my presentation.

Cultural concepts both shape and are shaped by the unfolding action of the interaction, and the use of language produces and reproduces roles, expectations, and other things taken for granted by those involved (Silverstein 2004). One can see this in the conversation earlier related with Volodya and Slava. An approach that understands culture as a theory of the world does not get the system of these kinds of cultural concepts. A Geertzian ethos and worldview approach assumes the transparency of language. A linguistic anthropological approach based on Peircean semiotics assumes a productivity of language to make the world, its participants, and their roles in it. Volodya and Volokha produced relationships with each other, the deer, and me through their production of signs, talking. Of course signs are not limited to speech. They can include photographs and drawings, gestures, even dances. If something means something to someone, then it is a sign. Most of the time this happens when people speak or write—that is, use language. While social identities (e.g., race, class, gender, ethnicity) are meaningful in a macrosociological context, they emerge as real, are experienced as relevant, in conversation. Actors reproduce, confirm, or change and challenge these "macrosocial" identities every time they put pen to paper, touch thumb to key, or start talking (as well as when they read and hear and see meaningful bits; that is, signs). Studying language in this way has made real progress in understanding cultural life, the distinctive roots of human conceptualization. People think by talking, and talking is using language. Linguistic action is special because it is both social action and analysis of that action. Speaking both gets things done and is used to examine those things getting done. These orders of metacommentary are infinitely fractal. The "cultural" in language lies in the connection between microinteractional experiences and macrosociological contexts.

The connotation of a word or phrase, in Peircean terminology, is the indexical quality of a sign. An accent indexes the person's native language, social class, or geographical home. Volodya's way of breathing as we crossed the tundra did not index some kind of embodied knowledge helping to walk quickly across a bog, as I first thought. It indexed a lifetime of relating to, living with, and communicating with reindeer. Related to the index, in Peirce's theory of signs, is the icon. An icon is a sign with a meaning that is a product of resemblance. Thus, while Koryak-accented Russian is an index of growing up speaking Koryak and learning Russian as a foreign language, it is also iconic of being Koryak. Such a person sounds like a Koryak. Accent, then, is one example of an indexical icon (Silverstein 2004). Koryak dance moves are another example, as I discuss in chapters 2 and 3. The dancer's moves are iconic of animals, but more important, they are iconic of movements of elders, and these skilled movements index relationships that were necessary to acquire the skills to dance like a Koryak.

Culture, Tradition, and Language

The central concept of culture has come under renewed scrutiny in recent years. Further, it has gained salience outside the discipline among other scholars as well as with lawyers, national governments, international agencies, and indigenous activists.[18] Anthropologists appear to have a love-hate relationship with the term *culture* and the assorted models of being human associated with it. Some claim that *culture* is too loaded with dangerous connotations of essentialism (every problem is explained as being caused by a group's culture) or that it is a crutch for sloppy thinking, although anything can suffer from sloppiness. Others find it most annoying when sociologists, or worse, politicians, set the terms of public discussion about culture in ways anthropologists find simplistic or possibly racist. For my part, I hold that culture is a useful idea, and that properly worked out, it aids our understanding of what people mean by "tradition," "language," "customs," "religion," and other hot topics among indigenous Kamchatkans. Most important, this reflects local usage and local priorities. I first went to Kamchatka looking for ethnicity and identity politics. I quickly learned that few people in Koryakia were interested in identity politics. Most found it irrelevant or distasteful. Many people, however, were interested in talking about "our culture," "our traditions," and sometimes comparing them with "your" or "their" traditions and cultures. After much reflection and analysis, I have found that the subtext to local discourses about culture and tradition is often very subtle and sophisticated.

In his introduction to the *Handbook of American Indian Languages*, Franz Boas (1911) cogently demonstrates that culture, physical type, and language are three different analytical categories, which do not necessarily divide people up along the same lines. Sapir (1921:207–220; 1933) reiterated the point, and Barth (1969) makes the same argument again, showing how such models are embedded in particular social and political orders. The point of this argument is often ignored and is worth repeating today: groups of people defined by culture, by language, or by biology (whether phenotypes or genotypes) do not correspond to one another; such groups never overlap completely. To assume groups like "the Koryak" and then go on to explain them is to fall into the reifying trap of nationalistic social science (Handler 1988). The Boasian separation of culture, biology, and language remains an important caveat for understanding the complexity of multiple typologies at work in everyday life. Just as biology and culture can only be integrated through a focus on the actual processes by which persons develop in an environment, so the connections between language and culture can only be understood in terms of actual, situated practices of speaking (Hymes 1974).

Sapir suggests in several writings how language is implicated in the study of culture and how understanding the workings of language is necessary for a comprehensive understanding of culture (1921, 1949 [1927], 1949 [1928]). The connections between language and culture were most famously formulated by Benjamin Lee Whorf (1956), though the details of

Whorf's formulation are famously misunderstood (Lee 1996; Ridington 1991). Whorf understood that language is part of culture and not an analogy for it or simply a marker of a cultural group (1956:139). Rather, Whorf argues that a close semiotic analysis of language and linguistic categories (e.g., time, evidentiality, number) will reveal a patterning of meaning as found in other cultural categories and practices. These common patterns are associated, and one does not necessarily cause the other. Whorf was too careful a scientist to make such crude claims as that language determines worldview. He did suggest that the grammatical categories of a language provide an interesting insight into cultural metaphysics; the unconscious patterning in language is connected to the larger patterns of culture, for example, in "common sense" ideas of space, time, number, cause and effect, and so on. Margaret Paxson (2005) provides an excellent example of the analytic power of this kind of approach in her discussion on the patterning of Russian grammatical categories and their harmony with local cosmology and social organization in a small peasant village in northern Russia. In a similar vein I have found that looking at how categories such as "culture," "language," and "tradition" are used in Kamchatka provided insights to the workings and effectiveness of symbols.

The way people speak often serves as an index of culture in discussions about culture, and linguistic differences are taken as indices of cultural differences in Kamchatka, as I found in conversation with everyone from politicians and school principals to teenagers in the village and reindeer herders in the camp.

One evening during my second visit with Volokha and the Middle Pakhachi herders in the spring of 1998, I tried to engage him in a discussion of ethnicity as part of my attempt to sort out local understandings of ethnic identity. We made a fire and ate salted fish packed in oil with onions, frybread, and moose, and we drank hot, sweet tea. I said to Volokha, "In the southern part of the region, the Koryaks say that they are all baptized, civilized, and that real Koryaks live in the north. I came up here and you're all Chukchi."

He laughed. "They [Koryaks] are few," he agreed.

"Is there is a big difference between Chukchi and Koryaks?"

"Oh yes, a big difference," he insisted.

"How?"

"Koryaks are greedy."

I didn't find that a useful ethnic marker, so I asked about language.

"They speak differently."

"How? Different words or just an accent."

He answered, "With an accent," then added, "Pure Koryak is incomprehensible." Volokha was probably referring to Nymylan Koryak spoken by maritime Koryaks in that part of Kamchatka, which linguists class as a separate language, Alutor. This conversation is important because the Chukchi people in Middle Pakhachi and Achayvayam are notorious in their chauvinistic conservatism. This meant a continuation of practices called traditional by all and abandoned by most other Koryak and Chukchi communities. It also meant that ethnic identity was more salient in Pakhachi than in other villages I visited, as I participated in ordinary people's conversations about culture and tradition. Most Pakhachi people were proudly reindeer Chukchi and disparaged maritime Koryaks as inferior in one way or another. Despite awareness that they spoke a variant of Koryak (called Chavchuven) and not Chukchi, Koryaks were completely different from Pakhachi Chukchi by their incomprehensible Koryak language. That said, these kinds of attitudes seem limited to only these two villages of Middle Pakhachi and Achayvayam. People in other villages were quite blasé about linguistic or cultural differences, acknowledging them without making value judgments.

Languages and ways of speaking are emotionally powerful symbols in themselves, condensing a range of meanings into the simple act of saying "hello" (*privet* in Russian; *amto* or *may* in Koryak). In the multicultural center that is Palana I was taught that greetings in Koryak were gendered. Men say "*amto*," while women say "*may*." I noticed that Russian men working in the administration would occasionally greet one another jokingly with *amto!* as a sign that they were fellow "Koryaks"; that is, residents of Koryakia. This struck me as a good example of Russian administrators appropriating Koryakness for their own purposes to legitimate their position of trying to set up the KAO as a fully independent political territory, separate from Kamchatka Oblast. In my own experiences of greeting and talking with a variety of interlocutors in Palana, I found that my use of the Koryak term was marked as indexing my role as ethnographer—that guy interested in Koryak language and culture. Often the informal Russian *privet*, more akin to "hi" than "hello," was more appropriate for the friendly greeting on the streets of a small town in order to avoid falling into the role of a clown. Traveling to various native villages, I found that the simple gendered distinction between *amto* and *may* did not hold. In the reindeer-herding village of Middle Pakhachi, for example, *may* was used to call out to a spouse. In any sort of domestic context, a man or a woman could call out "*may!*" in order to get a spouse to turn around or look up. In Nymylan villages like Lesnaya or Paren', I found both men and women using *may* as a greeting. Once I asked my Middle Pakhachi friends about this difference, and they confirmed that it struck them as weird to be greeted with *may*. "I thought she was yelling at me, trying to call me over," Anna explained. "Later I figured out that is just how they greet one another." And yet it seemed that *amto* was little used in reindeer-herding communities like Middle Pakhachi or Manily. Often visitors just came in and sat down and were greeted with a quiet "*yeti*" (you've arrived), acknowledging their presence without requiring a reply.

My problem with greeting people appropriately in Kamchatka is common to most students of foreign languages, especially languages very different from English. Whorf points out that understanding the proper forms for plurals in Hopi did not allow him to deploy plurals and singular forms correctly in sentences (1956:138). He still had two more years of work learning the appropriate way to say things not constrained by grammar or morphology so much as by idiom, usage, and a way of speaking. My problem in properly using one of the first words anyone learns of a foreign language was compounded by two axes of variation in code (sounds, vocabulary, grammar) and way of speaking. One axis is across space; different speech communities (villages or village factions) spoke different variants of Koryak and Alutor, but there was nothing surprising about this, nor were the variants particularly difficult to understand. The second axis was social but not in the commonly documented sense of social class or group status (such as high class vs. working class accents in London or New York), and it took me several months to understand how it worked.[19] The social axis of linguistic variation in Koryak is political—standard Koryak is that version of Koryak codified in grammars, dictionaries, and textbooks. It is taught in schools, heard on the radio, and printed in the newspaper. However, like standard Chukchi (Dunn 2000a), it is not based in a language community of everyday use but in the elite group of Koryak language professionals, most of whom now live in Palana. Thus the linguists' term *Palana Koryak* describes variation in the geographic axis and refers to a variant of Alutor, sometimes locally called Nymylan Koryak (Fortescue 2005; Zhukova 1980; Zhukova and Kurebito 2004). In spite of that, people in villages other than Palana used the term *Palana language (palanskii iazyk)* to refer to the standard or official variant of Koryak found in newspapers and taught in schools throughout the okrug. Dunn reports that standard Chukchi is supported by the authority of textbooks and the written word as well as the state institutions with which it is associated—schools, the press, and official plaques in Anadyr (Dunn 1999:16, 19–20; 2000a:392). I found the opposite in Kamchatka: far from speakers of colloquial Koryak telling me that they were "wrong" compared to official authorities, instead the textbooks and Palana language generally were almost universally condemned as "not *my* language" or not "how we really speak."

A Semiotics of Tradition

Tradition may be as contentious a category as culture is among anthropologists. I cannot avoid it, however, as nearly everyone in Kamchatka defined my task there as studying their traditions (*traditsii*) or customs (*obychi*). Sapir's discussion of "custom" in the *Encyclopaedia of the Social Sciences* highlights the importance of the term *tradition* as an index of historicity (1931:658). Traditions are commonly thought of as being rooted in the past, and to document their invention is supposedly to discredit their authenticity as real traditions (e.g., Hobsbawm and Ranger 1983). As I elaborate in subsequent chapters, my use of the term is not connected to the stultified and boxed-in culture typically ascribed to Koryaks by ethnographers and folklorists. I mean the term *tradition* in Roy Wagner's (1981:37ff.) sense of "context" or background upon which people "invent." There is certainly a difference between Koryak (or Chukchi or Itelmen or Even) traditions and Russian traditions. For Koryaks in the late twentieth century, traditions and "traditional life"—the examples they pointed to when I inquired about their culture—are in the trust of grandparents. This does not refer to a generation but to an age-grade. Thus the early Soviet ethnographers were most likely referred to the grandparents when they were doing their research in the 1920s and 1930s, when the grandparents I talked to were small children, and ethnographers in the future will be referred to grandparents who were young and inexperienced when I was asking such questions in 1998.

Among people in Kamchatka, particularly among indigenous people, traditions are what the elders do and say, not a disembodied set of knowledge codified in texts (sacred or folkloric) and supposedly belonging to a lost golden age or continuing through history essentially unchanged. Since the elders are the embodiment of tradition, change is built into this folk-model of culture and tradition, as I discuss in detail in chapters 2 and 3, where I analyze local practices and discourses surrounding Koryak dance groups. Dance in Kamchatka is a good synecdoche for culture in Kamchatka because it is available to anyone. There are no secret or esoteric dances, just as religious knowledge, oral traditions, hunting techniques, sewing, or any other body of knowledge or technique that may be construed as particularly "Koryak" are all open to those who are curious to learn about them, natives or outsiders. Dancing engages the whole person and implicates the dancer in wider social relationships and cultural symbols. They are also the subject of much discussion and evaluation. They include explicit elements of movement and rhythm as well as other processes of embodiment, ideas of the person, and power (Cowan 1990; Farnell 1995). They are caught up in discourse about "traditions"—Koryak dances must resemble something attributed to antecedents—and yet are the epitome of the creative arts. Individuals are famous for their particular styles of dancing that are both Koryak (and thus makes sense as part of a tradition) and individual (identifiable as "his" dance or "her" particular style of movement). Dances are therefore iconic of traditions and simultaneously indexical of the relationships between younger dancers and elder "bearers of tradition." They point to a person's relationship with specific elders, whether that be a grandparent-grandchild relation or a researcher-subject one, as in the case of the ethnographer.

The definition of traditions as antecedents connects them to the past, but they are not bounded "entities having an essence apart from our interpretation from them" (Handler and Linnekin 1984:273). Indeed, Peircean semiotics shows that *all meaning* exists only through our interpretation of signs.[20] An antecedent, what comes before, should not be confused with a model of historical continuity or stability. To mark a symbol or set of symbols (for that is what dances are) as "traditional" is not to describe something as handed down from the ancestors or continuous with the past. Rather, it asserts that the symbol is an index of past practices. Thus to claim that traditions are invented is not to claim that they are somehow inauthentic or spurious, although that seems to be exactly the claim some scholars make. I maintain, with Handler and Linnekin, that "it is impossible to separate spurious and genuine tradition, both empirically and theoretically" (1984:281). The anthropologist is presented with claims (data) from "natives" (people living in Kamchatka, in the present case) about various activities and ideas being traditional or not. I take such claims not so much as referring to historical ontologies but as claims of authority and social power.[21] Hence my discussion in the next section of authentic traditions is a description of Kamchatkan discourse about culture, and my trope of "genuine and spurious culture" is an analysis of models of culture that have political and social power in Siberia.

Outline of the Book

I have been alluding to chapters that elaborate on the ideas already introduced. The following chapter provides historical background to contextualize our present understanding of cultures in Kamchatka and a discussion of culture groups and their connections to government policy. Chapter 1 summarizes a certain authoritative model of indigenous culture found in Soviet and Russian ethnographies and in the discourse of educated people (elites) in Kamchatka. Although experts on Siberia will be familiar with this material already, these publications deserve examination because they lie behind much explicit commentary on local traditions that I present in subsequent chapters. Teachers and other educated people are familiar with these texts, and their model of culture finds its way into schools.

This explicit and conscious discourse on culture contrasts with the implicit and less reflective discourse on culture found in conversations about dancing. Discussed in chapters 2 and 3, dancing in Kamchatka presents an opportunity for observation, discussion, and interpretation of both unselfconscious activity and self-reflexive ideology. Unselfconscious dancing was apparent to me as I observed and participated in dancing at the Friday night village disco, at people's homes during impromptu parties, and during rituals honoring the spirits. More self-conscious dancing and talk about dancing was forthcoming during formal and informal interviews and when I had my video camera out for people of all ages to demonstrate their dances and teach me (the American ethnographer) about "our traditions." I found that the most interesting discourse on traditions happened in the context of describing and evaluating dances, dance groups, and individual performers, where people were focused on the specific signs (dance moves) and less on abstractions like "traditional dances." Many people participate in formal or informal dance ensembles performing indigenous Kamchatkan dance, and nearly everyone has an opinion on these groups, which range from the professional ensemble Mengo, in the administrative center, to the village dance groups of local children. I became interested in dance because people in Kamchatka were interested in dancing and talking about dancing. Chapters 2 and 3 explore a semiotics of indigenous dance practices and move toward an understanding of cultural continuity and change and the political economy of ethnic performances.

Chapter 2 plays the most with the ideas of cultures, genuine and spurious, taken from Edward Sapir's article of that name (1949 [1924]), in which he critiques what he sees as the "spurious" culture of contemporary America. I use these terms to analyze local categories of genuine and spurious ethnic dances and to differentiate good and bad models of culture introduced in that chapter and developed further in chapters 3 and 4. Sapir's "Culture, Genuine and Spurious" is primarily a critique of modernity and the soul-destroying meaninglessness of American culture. Sapir uses some standard Boasian tropes of the superiority of supposedly "primitive" Native American cultures to point out serious social and moral shortcomings in contemporary mainstream American culture and in modernity more generally. I do not think that Sapir would change his argument much if he were alive today. Indeed, consider his example of the meaningful and self-fulfilling activity of spearing fish on the Columbia and Snake rivers in the American Northwest (Sapir 1949:316)—now mostly impossible with the building of several dams—contrasted with the physically punishing, mind-numbing, soul-destroying work of cleaning fish for eighteen hours a day for four or five months on an ocean-going factory trawler working around the clock in the North Pacific. Sapir describes spurious cultures as those that reduce people to cogs in a machine, something one can see at work both in American capitalism and Soviet communism. A genuine culture is one that provides everyone with a meaningful place in society:

> The self must set itself at a point where it can, if not embrace the whole spiritual life of its group, at least catch enough of its rays to burst into light and flame. Moreover, the self must learn to reconcile its own strivings, its own imperious necessities, with the general spiritual life of the community. It must be content to borrow sustenance from the spiritual consciousness of that community and of its past, not merely that it may obtain the wherewithal to grow at all, but that it may grow where its power, great or little, will be brought to bear on a spiritual life that is of intimate concern to other wills. (Sapir 1949 [1924]:326)

This understanding of the proper relationship between individual and collective inspired by Freud and Nietzsche provides me with a platform from which to discuss genuine and spurious models of culture circulating in Kamchatkan discourse. Spurious models are those that fall into nationalistic traps of essentializing specific traits or insist on the correspondence of race, language, and culture. Spurious models of culture consider *tradition* to be static, definable in terms of a set of practices and beliefs. A genuine model of culture points out the relationships between memory and history in the realization of traditions, and the fuzzy-edged qualities of cultural margins

(I would like to avoid the term *boundaries*).[22] Many people in Kamchatka prefer to think of traditions as resources for creative play rather than as shackles that limit what one can do. Tradition and modernity are not necessarily opposed to each other, as is commonly assumed. A genuine culture, according to Sapir, is one that is constantly regenerated by playing with tradition. I argue that this is the proper way to understand *all* cultures. There are, however, many people in Kamchatka who think of traditions as being rooted in the past and available mostly by reading historical accounts. Throughout the book, I attempt to capture this tension between these two conceptions of culture and tradition—knowledge captured in writing or lived practices subject to constant change.

Authentic traditions are believed to be real in a sense that invented or faked traditions are not real. The claim that some traditions are invented implies that others are not, or it implies the romantic notion that there are other societies (non-Western? non-modern?) that have not succumbed to such fakery and have authentic traditions. I argue that traditions are equally invented and equally real. The anthropology of tourism has been one of the principal arenas for a fierce debate about the existence of authentic traditions or even experiences (Bruner 1993, 1994, 2005; Conklin 1997; Handler and Gable 1997; MacCannell 1999; Penney 2004). Drawing on debates about New Zealand Maori traditions, Hanson (1989) argues convincingly that the anthropologist cannot hope to sort out the "real" from the "fake," as the task is meaningless. I discuss authenticity as a local, socially real category operative in Kamchatka. Much work in anthropology and cultural studies has demolished the category of the authentic as something "really real," existing independently of the social and cultural contexts in which representations of authenticity are created (Baudrillard 1983; Eco 1986; Gable and Handler 1996; Handler 1986). When people in Kamchatka describe a dance as being "really" Koryak or Eveny, it is a simple affair to demonstrate how the referent of such a statement—Koryak or Even culture—does not exist as an independent, bounded, and neatly configured entity, let alone a real Koryak dance or real Even dance. My aim is not to defend the ontological reality of real Koryak dances or their authenticity or to sort out the *bona fide* from the fakery (cf. Bruner 1993, 1994; Heyes 2002; Kasten 2004). Nor am I interested in deconstructing local discourses of authenticity (cf. Gable and Handler 1996; Handler 1988; Hobsbawm 1983; McDonald 1989; Trevor-Roper 1983). Rather, I aim to describe the social and psychological reality that has the authority of being real, or true, or correct representation; that is, what value such performances have for local people, for whom the category of "getting it right" is part of social reality and a key symbol of culture and identity, which cannot be denied (Bigenho 2002).

Chapter 4 unpacks the theory of culture that relies upon authoritative texts, behind textbooks and teaching in primary schools and the Palana Teachers' College, and the parallel role of museums and ethnic craft production in teaching this model of culture to children. I show how the reified model of culture presented in chapter 1 is taught and used in self-conscious speech, while the more dynamic and implicit theory of culture evident in discourse about dance is often lurking in the subtext of teachers' and students' speech and actions.

Chapter 5 continues my discussion of schools, which are an important site where ideologies about language emerge. Koryak language is taught to some degree in most schools in the KAO, but that does not seem to be helping to reverse the trend of children not learning it, even as a second language. Languages do not die or *do* anything else. People do things with languages, including stop speaking them for complex reasons that rarely boil down to choice or straightforward oppression. I have found that the text-based theory of culture operative in schools is also connected to Koryak language revival efforts in the okrug. Attempts at standardizing Koryak are roundly rejected by people outside the okrug center of Palana, which hampers all efforts at getting children to learn and to speak Koryak.[23]

1. Discovering Koryak Culture through History

When I tell people in Scotland or in the United States that I am an anthropologist, they either ask if I am searching for the "missing link" or they do not have any idea what anthropology is. In Russia most people still associate the term *antropolog* with biological anthropology, and so I called myself an *etnograf*, an ethnographer. Ethnography is a household word among former Soviet peoples, as Bruce Grant (1995:18) found on Sakhalin Island; I also found that nearly everyone in Kamchatka knows what an ethnographer is and does. For people in Kamchatka, ethnographers recorded traditions, myths, and legends and spent the bulk of their time talking to the elders, doing what Western anthropologists disparage as "salvage" ethnography.[1] Culture, in the anthropological sense of "lifeways" and the different cultural permutations from one group to another, is everywhere a main topic of discussion in circles high and low. Although ethnography in Russia has similar primitivist roots to anthropology in other countries, it is no longer limited to "primitive others." The scholarly attention of an American was a point of pride among people in Kamchatka, at least in the 1990s, and more than one Russian asked why I did not study their culture. Americans and other foreigners, however, are much less exotic in Kamchatka nowadays.

After all the criticism of Orientalism and the Western "gaze" and Othering by anthropologists, it is important to bear in mind that being "studied" and represented by an anthropologist is something my interlocutors in Kamchatka very much wanted, and wanted done properly. Some expressed clear happiness that an American came all that way just to learn about them. Others asked, pointedly, if I was going to build a villa with the money from my book, although most understood that scholars are not rich, even if my society is comparatively much richer than theirs. From the very early days, Boasian anthropology held it as axiomatic that every culture is interesting, in and of itself (Bunzl 2004; see Boas 1940 [1887]). My experiences in Kamchatka have helped me learn a great deal not only about specific cultures far away from my home but also about culture in general. The sins of Orientalism and Othering lie not so much in curiosity in other people as in romantic, unreflective representations that approach a caricature.[2] Boasian semiotics, which keeps the interpreter in view without navel-gazing, provides a solution to the problem of representing others without caricature.

Siberians are familiar with ethnography because of the close connections between ethnographers and the government, particularly in the early years of the Soviet Union (Anderson 2000; Grant 1995; Ssorin-Chaikov 2003). Soviet ethnography was intimately tied to government policy on "the nationalities question" and the status of the demographically small peoples of the North and Far East. This chapter provides a brief overview of some representative ethnographies of Kamchatka and government policy as it affected indigenous people there. Academic theories and government policies of the Soviet Union together constructed a world where people became constituted in bounded groups, defined by concrete, objective qualities that supposedly persist through history and are common to the group as a whole and each individual in it (Slezkine 1994b).

Government policies and ethnography in Siberia had a symbiotic relationship in the process of defining groups such as "the Koryak," one which dates from the first Russian incursions in the seventeenth century (Hirsch 1997; Slezkine 1994a). The rubric "Koryak" refers to a group of people who do not share a single common denominator except for the fact that they have been classified as Koryak by political, military, and scientific representatives of the Center for more than three hundred years. A critical reading of the standard ethnographies (e.g., Jochelson 1908; Antropova 1971) reveals clues that the group boundaries so important in Soviet and Russian administrative policies and anthropological theories are permeable on the ground, if they exist at all. As far as I can determine, there has long been considerable fluidity of membership in households and settlements. Chukchi could turn into Koryaks; nomads could settle down, and settled people could take up nomadic patterns of life. One can define cultures in the area (e.g., Itelmen and Even) on the basis of language, spiritual beliefs, or material culture, but when it comes to allocating individual humans to a group, many Kamchatkan natives see these categories not as absolute but as situationally contingent. Information from historical ethnographies supports this, often to the consternation of administrators and even the ethnographers themselves (Hancock 2001). On the one hand, Kamchatkan native people are confident of their ability to identify a person as Even or Koryak or Itelmen based on speech, or traditional costume, or dance style; but on the other hand, these identifications may be moot, subject to revision, and most often derived from what that person is *doing* at the moment. Ethnographers, unfortunately, have assumed ethnic groups and then have gone on to explain them.

Roy Wagner's (1974) question about the existence of groups in highland New Guinea is equally applicable to Siberia. The answer to the question "are there culture groups in Kamchatka?" is, of course, "yes." Yet I argue that one can claim there is no such thing as "the Koryak," in effect answering "no" as well. From my point of view there is no common dominator among the various communities so labeled, aside from the fact of their common labeling by Westerners, starting with the initial imperial conquests and up to the latest scientific investigations. More important, I want to challenge the question itself, this obsession with looking for groups, more than any particular answer. The accuracy of representing Koryaks as one ethnic group or two ethnic groups is not as important as the style involved in the construction of that representation.

The Soviet Union ideologically defined itself through the codification of Marxism-Leninism. Soviet ideology was internally contradictory in advocating both ethnic nationalism and historical materialism. Although Marxism holds that class, as defined by social relations to the mode of production, defines the objective groups within a society, Marxism-Leninism codified the stance that ethnic groups, or "nations," had been oppressed under the tsar as ethnicities, not just as disenfranchised laborers. Within the Communist Party of the Soviet Union, the nation—as defined by a unique history, a stable language, economy, and psychology within a bounded territory—was thought of as a real, existing entity and was invested with legal rights (Slezkine 1994b; Brubaker 1996; see also Bromley 1977). Universal class groups were defined as the "content" of historical reality, while particular nations were just empty "forms" laid over the universal content of class history (Slezkine 1994b). Thus the form of an ethno-territorial federation was filled with the content of the centralized Communist Party: "rejecting tsarist centralism as retrograde [Marxism-Leninism] rationalized a far stricter centralization under the new Communist leaders" (Starr 1997:252; see also Smith 1996). Now ethnicity is often the most ready identity for political action in the former Soviet Union and in the Russian Federation; regional separatism is often cast in terms of ethnic national "rights," if at all possible.

The Soviet and also Western obsession with ethnic groups understands the social world to be segmented into separate groups at one level or another. In this way the Russians and Soviets were not so very different from Western European empires cataloging the "peoples" within imperial dominion. Russian and Soviet theories of culture, emphasizing ethnic groups above all else, segmented complex and dynamic variations in cultural practices, beliefs, and ways of speaking into separate pigeonholes. Thus administrators and scholars examined an area with the question "what are the ethnic groups?" foremost in their minds (Banks 1996; Hirsch 2005). I suggest that a more useful representation of indigenous Kamchatkan cultures uses overlapping continua or fields, fuzzily defined, avoiding discretely bounded groups that would isolate people and communities allocated to one group from those in another. Instead of asking the question "what are the ethnic groups?"—which assumes there are such entities—a better analysis seeks to understand the interactive dynamics of social life, the speech communities of a given area of the world, and the different ways of speaking and acting in the area. This better approach follows an inquiry into signs, what they mean and what people do with them. A particular way of speaking may be associated with a speech community (e.g., this village, that herding camp, those three villages), or it may be associated with a situation (e.g., ritual, trade), but it should not be *a priori* assumed as a defining feature of a social (ethnic) group: maybe there are groups, maybe not (Hymes 1968).

Modes of Encompassment and Differentiation in Russia

The Koryak Autonomous Okrug was part of a complex typology of cultural groups (ethnicities or "nationalities") and administrative districts in the Soviet Union. The legitimacy of the Koryak Autonomous Okrug's legal and political existence was predicated on the unique qualities of Koryak culture and the special needs that Koryak people have living in a modern industrial state. The autonomous region was supposedly a way of compensating Koryaks and other native people for their oppression under the tsar and helping them to become equal participants in modern socialist society. The reality was the opposite. Non-natives held most of the powerful positions and generally benefited the most from the region.[3] Thus, calling the USSR an "affirmative action empire" (Martin 2001) is an over-generous assessment of Soviet policy to assimilate indigenous Siberians (and others) to an industrial, communist modernity as quickly as possible. The economic and political structures of the KAO served primarily to exploit the people and the region for the benefit of the Center; still, the contradictory imperialism of the Soviet state also supported the reification of Koryak culture into a legitimate form of collective identity, which could have provided a level for political organization and action.[4]

The Koryak Okrug came "readymade" with a "Koryak people" implicit in the okrug's existence. This logic is most salient in Koryak education policy, which follows a nationalist conceptualization of what a language should be, as I explain in chapter 5. Thus the KAO provides an example of a "nationalizing state" (Brubaker 1996). The Soviets set up a nationalistic political structure without a "fully developed nation" to go with it. In nationalizing states, nationalist projects (like cultural revival and native language education) are "not only eminently respectable but virtually obligatory in some contexts. This is often the case in new states, especially those . . . closely identified with one particular ethnocultural nation" (Brubaker 1996:64). Koryaks constitute the "titular ethnicity" (a common term in post-Soviet studies), but most nationalizing projects are cast in terms of protecting and reviving indigenous (*korennaia*) culture, so as to include Itelmen, Chukchi, and Even people as well. Although the details vary greatly, this general pattern is repeated across the former Soviet Union, as we can see in Tatarstan (Musina 1996), in Sakha/ Yakutia (Balzer and Vinokurova 1996:161ff.), in Chukotka (Gray 2005), and in other former Soviet republics (see Chinn and Kaiser 1996).

The principle of sociopolitical macro-organization in Russia, which shapes people's attitudes toward government at all levels, is a vertical hierarchy of center and periphery. The Soviets inherited a contiguous land empire with control tightly centralized in the hands of the tsar, whose capital had been St. Petersburg since the early eighteenth century. Lenin moved the Center back to its traditional seat in the Moscow Kremlin, and the Soviet Union replaced the tsar with an even more highly centralized, authoritarian government (Starr 1997). The Center in Moscow is associated with order, control, strength, and civilization. The periphery, which can be experienced only a few dozen miles from Moscow, is associated with disorder, wildness, weakness, and nature. The name of the periphery in Russian and Western imagination is often "Siberia." Kamchatka is also both spatially and metaphorically the very edge, the "far away country."[5] For example, a neighborhood on the far outskirts of a new city in Moscow Oblast received the nickname "Kamchatka" to symbolize its distance from the center of town (Vysokovskii 1995:21).

This hierarchy of center and periphery is visible in local Kamchatkans' lamentations about the lack of a "strong leader" in contemporary society. In civic and political affairs many people in Kamchatka pine for the days when one man called the shots and things were accomplished in a seemingly orderly fashion. The perceived disorder in Russian Federation affairs in the 1990s was attributed to the lack of such a "strong leader" at the center. On the other hand, people are critical of those with "pretensions" (*pretenzii*) to being better than others. For example, I was criticized once or twice for not being able to relate to "primitives" (*pervobytnie*). The point was that I was too much like the Center (civilized) to be able to relate to peripheral people, who were supposedly the subject of my research. More commonly, I was praised for being a "simple fellow/ordinary guy" (*prostoi paren'*), especially by native people living in small villages. A "simple fellow" is a good person, one who is unpretentious, gets along with other people, and is not haughty, deceptive, or sly.[6] In terms of political organization and political relationships, people in Kamchatka expressed preferences for a clear hierarchy, while in interpersonal relationships, they want egalitarianism. Margaret Paxson (2005) describes a similar ideology of social and political relations for Russian peasants in European Russia. This contradiction (or dialectic) of hierarchy and egalitarianism recurs in my discussion of Soviet theories of culture and administrative policies in Kamchatka.

Center-periphery relations operate at each level of social organization in nesting hierarchies like a souvenir *matrioshka* doll (Humphrey 1994). In Kamchatka the center is the administrative capital and largest city, Petropavlovsk-Kamchatskiy. In the Koryak Okrug, which in the 1990s was trying to negotiate its way out from under the encompassment of the Kamchatka Oblast, the center is Palana, at least politically. The okrug consisted of four rayons, each of which had an administrative center. Centers are associated with culture, order, and support. People in Middle Pakhachi often look to the Olyutorskiy Rayon center of Tilichiki for hospital care, but if the condition requires specialists, then patients most often go straight to Petropavlovsk-Kamchatskiy. Higher educational opportunities for Pakhachi youth are available in the okrug center of Palana but are better in the oblast center of Petropavlovsk-Kamchatskiy. However, everyone considers the best higher education to be available in the federal center—Moscow or St. Petersburg. St. Petersburg (Leningrad) is a special center for indigenous peoples of Kamchatka and Siberia because it is the location of the historic Institute of the North, now part of Herzen Pedagogical University, which has special programs and departments to train indigenous teachers and administrators. *The* Center in Kamchatkan people's minds is most often Moscow. This was made clear to me in a casual conversation over a cup of tea at a fishing camp, which ended with the current economic plight, as many conversations did in 1998:

> "There were some people shooting sovkhoz deer and carrying them off, but the director could never catch them. On the one hand, I can understand why he shot them [killing one man and wounding others]. If he gets a good lawyer, he might get off. I don't know. We have no information about what is going on now. The worst thing is that he was under that [tapping neck; i.e., the director was drunk]. It is such a big country, and it doesn't make sense that everything has fallen apart. Those *chinovniki* [bureaucrats—derogatory] just take care of themselves."
>
> "Yeah, Palana is full of bureaucrats who don't do anything," I agreed about the okrug capital.
>
> "I mean in Moscow, but they do all right in Palana, too."

Laments like these typically focused on the general disorganization and lack of discipline at all levels, demonstrated by widespread poaching and the perpetual backlog of unpaid wages, which were allocated by the Center through the Palana administration. I was oriented to the activities of people in Palana, who may be responsible for not disbursing federal funds allocated for local wages, but my interlocutor here was clearly focused on the Center in Moscow as being responsible for the economic malaise affecting Kamchatka and the rest of Russia.[7] Whereas people in the United States may often be accused of not being able to see the forest for the trees, being so concerned with their own particular plight that they do not see the larger, systemic problems underneath, people in Russia implicitly see their local government, state farm, or village as a synecdoche for all of Russia. In Roy Wagner's (1986) terms, they have a holographic political worldview.

Like the Koryak man just quoted, people in the most peripheral villages are in some ways more oriented toward Moscow than those in villages with easy access to nearby cities. In villages such as Paren' and Upper Paren' without regular telephone service, most news comes from shortwave broadcasts from Moscow, introduced by the opening line, "*govorit Moskva*" (Moscow is talking), and everyone is listening. Paren' maintained twice-daily two-way radio connections with the sovkhoz base in Manily, but detailed information arrives in national newspapers and magazines, even if several months old (making it hard to call this "news"). Here the metaphor of the matrioshka breaks down; these villages are disconnected from intermediary encompassing entities, local centers like Palana and Petropavlovsk-Kamchatskiy, but in any case people there remain oriented toward Moscow, the all-encompassing Center.

Russian and Soviet theories of culture and Lenin's nationalities' policy must be understood with the concept of distinct groups arranged in encompassing hierarchies in mind. Before the Revolution Lenin's nationality policies were part of an overall plan to subvert the authority of the tsar and break apart his monolithic hierarchy (Gleason 1990a:12; Hazard 1990:48). By the time the Bolsheviks came to power that had already occurred, and they set about reestablishing order through a hierarchy of revolutionary workers' "committees" (*sovety* or soviets) and a federated system of administrative territories. Soviets were organized into encompassing hierarchies, starting in local villages and towns and culminating with the Supreme Soviet at the top in Moscow. Eventually administrative territories became organized paralleling a territorial distribution of culture groups, couched in a rhetoric of ethnic self-determination, which had been initiated long before the Revolution (Rywkin 1990:63; Stammler 2005:129–31). The specific policies changed during the course of the twentieth century, but the ideological principles remained constant. Ethnic minorities in Siberia, especially nomads, were seen by Bolsheviks and others in the Center as being the most "backward" (in the rhetoric of the time) of all the peoples in the Soviet Union (Grant 1995; Gurvich and Kuzakov 1960; Slezkine 1994a; Ssorin-Chaikov 2003). Special programs were instituted for Koryaks and others to "develop" or "grow" to the advanced level of socialist society (Antropova 1971:109f.; Sergeev 1955; Gurvich and Kuzakov 1960:128).

Reindeer herders were confronted with the most dramatic changes to their way of life under Soviet collectivization in the 1930s. Koryaks had an individuated sense of ownership of deer that connected people with animals in moral and spiritual bonds, and collectivization was anathema to Koryak ideas of personhood. Nomads were classed as the most "primitive" peoples in the Union, and government policies were directed at establishing towns for herders and developing a settled way of life for them. "Production nomadism" continued as men herded deer collectivized into government farms, but nomadism as a way of life was eradicated by forcing children into schools in town, and wage-labor positions were created for women (Konstantinov 2005:121–31; Vitebsky and Wolfe 2001; Vladimirova 2006:206–11). In this way the family dynamics of a reindeer herder resembled those of a sailor, gone out to sea (in the tundra) for months at a time, while wife and children lived without husband and father back "home." Fishing, sea mammal hunting, and even berry collecting were similarly regimented, ironically similar to the colonial logic found in Africa, where British colonizers were wed "to the idea that work should be steady and regular and carefully controlled" (Cooper 1992:209). As the Soviets moved to "rationalize" indigenous production, they introduced mechanization in any way they could, chiefly through transportation, as part of industrializing subsistence herding, hunting, and gathering.[8]

The Koryak Autonomous Okrug was at the bottom of a hierarchy of administrative districts paralleling a hierarchical theory of culture and civilization. At the top were fifteen constituent Soviet Socialist Republics (SSR), of which Russia was the only federation, the others being associated with a "titular ethnicity." The next level of administrative territories in the hierarchy was the Autonomous Soviet Socialist Republic (ASSR), fifteen of which were in Russia (one being inside the Azerbaijan SSR). While an SSR had the constitutional right to secession, an ASSR did not. All SSRs were on the external borders of Russia, but several ASSRs were located in the Russian interior (e.g., Yakut ASSR, now Sakha Republic, and Komi ASSR, now Komi Republic). Ethnic groups with smaller populations were allocated National Oblasts (five in Russia, one each in Georgia, Azerbaijan, and Tadjik SSRs), which included official status for their native languages. The minority peoples of the North were allocated National Okrugs (e.g., Koryak National

Okrug, Chukotka National Okrug), which were subordinated to neighboring oblasts shortly after their establishment (Kamchatka Oblast and Magadan Oblast, respectively). Okrug policy and decisions of any import were subject to approval by oblast authorities (Kagedan 1990:165f.; see Stammler 2005:129–30 for Yamal-Nenets Autonomous Okrug). In 1980 National Okrugs and National Oblasts were renamed "Autonomous" in line with Andropov's declaration that the "national question" was more or less "solved" (Gleason 1990a:16). Western analysts saw these culturally designated territorial units as empty symbols because the "real power . . . resides less in territorial structures than in the CPSU [Communist Party of the Soviet Union]" (Kagedan 1990:166). However, that ignored the active enfranchisement of local culture groups within the CPSU in no small part due to the culturally designated territories. With the fall of the Soviet Union and the demise of the Communist Party as the structuring power, these territorial constituents became the main structures of administrative policy. Administrative structures had been too conservative to allow for the erasure of existing territories.[9]

Ethnonyms and other terms of group identity are highly problematic in the former Soviet Union. The tsarist obsession with ethnic group nomenclature has continued through the Soviet era to the end of the twentieth century (Balzer 1994). Everyone had one and only one ethnicity stamped in his or her internal passport (Russian, Koryak, etc.).[10] The English term *Russian* conflates two concepts differentiated in the original Russian: *russkii* refers to the ethnicity "Russian," while *rossiiskii* refers to "citizens of the Russian Federation." *Russkii* is an ethnonym, whereas *rossiiskii* is a political or territorial status, citizenship. People in Kamchatka also make the gross distinction between "native" (*korennoi*, an adjective related to the word for root, thus indicating "rooted") and "newcomer" or "incomer" (*priezzhii*, pl. *priezzhie*), highlighting important social and cultural differences between indigenous North Asian people also referred to as "aboriginal" and immigrants, whether they be Russian, Ukrainian, or Chinese. The term *priezzhii* as it is used in Kamchatka should not be understood as a gloss for "white"—that is, as a racial or ethnic term—because Buryats, Sakha, and other indigenous Siberians not local to Kamchatka are likewise classed as "newcomers," *priezzhie*, and most are of the same social class of professionals who migrated to Kamchatka for professional and economic opportunities. The number of non-native, non-newcomer people in the KAO is very small.

Since the early 1970s the indigenous people of Koryakia have been a demographic minority. As of 2002 they made up just under half of the okrug's population, the rest being mostly Russians and Ukrainians, most of whom arrived within the last thirty years, attracted by perquisites for working in the Far North. The curious thing in Kamchatka is that people do not oppose *priezzhie* to *korennye* (indigenes, natives) but to *mestnye* (locals; see glossary). My educated friends in Palana agreed with my analysis that *mestnyi* is a loaded synonym for *korennoi* (indigenous), denying Russians or others who may have been born and raised in Kamchatka the status of being locals (*mestnye*). This strict usage seems to be limited to Kamchatka, and the word is used somewhat differently in other parts of Siberia. Although this usage of *mestnyi* in Kamchatka indicates a distinction between Russian and native (i.e., Koryak, Itelmen, Even, or Chukchi, in official local nomenclature), this distinction is never systematic.

This usage gave me trouble more than once, especially in conducting linguistic documentation. I was trying to record elders who spoke *local* variants of Koryak or Nymylan or Alutor. In one instance I found myself quizzing an elder in Paren' and getting strange data because she did not in fact speak Paren' Koryak but Upper Paren' (Chavchuven) Koryak. Another time I nearly offended a sweet grandmother in Lesnaya when I asked if she was *mestnaia* (local to Lesnaya) when we were talking about different ways of speaking among different villages. Eventually I learned to use village names as adjectives as a way of referring to local language varieties (i.e., *paren'skii iazyk*, *lesnovskii iazyk*).

I realize that "indigenous" is a problematic category in anthropology, and it is no less problematic in Kamchatka. In any case, intense settler colonization in northern Kamchatka is barely a generation old, and people in Kamchatka readily make a distinction between locals/natives (*mestnye*) and newcomers/non-native immigrants (*priezzhie*). This distinction is more common in everyday speech than categories such as "Koryak" or "Nymylan" or "Alutor." Native identity in practice is self-ascribed and mostly a function of primary social loyalties and, to some degree, lifestyle where genealogical identities are mixed. There are, of course, many cases of immigrants (mostly men but also some women) who have been living in Kamchatka most of their adult life and have children and grandchildren there. Such people are not called *priezzhie*, which can have derogatory connotations. Although people who may originally have been *priezzhie* cannot become *mestnye*, they can become "one of us" or "ours" (*nash* in Russian). The term *Kamchadal* was also often used by people born in Kamchatka but not claiming to be Koryak, Itelmen, Even, or Chukchi. They may or may not have considered themselves creoles.[11] What became clear to me, as I tried to figure out how people in Kamchatka were sorted out into different categories by culture or ethnicity, was that most Kamchatkans did not care much about such things, except when quizzed by an anthropologist. There is plenty of bigotry or racism in Kamchatka, but it is mostly directed at strangers. People rarely seemed concerned about a universal typology of cultures and ethnicities, let alone determining membership of people in those groups.

The term *nationalism* (*natsionalizm*) refers only to ethnic nationalism, especially in Kamchatka, where it always has negative connotations. Only bad things result from nationalism as it is understood in Kamchatka, the Chechen wars being the most notorious example. The word *etnos* (ethnos) in Russian is a technical term, and most people use the ordinary term *narod*, which is best glossed by the German *das Volk*, a folk or people, a nation, an ethnic/cultural group. The Russian term for "native," *tuzemets*, is now archaic and little used (mostly in jokes or ironically). Now people in Kamchatka and across the North refer to people like Koryaks as *korennye*— "indigenous." However, in many parts of Russia (especially Siberia), this refers more literally to "native born" inhabitants who care about their natal land, as opposed to the immigrant workers who are more interested in expropriation (Rasputin 1996:365ff.).

"Discovering" Kamchatkan Culture Groups

As mentioned in the previous chapter, I was in Kamchatka in the fall of 1997 when people were celebrating "300 years of Kamchatkan unity with Russia," dating from the 1697 erection of a Russian Orthodox cross by Vladimir Atlasov on the site of a future Russian fort on the Kamchatka River. Atlasov's report to his superiors is similar to those of other seventeenth-century conquistadores encountering and subjugating other peoples for other empires. He clearly described the route of his travels and the wealth he captured from the indigenous settlements, which he subjected to the *yasak* tribute (Atlasov 1988[1701]).[12] *Yasak* was an imperial tribute in furs levied on every adult male of the indigenous Siberian population and paid directly to the personal accounts of the tsar. Native people who had converted to Orthodoxy were taxed like Russian peasants. Yasak was levied only on *inozemtsy*, a term that means "aliens, foreigners" (literally "of another land") and indicates tsarist attitudes of total dominion over northern Asia. Assurance that all properly due yasak was collected and delivered to the crown depended on an accurate tally of alien (*inozemtsy*) men and their locations, and that is what Atlasov provided, with information about which groups (settlements) submitted peacefully to the tsar's domination and which ones did not. Their group identity was also important because hostages were often taken from recalcitrant tribute payers to ensure compliance the following year (Al'kor and Drezen 1935:25; Forsyth 1992:41). It is most likely that Atlasov's information about the cultural identity of these people on Kamchatka came primarily from his Yukaghir Chuvantsi allies. Complex continua of cultural and linguistic variation in Kamchatka were reported by Atlasov as three categories: reindeer-herding Koryaks, Alutors living in semi-subterranean houses and speaking a language "quite similar to that of the Koryaks," and Kamchadal (now called Itelmen), living along the rivers to the south of the Alutors (Atlasov 1988:8). The primary features distinguishing one group from another were economic activities, house styles, and language, and he included different battle tactics customary for each group (Atlasov 1988:6).[13]

About forty years after Atlasov's military expedition, Stepan Krasheninnikov arrived in southern Kamchatka in 1737 as part of the Second Kamchatka Expedition (1735–41) under the general command of Vitus Bering. He was the first scholar to study Kamchatkan peoples, working in the German tradition of natural history. In 1740 he was joined by the German scientist Georg Steller, who later went with Bering on his ill-fated voyage to America. Steller died in 1746 while still en route back to St.

Petersburg. He had systematized his notes and begun a manuscript on Kamchatka, and Krasheninnikov was tasked with writing the definitive description of Kamchatka, incorporating Steller's material, which he did in Russian (Krasheninnikov 1755). Steller is much more famous for his account of his trip to Alaska with Bering, since his description of Kamchatka was posthumously published in German in 1774 and received little attention compared to the fanfare and eager reception greeting Krasheninnikov's work, which was translated into English, German, and two French editions before the end of the century. The 1990s have seen many publications on regional topics and history by Kamchatkan publishing houses (both commercial and scholarly), and Krasheninnikov's 1755 book was republished in a facsimile edition in 1994. A Russian translation of Steller's book, drafted in the late 1930s, was published five years later in 1999. There is some dispute as to who was responsible for which parts of these two books, but comparison shows very similar accounts (Krasheninnikov 1972; Steller 2003). I discuss Krasheninnikov in detail because he is read and discussed in Kamchatka. I found the two-volume 1994 facsimile edition of his *Description of the Land of Kamchatka* in the home of nearly every educated Kamchatkan, whether indigenous or not, and Krasheninnikov's account frequently came up in my conversations.[14]

Krasheninnikov seemed to have some difficulty in delineating one indigenous group from another, even when considering ethnonyms for selves and neighbors: "The reindeer Koriaks call themselves tumugutu. They call the Russians, melagytangy, and the Kamchadals, khonchala. They do not know the Kuriles at all. The Koriaks who do not change their dwelling place at all call themselves chauchu; they also call the Russians melagytangy, the Kamchadals nymylaga and the Kuriles kuinala" (1972:197). This description reveals Krasheninnikov's ignorance of native languages. The reindeer Koryak word *tumugutu* is best translated as "friends/compatriots/comrades" (the Soviets seized upon it to translate their socialist term *tovarishch*). One can imagine a scene where the Russian is gesturing at a group of native people, asking them who they are, what they call themselves, and a native replies, "Who us? We are all friends." Jochelson (1908:407) dismisses Krasheninnikov's data as incorrect, and he also points out that *chauchu* is best translated as "rich in reindeer" and refers to reindeer-herding people, not settled communities![15] When nomadic Koryak speakers call Itelmens/Kamchadals *nymylaga*, they are simply calling them "villagers," from the root *nym-* (village, settlement). Jochelson's point is merely that Krasheninnikov got the names of the groups wrong. Perhaps he did, but more important, I believe this scholarly confusion results from the problem that these ethnic groups existed more in the minds of the ethnographers than in the minds of the natives or anywhere else.

I found current use of *melagetaŋen* to be more flexible than this description of past usage. The Koryak word *melagetaŋen* is still used to refer to Russians and white people in general. Nowadays, however, it has negative connotations similar to those of *priezzhii* (newcomer)—meaning a (hostile) stranger or outsider. People referred to me as *melagetaŋen* only when I was a stranger to them or they were clearly annoyed with me. Otherwise, I was *merekan* (the American) or "Alex." The negative association with *melagetaŋen* was made clear to me when I was watching some home videos in a native village. A common way for people to introduce me to their village was to show me video tapes of their fishing camp, rituals, and even funerals. One woman asked, "Who is that *melagetaŋen*?" not recognizing some white guy on the TV screen. Her sister exclaimed, "What *melagetaŋen*!? That's our (*nash*) Misha!"

The man in question had moved to the village with his in-comer parents as a young child, had grown up there, married a Koryak woman, and had children and most likely will die in Kamchatka. Thus while a white cannot become *mestnyi* (local) in Kamchatka, he can cease being *melagetaŋen* or *priezzhii* and become "ours" (i.e., "with us").

Distinguishing Koryaks from Chukchi was nearly impossible for Krasheninnikov: "If one draws no distinction between the Chukchi and the Koriak peoples, which can be justified since the Chukchi are actually Koriaks, the territorial limits of these latter extend much farther" (1972:282). He goes on to state that Koryaks live under the dominion of the tsar and pay yasak, while the Chukchi do not. Thus, he is following Cossack categories, where the most important distinction is between yasak-paying and nonpaying natives. He mentions that Chukchi raid Koryak herders and steal their deer, but he also provides a description of a Chukchi semi-subterranean house, which seems to be identical to Koryak ones documented by Jochelson (1908:452ff.). People who lived in such houses did not herd deer or did so only as a peripheral activity. They lived mainly from fishing and hunting and did not necessarily attack reindeer herders but traded sea products for deer skins and meat, which Krasheninnikov notes (1972:284). The most curious aspect of Krasheninnikov's description of the peoples of Kamchatka is that he persists in using the folk taxonomies Koryak, Kamchadal, and Chukchi despite his own observations that this nomenclature is an inadequate characterization of the cultures of the area. Still, Krasheninnikov's skill as an ethnographer should be acknowledged, because he provided the detailed observational data that allow us, retrospectively, to critique his generalizations, as I do here. I also cannot find objective criteria by which to distinguish Chukchi from Ko-ryaks, especially considering the ethnographic material I have

collected on Chukchi and Koryak traditions in villages like
Middle Pakhachi, where the majority of inhabitants are al-
most chauvinistic in their Chukchi self-identification (see also
Kerttula 2000:23).

Travelers' Tales and Government Reports

By the close of the eighteenth century most of Kamchatka was
effectively encompassed within the Russian Empire. Petropavlovsk-Kamchatskiy remained a small but important town and
port, serving as a way station for departures from Okhotsk to
Alaska. Gizhiga (now in Magadan Oblast, see map 1), along
the northern shores of the Okhotsk, was an important post
for controlling the northern reaches of Kamchatka and was
frequented by sundry travelers. In the nineteenth century it
was the main point of entry for the region occupied primarily
by Koryak people. Descriptions of Kamchatka from the late
eighteenth and early nineteenth centuries are mostly travelers' tales (Cochrane 1825; De Lesseps 1790; Dobell 1830;
Sauer 1802). These accounts highlight the adventures of the
author, although some interesting ethnographic tidbits may
occasionally be gleaned from the impressionistic narratives. For
example, De Lesseps comments that the local Russian settlers
and Cossacks (more a profession than a specific ethnic identity)
in Kamchatka were "not distinguishable from the indigenes,
but by their features and idiom" (1790, 1:15).

Another enduring theme in travelers' accounts, whether
those of eighteenth-century explorers or late twentieth-century
tourist-adventurers, is the remoteness and isolation of Kamchatka, despite evidence of considerable cosmopolitanism. De
Lesseps (1790, 1:10–12) describes Petropavlovsk-Kamchatskiy
as an important port in North Pacific trade routes, moving
furs about the Pacific in a profitable trade. Cochrane found a
Portuguese brig bringing flour from Macao and an American

ship, officered by Englishmen and crewed by native Hawaiians, provoking him to comment, "It is not a little singular that the first voyage undertaken by them should be to Kamchatka, almost the least known part of the world" (Cochrane 1825, 2:425; cf. Dobell 1830:87–89). While this may have been true of his London readership, Kamchatka seems to have been well known to entrepreneurs in the North Pacific and travelers worldwide. While staying overnight in a small Koryak village on the north coast of Penzhina Bay, De Lesseps was told by his Koryak hosts that they had seen Englishmen some years before and were curious why the French had not visited earlier (1790, 2:29).

Later in the nineteenth century and well into the twentieth such travelers' tales continued to be published, the most celebrated being George Kennan's adventure story *Tent Life in Siberia* (1986 [1870]), which went through fourteen printings before being expanded in 1910 and is still in print today. More common were the sober accounts by government administrators, either dispatched to the peninsula for the express purpose of updating the government on current conditions or publishing comments they noted down in parallel to their official duties while traveling in the region (Dittmar 2004 [1856], 2004 [1890]; Margaritov 1899; Sil'nitskii 1897, 1902). The common theme running through these reports is the wealth of natural resources, especially fish (salmon), and the lack of infrastructure and need for greater involvement of Russians in Kamchatkan fishing. Sil'nitskii points out that Japanese fishermen had already set up extensive processing facilities in Kamchatka by the beginning of the twentieth century, and he warned that "most of the fish wealth of this country is moving through the hands of the Japanese, since we are not taking any measures to protect our wealth from the Japanese, and at the same time we are not developing the Russian fishing industry on Kamchatka" (Sil'nitskii 1902:23). This situation only grew worse for Russia after the treaty of Port Arthur in 1905, where they formally ceded to the Japanese fishing rights in Sakhalin, the Kuriles, and Kamchatka. The general view of indigenous cultures in these reports is virtually unchanged from that of Krasheninnikov. Indeed, most of them cite Krasheninnikov either to illustrate further cultural "loss" or, on the contrary, lack of change. This choice between cultural stasis or cultural loss betrays a view of indigenous traditions that runs throughout the nineteenth and twentieth centuries, to which I return in subsequent chapters.

The Professionalization of Ethnography

In the nineteenth century we see a change from explorers to exiles as ethnographers. From the beginning of the nineteenth century well-educated (and usually leftist-thinking) political exiles had been part of Siberian society, but it was not until the 1890s, under the aegis of the philanthropist Sibiryakov, that this educated elite conducted systematic and careful research about the people with whom they had been living for some time (Shimkin 1990:41). Bogoras and Jochelson are numbered among this first cohort of eight researchers who knew local languages and cultures from years of firsthand participant-observation a generation before Malinowski was "exiled" in the Trobriands. The other noteworthy exile-scholar was Lev Shternberg, whose first publications caught the notice of Friedrich Engels. Shternberg eventually became the first professor and dean of ethnography in the Soviet Union at Leningrad State University shortly after the Bolshevik Revolution (Shimkin 1990:42; see also Kan 2001). Shternberg and Bogoras are generally considered the founders of Russian/Soviet anthropology, although their reputations suffered during the height of Stalinism in the 1940s and 1950s (Slezkine 1994a).

In Kamchatka even Bogoras's fiction, such as the novel *Eight Tribes*, is referred to as an authoritative description of Koryak and Chukchi traditions at the turn of the twentieth century.

Vladimir Jochelson was an elder compatriot of Bogoras. He had lived some years among the Yukaghir on the Kolyma River and Boas selected him to supervise the Siberian party of the Jesup expedition (Freed et al. 1988; Vakhtin 2001b). In 1900 and 1901 he traveled among the Koryak collecting artifacts for the American Museum of Natural History and documenting Koryak culture. Just as Stepan Krasheninnikov did, Vladimir Jochelson assumes Koryaks as a coherent object of study and then goes on to define them. He opens his chapter on "The Koryak Tribe" with a discussion of ethnonyms, explaining that the Russian word *koriak* comes either from a Yukaghir word or from a Cossack understanding of the word for deer in a southeastern Koryak dialect (1908:406). Significantly, Jochelson documents that "the Chukchi call the Koryak tañngitan; and the latter, in turn, call the Chukchee by the same name" (1908:407). He glosses the Koryak word *tañngitan* as "warrior" and mentions that Lower Kolymsk Yukaghir also use a word for the Chukchi that can be glossed as "warrior." This seems to suggest that ethnic groups are defined by those that attack one another. However, this would not work (nor does Jochelson suggest such a criterion), because there are records of warfare among various groups he considers to be Koryak, and "every stranger was regarded as a possible enemy" (1908:761). Jochelson concludes his description of Koryak self-appellation by admitting that groups most often referred to themselves as a group and to others by the place in which they reside (1908:408). Thus there are "Taigonos People" and "People of the West."

After ethnonyms, the secondary means of distinction for Jochelson was physical type, which includes cephalic index (head shape), stature, hair and eye color, and skin color (1908:408–12). His description of skin color includes contrasting the "bronze scale of tints" found among Koryaks with the "light yellow (the color of a lemon-rind)" of the Tungus and the European "bluish-milky or rosy-white color" (1908:412). Jochelson does not present comparative data to define Koryaks as a physical type but again assumes the group and then describes its characteristics. This is conceptually the same move as in Krasheninnikov's (1972:283) remarks on the differences between physical types of reindeer-herding and settled Koryaks, where he also states that Chukchi most resemble Itelmen physically. Jochelson's uncritical discussion of physical type in Kamchatka is remarkable, considering that his wife Dina Brodsky wrote her doctoral dissertation on the topic soon after completing the expedition, although he confesses that most of the data had yet to be processed (Jochelson 1908:409).[16]

Jochelson reserves his presentation of the territory inhabited by the Koryak for a separate chapter, following the one on "The Koryak Tribe," although he had already described the general outlines of the territory of the Koryak in the very first pages of that volume (1908:383f.). He discusses reindeer-herding nomads separately from settled communities. His description of territorial groups uses yasak "clans" as defined by the Russian administration as a starting point (1908:431ff.). These "clans" (*rody* in Russian) were administratively defined groups and more or less arbitrarily imposed on Koryaks by Russian tax collectors (Gapanovich 1932:44). In several instances Jochelson notes that people supposedly "belonging" to one "clan" had moved and were living in a different area. Nearly a century later I found a similar pattern of mobility—persons or small groups (family, brothers, etc.) could often be found living in villages far from where they grew up and still maintaining kinship and friendship ties among several villages. This mobility was and is common in Kamchatka generally and is part of the continual mixing and reconfiguration of social and linguistic groups, further confounding any historical coherence of ethnic or culture groups over time.

Ethnographers and Soviet Missionaries Govern Ethnic Groups

After the Soviets consolidated their hold on power and established regular administration over Kamchatka and the surrounding areas in the 1920s, the first requirement was a scientific knowledge of the people at the farthest reaches of the empire and their socioeconomic situation, needs, and wants. Vladimir Bogoras and Lev Shternberg trained the first generation of Soviet ethnographers and together developed a devoted following of students and colleagues. Thus Siberian peoples and cultures lay at the foundation of Soviet ethnography, just as American Indian culture played a foundational role in the development of American anthropology. The anthropologists embraced the Revolution by committing themselves and their careers to the development of socialism among the peoples of the Russian Far East and to improving their lot (Slezkine 1994a). Bogoras had participated in the Jesup North Pacific Expedition with Jochelson, and he maintained a professional relationship with Franz Boas and other scholars abroad. Both men regularly presented papers in German or English at anthropological conferences in Europe and the United States, and Bogoras contributed articles to the *American Anthropologist* and the *Handbook of Native American Indian Languages*.[17] In spite of that, Bogoras and Jochelson use a theory of culture more akin to Edward Tylor and James Frazer and seemed little influenced by the later work of Boas and his students. Their theory of culture focused on the existence of "survivals" present among contemporary primitives, defining them as such. These survivals marked groups in the Soviet Far East as exemplars of earlier stages of cultural development, and the primitives were presented in terms of a notion of "backwardness" that had come into general intellectual fashion near the end of the nineteenth century (Slezkine 1994a:125). The backward state of the natives was not considered to be necessarily bad, since it portrayed those individuals as a personality type close to primitive communism and thus made them seem ripe for development into "socialist men and women."

Bogoras's and Shternberg's students were the first wave of professionally trained ethnographic researchers to work in the Russian Far East. Their education emphasized long and intimate firsthand knowledge of the people in question, and theories followed the common evolutionary perspectives in circulation at the time. Bruce Grant summarizes the career of Bogoras's star student, Erukhim Kreinovich, who went to Sakhalin Island to assess the situation among the Nivkhi and begin socialist cultural construction (1995:76–79, 96–99, 104). Another prize student, Sergei Stebnitskii, was sent to Kamchatka to study the language; he established a writing system and began education programs in Koryak so that people could learn and embrace Soviet ideology. Stebnitskii's academic work was mostly linguistic descriptions of Koryak but also includes ethnographic descriptions (1930, 1937, 1938a, 1938b, 2000).

Soviet anthropology intensified the Russian tradition of producing information for state policy (Hirsch 2005:59ff.). The careful delineation of language groups and indigenous territories and the proper differentiation of groups from one another were the main preoccupations of Soviet anthropologists over the course of the twentieth century. Ethnographers participated in the front line of government policy implementation. Bogoras understood anthropology as a practical science with immediate applications for improving the lot of its subjects; as he wrote in 1925, "We must send to the North not scholars but missionaries, missionaries of the new culture and new Soviet statehood" (Bogoras in Slezkine 1994a:159–60). Culture was material, and like any other material, it could be molded, transformed, or changed into the desired configuration. The Soviet "missionaries" had an objective similar to that of Spanish missionaries in early colonial society: to capture "native minds and souls" (Rafael 1992:64). Although Soviets disavowed any interest in "souls," native minds were a high priority. Also as in missionary activity in the Philippines and elsewhere (including Orthodoxy in Siberia), linguistic exchange was a key part of the program; the translation of Soviet (Christian) dogma into local languages was essential.[18] Soviet proselytization was largely successful. Indigenous communists quickly emerged from the tundra and taiga to carry the banner as local administrators, teachers, and writers (Bloch 2004; Gray 2005; Hirsch 2005).

The civil war fell especially hard upon the small ethnic minorities of Siberia and the Far East. Direct experience of combat was rare, although there was some fighting between White and Red forces on Kamchatka. More common was material privation due to state neglect, exacerbated by increased exploitation by local Russian traders who had become agents of the state under Soviet rule. Ethnographers were fearful that these peoples would be wiped off the face of the earth inside the space of a generation. Playing to Communist goals of industrialization and improving production, ethnographers demanded that the government save indigenous peoples or risk losing any chance of securing the vast mineral, timber, and fur wealth of the Far North and East (Sergeev 1955:215f.). Using an argument similar to those made in the nineteenth century for native policy reform, they asserted that only these people, long adapted to the severe local conditions, could show the

Soviets how to adapt and work in the environs of Siberia and the Far East. In Kamchatka the Soviets practiced a contradictory approach of remaking indigenous primitives into modern socialists, while "promoting" native culture. Koryak reindeer herders, for example, were categorized as primitive because of their nomadic way of life and lack of social differentiation. Reindeer herders in northeast Asia have a personal understanding of property—each deer has a personal human owner, and deer and people are interconnected through webs of kinship, spiritual power, and daily practices. Soviet collectivization of deer was at first voluntary, then compulsory. Owning and herding deer lay at the core of these people's way of life and their symbolic universe (King 2002b, 2003). The Soviets believed that they could destroy this symbolic universe—organized by connections between deer and people—replacing it with a European symbol system in the form of Marxism-Leninism, and still promote "native culture" and reindeer herding.

When Stalin's Terror swept across the Union and into Kamchatka, natives and ethnographers alike were repressed. Rich herders were arrested, shamans were deported, and ethnographers disappeared. Bogoras and Shternberg were deemed not real Marxists, let alone Bolsheviks. Their work was discredited, although Shternberg's to a lesser extent, due to his integral role in the development of Engels's theory of primitive communism in *Origin of the Family, Private Property, and the State*. Several of their students were repressed. In 1937 Kreinovich was arrested, beaten, and tortured. He spent ten years in one of the notorious Magadan prison camps but lived to be rehabilitated and set free (Grant 1995:104). Stebnitskii and his junior colleague Georgi Korsakov, with whom he collaborated on a Koryak dictionary, were not so lucky; both were killed in the war, Korsakov in 1941 and Stebnitskii in 1942. Stebnitskii is now honored in Kamchatka as a hero of the Koryak people

(Kosygin 1993), and the work of Bogoraz-Tan (as he is known in Russia) is almost reverentially cited as hard fact by native and non-native scholars alike.[19]

Socialist Deep Structure vs. Ethnic Surfaces:
A Soviet Theory of Culture

At the Sixteenth Party Congress in 1930 Stalin asserted that "in actual fact, the period of dictatorship of the proletariat and the work of socialist construction in the Soviet Union is a period of prosperity for the national cultures, socialistic in content and national in form" (Kuoljok 1985:13). This evolved into a dialectic of encouraging ethnic differences in order to promote social development toward communism (Hirsch 2005:13ff.). Soviet logic held that encouraging diversification in "national forms," such as language, music, way of life, and economic specialties (e.g., reindeer herding, fishing, cotton growing) would draw these different peoples closer together over time in an increasingly homogeneous socialist state. In this formulation, culture figures as extraneous meaning sprinkled on top of a material or sociopolitical foundation, much as salt is sprinkled on bland potatoes or sugar on bitter medicine (Grant 1995:82).

Although "form" is superstructural (in Marx's terminology), it is not simply the effect of infrastructural causes. The form influences the content by enabling or hindering the content's expression. Moreover, the specific forms of the socialist economy had to be chosen to fit the existing cultural forms of the population in question. For example, having traditional maritime hunters herd reindeer or reindeer herders go fishing was not successful (Antropova 1971:128–51). The same content (socialist economic relations) can be had with varying forms appropriate to the circumstances: traditional reindeer herders collectively herding deer in a scientifically rationalized manner and traditional maritime hunters and fishermen hunting and fishing in an industrialized collective enterprise. Policy was supposedly informed by ethnographic research, which followed a theory of culture that found fuller formal expression only from the beginning of the 1950s (e.g., Gurvich and Kuzakov 1960; see also Banks 1996).

The internal characteristics and variation of "national forms" were elaborated in the Soviet theory of ethnos (*etnos*), which became codified in the 1950s and 1960s.[20] Bromley provides a succinct definition of ethnos as "a historically evolved group of people having a unique inherent set of common and stable cultural (including language) and psychic features as well as self-consciousness, including *awareness* of their separate identity different from other similar entities, and their own self-given name or ethnonym" (1977:41, emphasis in original). Language, territory, and self-consciousness were the critical features defining an ethnos. This is a reifying and essentialist understanding of culture. Bromley (1977:11) seems to understand "culture in the broad meaning of the word," embracing all areas of human experience, a view similar to Tylor's in the nineteenth century (Stocking 1968:74). However, culture as a term rarely functions this way in Soviet-era Siberian ethnographies. More commonly, it functions as a synonym for ethnos. Thus the Koryak ethnos is the carrier of Koryak culture: one people, one culture.

Although Bromley examines the problem of the lack of fit between the theory of ethnos and what ethnographers find on the ground, he does not reject the concept's analytic utility (unlike Barth's [1969] rejection of ethnicity as a natural fact). If one can see that a given language and a discrete culture do not always overlap on the same bounded territory on a map, how does an ethnos achieve "ethnic unity"? (Bromley 1977:24). The solution to the problem of defining an ethnic community in objective terms is endogamy (Bromley 1977:25). Thus ethnicity is turned into race, a biological category. For example,

Kozlov's (1988) investigation of "ethnic processes" (ethnic change), is primarily a statistical examination of mixed marriages between ethnically defined populations, racialized into statistically significant categories (see also Grant 1995:16).

The Soviet theory of culture remains remarkably persistent. The encyclopedic *Peoples of Siberia* (Levin and Potapov 1964 [1956]) is presented within this framework. Canonical ethnographies like Antropova's (1971) *Kul'tura i byt koriakov* (Koryak culture and everyday life) and Taksami's (1967) *Nivkhi* assume that their subject matter is the ethnos named in the title. Theoretical revisions critique the typologization of ethnic communities into a hierarchy of ethnosocial entities but do not challenge the basic ideas behind the ethnos (Schindler 1991:73). In the post-Soviet opening up of Russian anthropology to other theoretical frameworks, this simplistic understanding of culture and ethnicity has come under fire. Tishkov (1992, 2003) rejected the concept of ethnos but has not questioned the basic assumptions behind the idea of ethnos: existence of an identifiable, bounded group, with a separate language, way of life, and unique history, corresponding to residence in a "homeland" or particular territory. Elfimov's (1997) more recent interviews with four other leading Russian ethnographers demonstrate that the idea of ethnos presented above continues to be important to Russian ethnographic research and analysis. Most interesting for me, ethnos is the operative theory of culture in Kamchatka today.[21] The Soviet theory of ethnos has "filtered down" to mainstream society, as becomes clear throughout this book.

Culture Groups in Theory and Practice

The manifestations of ethnos on the ground and the discrepancies between the preceding definitions and social "reality" led to the development of an unduly complicated typology of social forms (Kuoljok 1985). At the bottom were tribes. Defined much like an ethnos (although particular details were disputed among scholars), they looked like a clan- or lineage-based society. Tribes were small and all members shared common descent. The intermediate category was the *narodnost'* ("nationality" or "a peopleness"—a neologism developed by nineteenth-century Russian ethnographers [Hirsch 2005:36ff.]). A *narodnost'* was a precapitalist, class-stratified society, most often with a developed state structure, common language, and national religion. The top tier was reserved for the "nation," which had distinct social classes, a state structure, a large population (millions), and a strong national feeling. In Kamchatka, Paren' or Palana Koryaks would be examples of tribes, but "the Koryak" is a *narodnost'*, hence the Koryak Autonomous Okrug.

These categories force people into the Koryak group or the Russian group or the Even group but do not allow for multiple or shifting identities for individuals or fluid movement among populations, let alone hint at the kind of creativity in working with traditions that I saw every day in Kamchatka. Such pigeonholing parallels state policy, where ethnicity was stamped on every person's identification card. Children's ethnicity was determined by that of their parents and thus became biologized like race in the United States: "By the end of the [1930s] every Soviet child inherited his nationality at birth: individual ethnicity had become a biological category impervious to cultural, linguistic, or geographical change" (Slezkine 1994b:444). If children had parents of different ethnicities, then they were allowed to choose only between the two ethnicities of the parents and not, for example, identify with an ethnicity defining the context in which they grew up or even that of a grandparent, if a parent had had ethnically mixed parents (Karklins 1986:37ff.). This policy required that each ethnos be properly identified, and their own self-appellations be used. Lamuts became Evens, Gilyaks became Nivkhs, and Koryaks became Nymylans (for a time, at least). The Soviet obsession with getting the names right was connected to the practical problem of how to write a person's ethnicity on his or her identity card. In Kamchatka the term *mestnyi* (local) was used for an indigenous Kamchatkan person. Specific ethnonyms like Koryak or Nymylan or Alutor or Chavchuven are associated with real differences in dress, ways of speaking or making a living, but the correspondences are never neat, and there is significant variation within the group of people who may be identified (or self-identify) as Koryak or Alutor or Chukchi. Thus while the use of ethnonyms is interesting, it is a waste of time to try to draw up a system of names corresponding to real groups that are internally coherent and have significant differences among them.

The best known and used Koryak ethnography in Kamchatka is by Valentina Antropova (1971).[22] She wrote the chapters on Koryaks and Itelmen for the monumental *Peoples of Siberia* (Levin and Potapov 1964) based on published and unpublished sources. Her monograph on the Koryak includes material collected during three summers of fieldwork in Kamchatka. Her book was used as a textbook in the Palana Teachers' College and is used as a basic reference in the only other book about Koryaks by a Western anthropologist (Rethmann 2001). Antropova's introduction covers (in order) the history of scholarship, population, language, names and self-consciousness, and "local groups" (1971:3–20). Thus the Koryak ethnos is established by historical precedent and the conjunction of a bounded population speaking closely related languages on a determinate territory and self-conscious of their own identity. The curious thing is that her own discussion points out that several different communities are being referred to as "Koryak" in these terms. Where Krasheninnikov and Bogoras described a single language, Antropova describes the scholarly consensus on Koryak as three different languages—Chavchuven, Alutor, and Kerek. Soviet linguists have refined these categories into more specific ones. Chavchuven and Alutor are themselves divided into several different dialects (Antropova 1971:16). Although the name *Koryaks* is attested to in documents from the seventeenth century, a sort of validation by precedent, scholars have never been able to identify a single ethnonym (or any one trait) covering all people so labeled. That is why the early Soviets sought to replace the term *Koryak*, supposedly referring only to deer herders (from the Koryak root *qor-* for deer), with the term *Nymylan*, but the latter had a parallel weakness in that it refers only to villagers. Thus *Nymylan* was no better than *Koryak* and lacked any history of local, administrative, and scholarly usage; it never caught on and was abandoned by the 1940s. Use of the term *Nymylan* in Kamchatka now refers to maritime Koryaks living along the Okhotsk in villages like Lesnaya and Paren', especially. On the Pacific side of Kamchatka, people used Nymylan only occasionally, and instead *Koryak* or *Alutor* were more common. In Soviet writings on the language the 1930s and 1940s, the name *Nymylan* referred to the variant of Koryak language spoken by reindeer herders (e.g., Korsakov 1940, 1952; Korsakov and Stebnitskii 1939; Stebnitskii 1934, 1937).

Since Atlasov's first descriptions, Koryaks have been divided into two groups defined primarily in terms of economic focus and residential patterns: nomadic reindeer herders versus settled hunters and fishers. In the twentieth century ethnographers began to record the economic practices of the Alutors; they had a more diversified economy that incorporated small herds of deer with fishing and hunting. Antropova writes much about this, and she implicitly creates a third, mixed economic category of Koryaks. Indeed, Antropova's thoroughness in describing the ethnographic literature on northern Kamchatka gives the reader a remarkable sense of the diversity among communities referred to as Koryak and the fluidity among these communities: "Aside from the indicated nine local groups, there were settled Koryak populations, which even in the end of the nineteenth century were difficult to count in this or that group" (Antropova 1971:19). The picture that emerges is a complex pattern of interwoven continua in language, economic practices, beliefs, material culture, and daily practices.

The territory occupied by Koryaks is not contiguous or easily bounded. Krasheninnikov, Jochelson, and Antropova all note that Koryaks and Itelmens lived in roughly the same area in the central part of the peninsula and that in the north Chukchi, Koryak, Even, and Yukaghir people migrated in nomadic bands in areas that could be only roughly generalized. Of course particular social groups were and are associated with specific territories, but these groups do not necessarily correspond to single or even multiple cultures. Reindeer herders have a sense of territory and pasturage, but this did not follow hard and fast boundaries.[23] Territories not only overlapped, but one could find people originally from one culture living in a community of another culture. Jochelson, Antropova, and contemporary ethnographers in Russia and Kamchatka refer to this as "assimilation," thus accounting for movement of individuals without questioning the boundedness of their culture groups or the categories. Assimilation assumes the existence of bounded groups *a priori*, defining who is in and who is out, instead of starting with an analysis of people and communities and examining the social and cultural dynamics of interaction among persons (human and nonhuman).

The most likely venue for the political mobilization of ethnic and cultural identity in Kamchatka would be through the actions of the Association of Indigenous Minority Peoples of the North, Siberia, and Far East of the Russian Federation, officially known in English as the Russian Association of Indigenous Peoples of the North (RAIPON).[24] The Association, as it is known in Kamchatka, was founded in the twilight of the Soviet Union under the leadership of the famous Nivkh writer Victor Sangi. The first federal-level conference was held in Moscow in 1990, and there have been five more since then. The Association's organization follows a familiar Soviet pattern: native people in each village get together and elect delegates to meet at the rayon center. In the rayon centers delegates are chosen to represent local interests at the okrug congress (s"ezd) in Palana. I attended the Third Okrug Association Congress in Palana in May 1997, where a new president of the Koryak Okrug Association was elected.[25]

According to people with whom I talked, the movement behind the Association was initially strong and resulted in native Kamchatkans being able to air their complaints about the appalling and previously unpublicized social and economic conditions common among indigenous people of the Russian North. There were ambitious plans for legal change and special recognition of indigenous northerners in the Federal Duma, but the most important aspects of that legislation became bogged down. At the okrug level many would-be activists were already disillusioned with the Okrug Association in 1995. Some dedicated individuals were (and are) working in Palana, Ossora, Tilichiki, and other parts of Kamchatka to advance native causes through political and legal channels, but they cannot muster much support among fellow *mestnye*.

The Koryak Autonomous Okrug had less success than its Chukchi neighbor in gaining administrative autonomy from its encompassing oblast, although politicians of several different inclinations, from communists to native activists, assured me that the KAO had a measure of administrative autonomy from the Kamchatka Oblast and that it would eventually have direct and complete relations with the Center in Moscow, like all other federation-level territories.[26] In terms of the post-Soviet political logic, the Koryak Okrug's existence was predicated on the vitality of the Koryak nation, although some incomer local politicians openly denied this, insisting that the name Koryak Autonomous was an obsolete survival of 1930s Soviet nationalities policy. They claimed that the KAO was simply an administrative territory in Russia like any other province. Most native activists resisted these claims, asserting legal rights granted to indigenous Siberian peoples under Russian federal law. As I discuss in chapter 5 on the role of Koryak language education and okrug administration, newcomer administrators and native activists sometimes cooperated to support special programs for the indigenous population. The special status of the KAO as an ethnic territory is also reflected in cultural education (examined in chapters 4 and 5), state sponsorship of ethnic arts (*narodnaia tvorchestvo*, discussed in the following two chapters), and special programs supporting traditional economic activities such as reindeer herding or salmon fishing (King 2003).

The entire population of indigenous people was only about one-third of the total Koryak Autonomous Okrug population in the late 1990s. In those days of new Russian democracy, one would think that symbols of indigenous culture or programs directed to indigenous people's concerns would be the purview of a small number of Koryak activists. There is no Koryak national party, although there was an incipient Koryak "nationalizing state," to use Brubaker's (1996) term, in the form of the Koryak Autonomous Okrug, but native people in political office have not acted much differently from non-natives. The last appointed governor, Sergei Leushkin, was condemned by many for not paying wages and letting basic infrastructure fall apart. People had high hopes for indigenous issues when the first democratically elected governor of the okrug, Itelmen Valentina Bronevich, took office in 1996. Her election as governor of the KAO in 1996 presented the best opportunity for politics and activism grounded in cultural identities. It did not happen. Many complained that her term saw only worse times for natives in Kamchatka and that she merely took care of her cronies, irrespective of ethnicity, but this never led to a denial of her nativeness, even though she seemed to have "left" the okrug and was living more in the main oblast city of Petropavlovsk-Kamchatskiy. Indeed, people used her as an example of native people not sticking together and a reminder that people cannot be judged by their ethnicity or where they were born but only by what they do. Bronevich lost her reelection bid in 2001 to the former director of the Koryak mining enterprise, Vladimir Loginov, who was born in Kamchatka to a famous Kamchadal name, but he was eventually removed by President Putin in connection with misusing okrug funds. Since my first trip in 1995, every winter continued to be the hardest in memory in terms of social and economic conditions. The winter of 1998–99 saw the most people going hungry and doing without electricity or sufficient heating. The winter of 1999–2000 was no better and even saw many cases of dysentery in Palana. In the twenty-first century, conditions have at least not worsened, except in Olyutorskiy Rayon, which was struck in April 2006 by a devastating 7.9 earthquake that destroyed heating, water, and power infrastructure in most villages, including the administrative center of Tilichiki and the airport across the bay in Korf. This resulted in the closure of Korf as a residence and the resettlement of hundreds of people to Petropavlovsk and other towns in the okrug.[27]

The "national question" in Kamchatka is about economic and moral decline among the indigenous people, which is common across the North (Pika 1999). They had supposedly achieved self-determination but lacked decent housing, social services, and economic opportunities. People in the Koryak Okrug expressed their frustration at this state of affairs (common across Siberia) by never reelecting a governor (rare in Russia), and in the autumn of 2005 they voted overwhelmingly to get rid of the entire okrug administration by merging with Kamchatka Oblast to form a new province called Kamchatka Krai.[28] Considering that nearly half of the KAO population is indigenous, and that about three-quarters turned out to vote and almost 90 percent of those voted in favor of the merger (higher than turnout and support were in Kamchatka Oblast), it is clear that cultural identity is not a very effective means for political organization in Kamchatka.[29] Ethnicity is not a status group or party in the Weberian sense, certainly not in Kamchatka. There is no group called Koryak doing things *as a group*. Ethnic identity in Kamchatka is not primordial. It is malleable. People change it, even on their passports, most easily when a person registers for his own identity card at the age of sixteen. This contradicts the Soviet/Russian understanding of culture as codified in the theory of ethnos, and it weakens native political activities vis-à-vis Russian administrators.

Local people often think of their culture in explicit terms that echo the theory of ethnos, although the technical term *etnos* was rarely used, *kul'tura* (culture) or *nashie byty* (our customs) being more common. However, as I argue in subsequent chapters, many native people in Kamchatka talk about their culture in ways that seem to express an unconscious theory of culture more similar to that articulated in cultural anthropology than to that of Soviet ethnography. Many native people do not think of their culture in terms of encompassing hierarchies or bounded groups. They have a more localized, nontaxonomic understanding of continuity and difference, comparable to that reported from many other regions of the world, including Africa, Amazonia, and Melanesia. While the distinction between incomers and "locals" is not fluid, it is also not taxonomic. Incomers can cease to be incomers without becoming *mestnye*. As in my example with the usage of *melagetaŋen*, the newcomer-local distinction is not totalizing. There are people who are "ours" although not necessarily "us."[30]

2. Genuine and Spurious Culture in Kamchatka

A performance incorporating native or local (*mestnye*) themes was organized jointly by the okrug art school and the House of Culture to celebrate Earth Day 1997. The concert consisted of a series of dance routines and skits by students, punctuated by narration about humanity and our relationship to the earth. Koryaks and natives were portrayed as close to nature, living in harmony with the climate, its seasons, and the ecology of the region, and contrasted with the environmental depredations of Western, urban culture. After one particularly nice performance of (more or less) native-looking children doing a Koryak-looking dance, loud, Western dance music took over before the Koryak song ended and before they were completely off the stage. A girl dressed in apparently urban apparel carried a small boom box and set it center stage forward. The stage filled with youth wearing what looked like a rural teen's imagination of urban fashions worn in the 'hood. Card playing, some attempts at break dancing, tumbling by some boys (stylized fights), and general mayhem ruled the stage while the music blared on. They left garbage behind. The native actor who had played a caveman in an earlier scene entered the stage, this time in a Koryak costume (he appeared in several performances, drumming and singing for student dances), picked up the trash, and kicked some of it off to the side before the next segment. I open with this event because of the clear primitivist ideology expressed in the performance and shared by the audience members I talked with afterwards. Native Kamchatkan cultures were presented and understood as primitive (*pervobytnyi*) and close to nature (*priroda*), and they were thus positioned as morally *superior* to the destructive and morally suspect urban culture connected to Russian/European music and dance. In many ways this use of Koryak culture to critique dominant Russian culture parallels attacks by Sapir and other Boasians upon mainstream American culture (Sapir 1949 [1924]; Stocking 1992). The striking thing about symbols of native culture in Kamchatka, however, is the salience of dance. Native dance forms are synecdoches of native cultures in general. Thus a Koryak dance indexes Koryak culture and tradition; an Eveny dance indexes Eveny culture, and so on. This indexical use of dance is pervasive in Kamchatka and seems to have a long history.

Folk dances seem to have been presented for a very long time in Kamchatka as particularly salient demonstrations of local culture appropriate for visiting guests. The eighteenth-century traveler Jean Baptiste-Barthelemy De Lesseps describes one such dance in the *ostrog* of Karagui (Karaga village): "To divert our attention, it was proposed to us to try the abilities of a celebrated female dancer, who was a Kamtschadale, and lived in this ostrog" (1790, 1:240).[1] The woman apparently went into a shamanic trance following an energetic performance, but the Frenchman, who was usually sympathetic in his descriptions, was nonplussed: "In spite of the praises that were lavished upon the talents of these actors, the scene, I confess, afforded me no amusement, but on the contrary, considerable disgust" (De Lesseps 1790, 1:243). Captain John Cochrane, an Englishman in service to the tsar, was similarly regaled with a demonstration of local dances:

> Napanas contains 8 dwellings and an excellent Toion, who induced the people under his command to show me the national dance. The poor fellows willingly obliged me, showing the improvements they have made upon the practice of bears, or rather, perhaps, on that of goats. The dance consists in a variety of distortions of features and limbs, all doubtless derived from the ridiculous and wanton customs of their ancestors. The dance of the Cossacks is equally bad, if not worse. (Cochrane 1825, 2:13)

It is not surprising that the good captain was neither impressed by the mimetic faculties of Kamchatkan natives nor entertained by their choreography. Peter Dobell, who was in Kamchatka in 1812, about nine years before Cochrane, provides a similar description of two Kamchadal women who "performed in a manner that excited my admiration and astonishment. Every feature of the face and muscle of the body seemed in motion at the same instant; . . . as if seized with a sort of frenzy. . . . The whole frame was violently agitated, and distorted into a hundred different postures; some of the gestures were by no means ungraceful, but, at the same time, not altogether decent" (Dobell 1830:78). This last comment explains much of the nineteenth- and twentieth-century Europeans' reactions to Kamchatkan dances, which often entail body movements that Europeans find lascivious. Although not all the moves were explicitly connected to human sexuality, many were, and in this respect indigenous Kamchatkans had the jump on European trends in popular dance by a couple of centuries. I find it fascinating that local hosts were ready to present folk dances to distinguished travelers as a display of their culture. It should be clear then, that the Soviets were building upon existing forms when they seized upon dancing as a cultural "trait" that could be made safe for ideologically appropriate displays of multiculturalism, and it continues to be the hallmark of Kamchatkan indigenous culture, readily performed locally and abroad as a demonstration of the creativity, distinctiveness, and continuing vitality of Koryak and other indigenous Kamchatkan cultures.

For a final example I personally experienced, the librarian in Middle Pakhachi volunteered to round up some of her friends and relatives to demonstrate traditional dancing for my video camera, and she organized a dance party one afternoon in her reindeer-skin tent (yayaŋa), which her family set up on the tundra at the edge of the village for their elderly mother. She was interested in helping me learn about "native culture and traditions," as I phrased it. The librarian personally demonstrated her deceased father's dance, for which he had been famous. My friends in Middle Pakhachi insisted that I visit another elderly man whom they considered to be one of the best dancers in the village. After a short visit and some token gifts (tobacco and tea), he readily obliged to dance for us and my camera.

Anthropologists have been studying dancing for a long time, but this has usually been as an aspect of expressive culture or incidental to rituals (e.g., Bateson 1936; Boas 1897; Lowie 1935; Schieffelin 1976). A focused study of dancing was marginal to social science disciplines until recently (Ness 1992:2; Spencer 1985; Thomas 1995:3). Dance theory grew out of a tradition in the humanities and is now a key part of cultural studies for its focus on the body, kinesthetics, and "embodiment" (Daly 2002; Desmond 1997; Dils and Albright 2001; Dyck and Archetti 2003; Graff 1997; Martin 1998; McNeil 1996). Gender, ideology, power, and identity are common analytical categories in dance studies. It is no longer possible to describe the anthropology of dance as marginal or ignored with the recent growth of publications (Buckland 1999; Doi 2001; Farnell 1995, 1999; Hughes-Freeland 2008; Kisliuk 1998; Mathur 2002; Pegg 2001; Royce 2004; Sutton 2002; Wulff 2007), including the revised republication of two key theoretical works (Royce 2002 [1977]; D. Williams 2004 [1991]). My discussion here, however, concerns speaking about dancing and not dancing itself. I am therefore interested in dance as a symbol in discourse about indigenous culture and tradition in Kamchatka. In Peircean terms, it is an iconic index, containing elements of mimesis or resemblance as well as a direct connection to other things, such as social relationships, ethnic identity, and a cultural epistemology.

I have found that nearly everyone who is physically able enjoys dancing and watching others dance in sundry venues. People I talked to in Kamchatka readily identify dances, dance moves, and dance rhythms in terms of cultural styles. There are no generic or culturally unmarked dances. Discotheque dancing is classed as "Western," or "European," or (when talking to the ethnographer) as "your style." Western dance forms are popular among children and youth, but so are dance forms attached to local traditions. Indigenous or, more commonly, "local" (*mestnye*) dances and moves are classed as being associated with one of the many cultural styles in Kamchatka, which include Itelmen, Even, Chukchi, Nymylan, Chauwchu, and Koryak (labels that are not necessarily mutually exclusive). Regional and village styles can be identified and cataloged by artists, local folklorists, and ethnographers (Zhornitskaia 1994).

Dancing and dance groups are often a key part of cultural revival movements by indigenous peoples across the North (Bogeyaktuk and Steve 2004; Crowell 2004; Fienup-Riordan

1996; Ikuta 2007, 2010; Krupnik 2005; Shnirelman 2001; M. Williams 1996) and around the world (Doi 2001; Kaeppler et al. 1993; Kinase 2002; Pegg 2001; Royce 2002; Yamada 2001). This is due in no small part to the ability of dancing to condense a great deal of symbolic power into a dramatic spectacle. At the same time, dancing indexes much that is typical of ordinary forms of movement in the culture (Hewitt 2004; Ikuta 2010; Ness 1992). It is at once sacred and secular, sublime and banal. Changes in dance forms are indexical of larger cultural change (Doi 2001:20). Dance and professional dancers have much greater esteem in Russia and the former Soviet Union than in most parts of the West (Doi 2001:ix). Early Soviet authorities and propagandists made use of Russian enthusiasm for dance as part of their cultural construction project. Dance, both professional and amateur, was a key part of crafting new nationalities/ethnicities, "civilizing primitives," and developing a common Soviet cultural expression (Levin 1996; Pegg 2001; Swift 1968:158ff.). Dance groups were one of a very few icons of cultural difference in form across the common socialist content, and they frequently performed as representatives of their culture or "nation" in grand festivals. This use of dance groups as cultural representatives is also common among Native Americans in both North and South America (e.g., Bigenho 2002; Ikuta 2010; Krupnik 2005).

Hololo Dancing

The next chapter focuses on discourse in Palana and cultural elites performing in professional and semiprofessional venues. Russian culture permeates Soviet and post-Soviet sociopolitical organization through dominant center-periphery macrostructures. These center-periphery relationships were replicated inside the KAO to a certain extent, with Palana at the center and small native villages on the periphery, whether they are sixty or six hundred kilometers distant from the town. People in Palana regularly wondered at my presence in the administrative center because my avowed interest in Koryak culture and language should have sent me straight to a small village like Middle Pakhachi, Paren', Manily, or Lesnaya, all villages where I did indeed live and talk to people for several weeks or months at a time. Here I turn my attention to the work of a very energetic and powerful woman—Nina Nikolaevna Milgichil—and her dance troupe Fakel, in which performers are mostly children but also include three or four adults. Manily is a Soviet village, an amalgamation of several Nymylan villages along the northern coast of Penzhina Bay and reindeer-herding peoples from the interior. Unlike those in Tymlat and Lesnaya, Penzhina Bay Nymylans no longer perform annual hunting rituals, although the spirits are thanked through small offerings and gestures at the time of a kill. Manily seemed grim in the 1990s, especially as it had benefited from greater attention and infrastructural development than villages like Lesnaya and Tymlat in the 1980s. I first visited Manily for only a short time in 1998, while on my way to and from Paren', across the bay. I made a point to return to Manily for several weeks in 2001, however, and worked with Nina Nikolaevna and her husband Vasili Borisovich transcribing old recordings made in that area a century earlier. My wife and I stayed in the Milgichils' small home, and we had many opportunities to talk about life in the village, which was wracked by social anomie and had recently attracted the unwanted attention of Protestant missionaries. Milgichil explicitly connected dancing and dance troupe performances to religion and healthy souls. After reanalyzing my material, I found that this ideology of the soul-fulfilling power of dance was implicit in comments I had recorded from many others.[2]

Dancing in Koryak traditional culture was a form of recreation as well as an integral aspect of many rituals. Different rituals—for bear hunting, opening the fishing season, or the first calf of the spring, for example—had unique dances associated with them.[3] Dances associated with rituals were a key part of celebrations hosted by an individual or a household. These dances carried a sacred power that imbued the performer and his or her fellows with the strength and ability to thank spirits appropriately, show respect, or renew vital forces (see Plattet 2005). As rituals have fallen into disuse through a combination of state coercion and social acculturation to Russian/Soviet atheism, the dances associated with them have also ceased to be performed in many places (see Zhornitskaia 1994:205). Entertainment dancing was small scale—a few people in one tent or house dancing to a drum to celebrate their good mood—and I took part in several such improvised dance parties.

The Nymylan ritual of Hololo is still performed in many native villages in the KAO. The entire affair comprises a suite of ritual acts that are part of a large celebration in honor of the spirits of hunted animals—bear, snow sheep, and seal in particular. A series of dances, games, feasting, and several small rituals of thanksgiving help to send back home the spirits of the hunted animals and to thank them for successful hunts during the previous year.[4] A single household usually sponsors the ritual, although closely aligned households (especially if the men are hunting partners) may jointly sponsor a Hololo. The ritual complex is a joyous celebration, dominated by feasting, partying, playing games and sports contests, and much dancing to singing with hand-held Koryak drums. The dancing begins with the first parts of the ritual in the morning but is most active and has the most participants in the evening. I was told that dancing and partying should go on all night until the rituals at dawn the next day conclude the festival, but at the few I attended in 1997 people tired out at two or three in the morning and sent guests home to sleep for a few hours before the late autumnal sunrise.

I first traveled to Lesnaya with my folklorist colleague Aleksandra Urkachan, who has many relatives there, to attend a Hololo ritual in the autumn of 1997 and to interview elders and others about their traditions and their lives more generally.[5] I returned to Lesnaya in October 2001 for a brief follow-up visit. In December of 1997 I was invited to attend two Hololo rituals in Tymlat on the east coast (figs. 5, 6). I was traveling with several people, and our flight to Ossora was delayed by snowstorms. To my amazement, both families in Tymlat held off their celebrations until I and another folklorist from the Tigil'skiy Rayon village of Khayryuzovo arrived. In both cases the local folklorists were interested in documenting the ritual in order to work with young people. Also in both villages, people were concerned that I get it "right," get the correct interpretations and understand the importance of the various elements of the festival, and also learn something about Koryak music and dance.

People in Kamchatka make a clear distinction between native (*mestnyi*) dancing, whether Koryak, Even, or another indigenous style, and Western or disco dancing. Syncopated Koryak beats contrast with the relentless back beat of Russian pop, but even with a straight 2/4 rhythm (also traditional), the dance moves and body positions are clearly different. Many elders and middle-aged people who are acknowledged as accomplished dancers by others in the village have told me that they cannot dance to disco music. "I can't dance to your music" was typically the way this was expressed to me. These same people also complain that youth are not learning native Koryak dancing, but just jump up and down to the rhythm of the drums at Hololo and other occasions. One festival

Fig. 5. Hololo dancing in Tymlat went on nearly all night. Photo by the author.

Fig. 6. At various times during the Hololo in Tymlat, both men and women approached the sacred branches tied up in the center of the apartment and danced in ecstatic communication with animal spirits. Photo by the author.

I witnessed in Tymlat included a dance contest, in which a daughter of one of the hosts judged a three-by-eight-meter room packed with dancers and three drummers (fig. 6). She held the prize over her head and urged the dancers with repeated cries of "dance with more native moves," which was primarily directed at the teenagers who were less adept. She had asked me to videotape the whole thing, which consisted of over an hour of sweaty dancing by people from fifteen to over sixty years of age.

While many people at these festivals, especially educated or folklore-inclined individuals, considered it most appropriate that I videotape the whole affair, including hours of a tightly packed crowd dancing, others invited me to participate directly in the festivities. This Hololo was not my first attempt at Koryak dance; I had been in Kamchatka for eight months into my second trip already and had had several opportunities to practice Koryak dancing. Many people, especially elders, immediately applauded my attempts, even more so after I was given a beautiful dance parka to wear. Others, mostly people in their thirties, were more critical, pointing out how my moves were incorrect and resembled Russians or Gypsies more than Koryaks.[6] I promptly received detailed instruction in arm and hip movements, posture, and steps. This was most likely the same kind of instruction that previous generations of ethnographers and folklorists (such as Gil' and Yetneut, discussed in the following chapter) received. The first part is demonstration with repetition. The correct form was demonstrated, and I was expected to repeat it. When I failed to repeat the form to my instructor's satisfaction, he or she would grasp my arm or side or push my leg with a foot and manipulate my body directly. I should emphasize that in all cases, my "instructor" was simply a man or woman of confident ability and concerned that I get it right. At the Lesnaya

Hololo I was instructed by an elder woman, and in Tymlat I got instruction from a woman and a man, both of about my age (late twenties, early thirties).

As Plattet (2005) and others have noted, dancing is one of the central features of the Hololo ritual (see also Kasten 2004; Urkachan 2002). Joyous and enthusiastic dancing communicates gratitude, happiness, and general good feelings between predatory humans and prey animals, who are considered the more powerful persons in this relationship (e.g., see Brightman 1993; Willerslev 2007; see Ingold 2000:61ff. for a general discussion). Some of the moves are iconic of these prey animals—seals, bears, and mountain sheep. Some of the dancing indexes the intimate relationship between hunter and prey, as when men who have killed a bear the previous year take turns dancing with a bearskin. All of the dances, however, index being Koryak (or Alutor or Nymylan or *mestnyi*), or rather *knowing* Koryak traditions. My dance teachers were thus taking on the responsibility of key informant (not their term) in order that I "get it right," in their words. In Tymlat in particular, *mestnye* dancers contrasted with newcomer spectators. I was not the only one with a video camera, for there were several Russian neighbors there videotaping as well. Few of the newcomers (Russians) attempted to participate in the dancing, however, and this also serves as an index for general nonparticipation in Koryak traditions. I argue further that Hololo dancing is an index of active participation in a moral community, connecting people to one another and people to animals and nonhuman beings in relationships of mutual respect and obligations.

The morally wholesome entertainment value of Hololo and other native rituals is not lost on native activists and village administrators. Some have tried to transform this household-based ritual into a village-wide festival and spectacle under the direction of the local house of culture. Such attempts were met with silent resistance and noncooperation in Lesnaya and Palana in the 1990s and continue to be (Kasten 2005:245). In the village of Tymlat the grassroots organization Aborigenka ("aboriginal woman") has had more success, in no small part because it earns substantial amounts of money through commercial fishing activities, whereas village houses of culture no longer receive money or materials from the center for local festivals or projects. The organization aided two Tymlat households with about a thousand dollars each to produce elaborate Hololo rituals, and Aborigenka supplied additional prizes for contests held as part of the festivities. This money was spent on food for guests, new paint and wallpaper for the hosts' apartments, and other supplies related to the festivals. Other towns have had herding rituals organized by the house of culture and the local state collective farm (sovkhoz) into a several-day festival associated with reindeer herding.

Fakel—Social Insecurity and Ritual Healing

Cultural revival is at the forefront of Kamchatkan discourse on indigenous groups. Public forums are dominated by groups such as the Russian Association of Indigenous Peoples of the North (RAIPON) and local officials and activists. Small dance ensembles play a significant part at the grass roots, and they are sometimes supported through official channels with subsidies for transport to perform at festivals of one kind or another. These rare opportunities to travel outside the village provide youth with real incentives to participate. Many of these groups are led by junior elders—middle-aged men and women who may have one or two grandchildren already but also have younger children of their own and still look to senior elders for guidance in defining tradition. While dance ensembles and other practices of explicit cultural revival may superficially seem to be purely recreational, they are part of a life and death struggle in rural Siberia. Koester's (2002) convincing argument for the vital role of song and dance in maintaining a good life and well-being among Itelmen in the southern part of the okrug holds equally well among Koryaks in the northern parts. Valeri Yetneut's death was remarkable in his community but not unique or even rare. Young people all across Siberia are dying in unprecedented numbers due to violence of one form or another, often in connection with alcohol abuse (Pika 1999). Many junior elders see this violence as a symptom of a moral crisis paralleling the economic and social crises of post-Soviet Siberia.

One such junior elder is Nina Nikolaevna Milgichil, who was working as a teacher in the music school in Manily when I talked to her in 1998 and again in 2001. She has formal training in choreography and teaching dance and a folkloric curiosity. She founded and for many years directed the dance ensemble Fakel ("torch" in Russian, for one of their dances with torches). She has also made a point of documenting knowledge from the elders in her own papers and notebooks, occasionally sending information to the folklore center in Palana for publication. Milgichil has also read every book she could on the subject of Koryak culture and traditions. She is a critical reader and does not hesitate to disagree with ethnographers or other authorities when the printed version deviates from what the elders have taught her. I gave her a copy of the recent translation of part two of Jochelson's (1908) ethnography of the Koryak (Iokhel'son 1997). She found much interesting material in it that fitted well with her understanding of Koryak traditions she had learned from elders in the mid to late twentieth century. She has learned a lot from the "grandmothers" (her word), especially from her mother's sister (Amchekh), who was widely respected for her knowledge and power. Milgichil is also a synthetic thinker, looking for how details fit into wider patterns of culture. As she explained to me in 1998, "Stories are just parts of the system. One story gives you this bit [gestures with left hand], another over here [gesturing with right], but it's hard to get the whole system." She was interested in Jochelson's discussion of Koryak religion because the only book she had that addressed the subject suffered from an enduring Soviet ideology and got many of the facts wrong (Kushanov 1993).

We talked often of religion; it had become a contentious topic for her in the 1990s. Protestant missionaries had come from the main city of Petropavlovsk-Kamchatskiy with a guitar and books. They organized meetings and targeted young people with evenings of songs and sweet snacks. They talk about God, but some people seemed to have gotten strange messages. For example, one man claimed to have learned that he was not allowed to work. Another refused to repay a debt, indicating, "God forgives." Although some of these missionary organizations are associated with churches based in the United States, they have an established institutional structure in Kamchatka. As in Manily, there are active Protestant congregations (locally called *sekty*, a Russian word) in Lesnaya, Tymlat, and Palana, and in all of these places young native people seem to be the primary (although certainly not exclusive) target of missionary activities. Cynics told me that young people are willing to join any group that will feed them. As Milgichil explained to me in one conversation on Koryak religion, myth, and ritual, she understood that children want a morality, and they were not getting any at home. Their parents are from the generation raised in the Soviet *internat* (boarding school for indigenous Siberians). They were not raised and taught by parents, so they do not know how to raise and teach their own children. In a nearly anthropological vein, Milgichil explained to me how ritual is an important part of religion, morality, and self-knowledge or self-respect. Although elders have stopped observing Koryak rituals in Manily, if someone does host one, many people are interested and they attend. Conflict arises from the Protestants' total prohibition on anything associated with indigenous tradition; the missionaries inveigh against speaking traditional languages, wearing fur clothes, performing the old rituals, or even performing in ethnic dance groups. Thus these missionary groups create sometimes bitter divisions among family and friends in villages that can be as small as seven hundred people.

Drumming and dancing in Kamchatka are linked in one way or another to spirits. Nearly all indigenous dance is accompanied by a skin frame drum, and drums have at least latent spiritual connections. Drumming is never far from communicating with spirits, and thus it is closely associated with shamanic power. The dance ensemble and public performances may have been ethnic spectacles denuded of spiritual power from the Soviets' point of view, but Nina Milgichil was using them in her own efforts at cultural revival and in her private battles against missionaries and social anomie. Sounding almost Durkheimian, Milgichil told me how two different girls had hanged themselves in the previous couple of years: "Young people see no way out, and their souls are empty. No one passed them anything. They do not know anything. When they see grandmothers doing something, anything, any kind of ritual (usually in secret), they call it shamanism. It's not, but they call it that because they do not know any better." The complaint that youth are no good any more is a common one. However, Milgichil is uncharacteristic in putting responsibility for this state of affairs squarely on the shoulders of the elders. Parents and elders must take responsibility for their youth, and if young persons have empty souls, it is not primarily their fault. Equally atypical for post-Soviet Siberia,

Milgichil does not wish for someone else to take charge, that the state or "they" would help out and fix things. She is doing what she can with her own time and resources to imbue youth with a sense of the sacred that would provide them with moral grounding and self-respect.

Milgichil does not describe herself as an elder, but she does have considerable authority in matters of culture and tradition because of the extensive knowledge she has acquired firsthand from elders who have now passed away. She described herself as a teacher in the music school, and she is very much a teacher in the broadest sense of the term. Like any good teacher, she is concerned for her students as whole persons and is trying to focus the warming rays of Koryak traditions to kindle their souls. In subtle ways she proselytizes her own indigenous religion in a quiet struggle over the souls of young people in her village. In our conversations about dance, ritual, and religion, Milgichil often rejected the label *shamanism* for her beliefs and practices and preferred to call it *Koryak religion*. By using this term she asserts that the "pagan" (*iazycheskii*, a locally used Russian term) beliefs and practices of Koryak culture were just as valid as those labeled Russian Orthodoxy, Roman Catholic, or Protestant. Russians have their religion, and Koryaks have their own religion too.

Most native Kamchatkans I have encountered dislike the terms *shaman* and *shamanism* (cognates in Russian) or at least are uncomfortable with talking about their traditions in those terms. Obviously some of this discomfort is connected to the murderous Soviet repressions of individuals labeled as shamans and to general policies discouraging sacred practices of all kinds. New Christian missionaries have picked up where the Soviets left off, at least in ideological terms, and they label nearly all indigenous traditions as shamanism. The "sects" (*sekty*) prohibit their members from anything remotely smacking of shamanism, including dancing, singing, or even playing a Koryak skin drum. As a result Fakel had lost some of its most promising dancers. In 2001 Protestant missionaries had converted several teenagers once active in Fakel, and Nina Nikolaevna was concerned about the children of the village who had left her dance group.

During a conversation in which Milgichil was lamenting the negative influences of Protestant missionaries in her village, I mentioned that a positive interest in shamanism was growing in Europe and America. I described an e-mail I had received from an Italian looking for a "real Koryak shaman" to invite to a conference, and my bewilderment as to how to answer him. When I returned to Kamchatka in 2001, I learned that he had found Maria Tepenovna Yetneut, Valeri Yetneut's mother, and that she was going to Italy. I commented to Nina Nikolaevna that I was unsure what a "real shaman" was or if Aunt Masha (as she was usually called) were one, but if these people in Italy thought she was a real shaman, that was fine with me. She certainly knew a lot about Koryak cosmology and rituals. Nina Nikolaevna frowned and disagreed with my use of the term *shaman*: "It is not shamanism. It is genuine Koryak art (*Eto istinnoe koriakskoe iskustvo*). Nervous people go into ecstasy. When I am dancing sometimes I lose myself too, don't notice anything else. Rituals require a leader, someone leading them—the oldest, wisest—the younger ones watch and learn, knowing that they will lead [in the future]. Maria Tepenovna learned and now she leads. There are some people who know healing herbs, but they're not shamans." The conversation quickly segued into the topic of native dance groups, underscoring the sacred power implicit in Koryak dances and their performances:

Mengo is not real [*nastoiashii*] cultural dance. It's stylized. Weyem is better. I also argued with them, and the last time they performed here they were good, had good stuff, the right moves. One needs to dance, sing, play from your soul. Each person follows his own lead. Fakel has that, not all in lock-step like a bunch of robots. When you play a drum, a good drum takes pains and care to make and to maintain. It is a musical instrument. When they hear a really good drum, they think it's shamanism. It's really Koryak art or music. You become one with the drum. It should be an extension of you, of your soul.

I am sure that Milgichil has not read Sapir's (1924) essay, but to my mind her passionate views on dance, ritual, and the healing role of the dance ensemble encapsulate perfectly what he meant by a genuine culture. Sapir and Milgichil both express the importance of a harmonic relationship between the needs of the group and the needs of the individual, one that is symbiotic. The individual should not be reduced to a robot, as Milgichil puts it, or reduced to a cog in the machine like Sapir's telephone girl (1949 [1924]:316). They both seem to value the pursuit of art with all of one's being to feed the soul, just as important as the food on the table provided from wage labor or salmon fishing.

One might also recall Marcel Mauss's (1990) conclusion to *The Gift*, and the importance of public rituals for a moral community. Nina Milgichil could be seen as working to foster a moral community through Koryak cultural dance and the public rituals constituting their performances. Like Mauss (more so than Durkheim) Milgichil locates the soul of a moral community in a relational (rather than collectivized) notion of moral consciousness. Dancing in a group does not foster an effervescent collective consciousness so much as it builds and

Fig. 7. Dancers in Fakel assemble for their impromptu performance for the visiting American ethnographers. Nina Nikolaevna is at far right. Her teenage son is at the center, looking at the camera. Photo by C. Kincaid (author's collection).

strengthens relationships of love, respect, and mutual support among those involved.[7]

Nina Nikolaevna's husband Vasili was officially director of the group, but Nina remained the spiritual leader. While I was in Manily in 2001 she organized a Fakel performance in her front garden for my wife and me, and we videotaped and photographed the ensemble. Originally she wanted just a few people, since the space was cramped, but word went round the village in a few hours, and nearly everyone turned up to perform for the Americans (figs. 7, 8). Nina Milgichil was pleasantly surprised that some of the teenage girls who had joined the Protestant sect also came and danced and talked to me about sewing their parkas and their involvement with Koryak traditions.

Milgichil's choreography departs from that of other ensembles by eschewing a total coherence of collective stage presentation. Dancers are not necessarily synchronized with one

Fig. 8. Fakel dancers performing Hololo are organized in pairs and threes, oriented to one another and not primarily toward the audience. Photo by C. Kincaid (author's collection).

another; a large group of a dozen or more performers crowds a small stage and people dance in small groups of two, three, or four. Individuals are encouraged to pursue their own styles and develop unique moves while remaining true to the dances of their elders. Nina's older son, for example (pictured on the cover and visible in figure 7 just behind his younger brother holding the drum), is famous in the village for a particularly beautiful style that seems to float across the stage or ground. Thus Fakel performs genuine Koryak dances in Sapir's sense because it does not force individuals to follow slavishly a stagnant vision of tradition but encourages individuals to fulfill their maximum potential through harmonious pursuit of a living tradition. Milgichil encourages other youth in the group to talk to their own grandparents, and these relationships are indexed in their performances. While performances by the professional troupe Mengo and Yetneut's Weyem would usually be choreographed down to the smallest move and gesture, Milgichil takes a more improvisational approach, enjoining each performer to bring her or his own self to the performance in a new way every time. Thus she inculcates a sense of agency and self-worth in young people through dance performances. While reviewing videotapes of performances, I was struck at how Fakel dancers seemed to focus more on relationships among themselves on the stage than play to the audience, while Mengo and Weyem dancers privileged performer-audience relationships in their moves and postures.

I have discussed Nina Nikolaevna Milgichil's work with young people in detail because it is not exceptional. Milgichil is exceptional in her eloquence and explicit ideology of moral renewal through cultural revival, but she is certainly not alone. At the Hololo in Tymlat the primary school teacher from Khayryuzovo had come for her own folkloric research to document the living ritual and sacred practices in order to invigorate the moral life of children and adults in her own village, which had long ago abandoned traditional rituals, as described in the previous section. There are many more examples of such young grandmothers and grandfathers taking responsibility for the moral life of young people. Most important, they and others were nearly unanimous in the opinion that young people responded positively to such initiatives.

Dance Ensembles in the KAO

Zhornitskaia (1983) provides a good survey of the ethnography of indigenous dances of northeast Asia as well as a history of house of culture dance ensembles in the area (1983:134–51). Kravchenko (1995) has written a celebratory history of Mengo and includes information on some of the other Kamchatkan ensembles too. The proliferation of native performance ensembles in the 1990s was a legacy of Soviet nationalities policy, which defined cultural variation as superficial to the basic structures of class. Native cultures were reduced to the "forms" of folk dance and music ensembles, which performed on stage in various festivals in Moscow and across the Union. Religious ceremonies honoring ancestors or other spirits, traditional economic practices, and social organization were all seen as "backward" and as challenges to the modernizing Soviet state and society. Performing ethnic dances and/or music on a stage, divorced from their original (usually sacred) contexts, was politically safe and even encouraged by the state, while other aspects of traditional culture were simultaneously and brutally repressed through the forced collectivization of herding and hunting and the imprisonment of community leaders and shamans.[8] The first of many All Union Festivals of Folk Dance was held in 1936, just as Stalin's deadliest and most repressive policies against indigenous Siberians were coming into full force (Zhornitskaia 1983:134–36). An informal group organized especially for the 1936 festival represented the Koryak Autonomous Okrug (then known as the Koryak National Okrug). Amateur ensembles of native Kamchatkans interested in presenting native dances on stage represented the okrug at other festivals, performing mostly Koryak and Itelmen dances. These Soviet-era groups were usually organized by a local house of culture, and during my fieldwork I found native people in Kamchatka continued to delight in performing and watching staged dance performances.

Nearly every village has a formal or informal dance ensemble devoted to indigenous dance, usually organized under the aegis of the local *klub* (club for music and recreation) or *dom kul'tury* (house of culture), a school, or through the energies of a particular family. The remote village of Upper Paren', for example, had an active dance troupe that was organized by the director of the village *klub*, initially for a Magadan Oblast folk festival of some kind. Named Muchigin Yayai

(Our Drum), the group did well at the festival and continued to perform on holidays in the village and at least one other festival in the nearby rayon center of Evensk. The dancers in Muchigin Yayai were all excited to have an anthropologist and a linguist in the village and volunteered to perform for my camera, so delighted were they for an audience (fig. 9).[9] I was told that performing, or even just rehearsing, had recently (1998) become more difficult with electricity rationing in the cold, dark premises of the house of culture.

Muchigin Yayai, in the small reindeer herders' village of Upper Paren', is another example of how people in small villages are using the Soviet folklore festival as a catalyst for cultural revival and moral renewal. The village vice-mayor introduced me to one of the principal organizers of the ensemble, Dusia, who agreed to round up the troupe for filming the next day. Dusia explained that they had formed the ensemble only a couple of years earlier: "All the years we have lived, we should have had an ensemble." A big, formally organized native festival in the local rayon center spurred them to develop a performing group. It was a collective effort: "We did it all ourselves. We got together in the library and discussed among ourselves, looked for good material in books there, tried to find and use our own poets." They drew upon locally published material for inspiration to stage skits and dances that would make a good presentation. It was difficult; staging performances for an audience was foreign to them and their experience of traditional native dance (see Zhornitskaia 1983:136). "[The director of the village *klub*] has some education, but none of us have choreographic training. It is not in our tradition to perform on stage, so we have to improvise something," Dusia explained to me.

Their group is small, only six or seven people in total, as is typical for groups in such villages. Their improvisations included dances by one or two individuals, quoting poetry over a staged scene of drinking tea in a skin tent, a pantomime of a Koryak legend accompanied by reading of a local poet's version of the story, and some individual songs. A young boy of about ten years of age performed his grandfather's song, accompanied by his own drumming on a Koryak drum. Dusia explained, "In our tradition, at a festival everyone sits in a circle and the drum is passed around. The youth quickly caught the melody and performs it fine." He did indeed; the performance as a whole was entertaining. Many of the skits included dancing as part of the story. They were well received in the rayon center during the festival and also at home in their own village. The ensemble performs locally on federal holidays: New Year's Day, International Women's Day (March 8), May Day, and Russia Day (June 12). One person came to me wanting to know when I was videotaping the ensemble. She had not seen them perform and wanted to very much. As in other small villages, the ensemble was a source of local entertainment and civic pride. Though originally formed to represent local Koryak ethnic dance and song in the multiethnic rayon center, where Eveny and Kamchadal performances could also be seen, dance groups continue for their own pleasure and artistic satisfaction. With electric power intermittent and transportation hard to come by, there is little public entertainment, and many in the village told me they wished the ensemble performed more often; but the local house of culture building needed major repairs, and there was no longer an appropriate venue. Because of that, I videotaped them outside in the summer sun, behind a building to shield my microphone from the wind (fig. 9).[10]

As Dusia explained, adapting the Koryak dances of their grandparents to the stage was a daunting task for the group of amateurs. Like Burning Man, Koryak performance arts are not for spectators but for participants alone. Traditionally, the

Fig. 9. The dance ensemble Muchigin Yayai in Upper Paren' performs for an American ethnographer, a Japanese linguist, and a few fellow villagers. Photo by the author.

only spectators would be those tired and resting or otherwise physically incapacitated. Everyone present had access to the performance forms, although some individuals were singled out as exceptionally skilled. The Upper Paren' ensemble's dance performances thus highlighted individuals as opposed to the synchronized ensemble dancing of Mengo and Weyem, discussed in the following chapter. Koryak performance traditions include singing individual songs, which may have come to a person walking the tundra either from an outside (spiritual) force or from an internal creative force. One young man in his twenties had composed several songs while working at the reindeer herd, and he sang a love song accompanying himself on a Koryak hand drum. He sang in Russian, and I noticed that his drumming had a Western pop beat. Later on Dusia pointed out that he did not know Koryak well enough to perform in that language, which she considered unfortunate and undesirable for a folk ensemble. However, Koryak performing arts are more than song and dance composed, produced, and performed in a traditional manner. The specific forms must also resemble those of the grandparents closely enough to be recognized as Koryak and not as Western or Russian; they should be iconic of tradition. In this case the young man's straight rock rhythm departed too drastically from the syncopated alternation of triplets and swing-two beats for Dusia and others to consider his drumming and singing as being "Koryak." Dusia's comment on the man's ignorance of Koryak language points up the connection between icon and index implicit in Kamchatkan semiosis—the poor resemblance of his music to Koryak traditional music indexed other gaps in his knowledge of tradition, such as speaking Koryak language.

This kind of instruction is not limited to professional folklore researchers. The villages of Karaga, Ossora, Il'pyr, Tilichiki, Talovka, Manily and others have children's ensembles organized by professionals in the local house of culture or in the school. These ensembles follow the Soviet logic of native cultural transmission. An institution is established for the formal recording and reproducing of specialized cultural activity, and those cultural forms are formally taught to the next generation in structured learning sessions. Children's dance ensembles are billed as extracurricular recreation, but they are not merely good entertainment for children in the village. Children "should know the ways of their ancestors," and Soviet rationalized institutions, such as a dance ensemble, are considered the most appropriate manner in which to pass on those ways. However, the social dynamics of a small village ensure that grandparents are involved, at least peripherally. Thus, despite the Soviet logic of these groups, they are not as professionalized, nor as thoroughly "socialist in content," as similar groups in more urbanized places like Palana or

Petropavlovsk-Kamchatskiy. My point is that I found Koryak culture alive and well in many small, rural villages while it was often declared dead or dying in more urban centers. That rural society is more conservative culturally than urban life should not be surprising.

Multiple Relations to Tradition, Elders, Culture
Tradition and innovation are connected to relationships between youth and elders. The acknowledgment of the genuineness of a performance both derives from and serves as an index of these relationships. Youth who perform "proper" Koryak (or Even or Chukchi, etc.) dances are those who have solid social relationships with particular elders. They have both technical skills (many, besides dancing) and a reputation for a solid moral grounding in the traditions of the ancestors. The youth who stand out as exceptionally skilled, however, are those who bring new shapes to these old forms. Thus the positive valuation of dances as "good" or "traditional" or "correct" is simultaneously a positive valuation of the dancers as persons. I am talking about more than just dance, which is merely a synecdoche for culture, which in turn should not be confused with an imaginary compendium of traditional knowledge. People who were doing more than just surviving in the hard times of the 1990s but thriving, raising a family, and getting through their days and years with their dignity intact drew upon the background provided by their traditions and the relationships with elders that have solidified that knowledge.

Peircean semiotics helps us understand the power of dancing in Kamchatka and the social context for judging performances as "really Koryak" (*nastoiashchii koriakskii*). Insofar as a choreographed dance resembles an elder's dance, it is an icon of tradition; the meaning of the dance-sign is based on its resemblance to its object (traditional dance). Important social meanings of a dance are indexical; they have a direct, real connection with elders themselves, evidence of a relationship between the dancer and her mother, her grandmother, or some other elder who cultivated those forms in the dancer. Performing a dance is also an index of knowledge (or lack of knowledge) of a specific culture. Many of the forms and extended meanings of postures and sequences are iconic of animals or traditional habits (tanning skins, fishing, hunting, etc.). I do not describe in detail the ethnochoreography of Koryak dancing, but an ethnography of speaking about Koryak dancing.[11] Here, I want to focus on the power of dances to serve as connections to traditions, typically as icons or indices.

Traditional dances in Kamchatka are not just mimetic; they are not really copies of anything but are improvised within a set of expectations (see Ingold and Hallam 2007). Most people are primarily concerned with a project of living well rather than with replicating preexisting forms, and living well involves a good measure of creative improvisation, which of course is not simply the production of novelty for its own sake (Ingold and Kurttila 2000). Since elders are the embodiment of tradition, these traditions will inevitably change as current elders pass on to the ancestors and are replaced by younger generations. The only cultures that do not change are dead ones.

3. Dancing in the Koryak House of Culture

In November 1995 the KAO Teachers' College was feted on the occasion of its fifth anniversary with a jubilee evening. The small theater in Palana was packed to standing room only, and bureaucrats' tedious speeches of congratulations were politely tolerated in between performances of music and dance by college students and other local artists. Many people were there specifically to see two dance ensembles that were performing—Mengo and Weyem. Mengo has more than twenty performers, and they filled the small stage with dazzling numbers. Energetic leaps, virtuoso drumming on native hand-held skin drums, and other native dance motifs were enthusiastically received by the ethnically mixed audience. The numbers they performed that evening were all native dances, and they were received with cheering and synchronized clapping.[1] Two dances in particular electrified the audience. "Drummers" featured the charismatic Sergei Kutinkavav, who has a strong, almost operatic voice, and the look on his face made me want to get on stage and join him. Looking around, I saw that the audience was also energized and entertained by the fast-paced moves. These forms are drawn from reindeer herding Koryak men's dances and are characterized by athletic jumps and tricks with a dance drum (drumming under the legs or behind the back, all without losing a complex beat). Another favorite dance was "Dance with Chawats." The Russian title includes the Koryak word *chawat*, "lasso," and it features an all-male cast of herders dancing athletic native moves and playing at lassoing a deer. Each dancer would take his turn in holding a medium-sized rack of reindeer antlers above his head as another man lassoed and threw the "deer" to the ground. Other features include tricks and jumping with lassos in hand and a lot of Koryak shouts and herder calls.

Judging from the audience reaction, however, Weyem was *the* favorite that evening. Weyem was founded by Valeri and Liza Yetneut, who had previously worked in Mengo. All the other dancers in Weyem had day jobs or were students at the Teachers' College, but they performed to a very high standard. When Weyem was introduced, they got the biggest pre-performance ovation, and the audience loved every number they performed, especially the "Chawchu Dance," which is a stage adaptation of various dance moves from reindeer herders in Penzhinskiy Rayon, Valeri's childhood home. The dance starts with three men drumming, followed after a minute by three women dancing onto the stage. Every time I attended a performance of this dance with audience-dazzling athletic stunts like drumming under a kicked leg and other drum tricks, it always received wild applause. The only musical accompaniment for this dance consisted of the Koryak drums played on stage and some singing by the dancers, whereas other dances made use of taped music that Valeri had composed on a keyboard synthesizer, imitating the sounds of an organ, drum kit, and bass guitar. For example, Weyem's Eveny dance switched from synthesizer music, with Valeri Yetneut singing a song with some Even words, to a tape recording of a grandmother singing unaccompanied, which marked a quiet yet powerful interlude in the performance. Yetneut made much use of native language in his performances.

House of Culture

The house of culture is a prosaic institution of civic life in post-Soviet Russia. It functions as a civic center for residents interested in "artistic do-it-yourselfism" (*khudozhestvennaia samodeiatel'nost'*) and once served as a core institution of Soviet agitprop (Levin 1996:58). One can find a house of culture (or a small *klub*) in every city and village in the former Soviet Union. Ideally, it has a performance space for theater, dance, and music as well as practice space and other rooms for everything from children's crafts and folk art to temporary exhibits of local painters and sculptors. In short, a town's house of culture is the place for everything concerning the creative arts. This Soviet institution built upon turn of the century progressive movements that established clubs and art centers for workers and ordinary people in cities like Moscow and St. Petersburg (Khazanova 2000). In Siberia it was part of a massive modernization project to bring primitive nomads into the fold of a socialist civilization (Grant 1995). "Culture bases" (*kul'tbazi*) were established in key areas to teach "primitive" Siberians the operations of modern technology, from flashlights to writing and medicine (Grant 1995:72–85; see Gurvich and Kuzakov 1960:134ff. for Kamchatka's culture base). The present KAO village of Kamenskoe was established as *Koriakskaia Kul'tbaza* and initially served as the okrug administrative center until that role was moved to Palana in 1937. Although Bruce Grant (1995) uses "house of culture" in the title of his book on Nivkhi ethnohistorical experience of the Soviet century, he unfortunately does not spend much time discussing the specific institution as it is operating on Sakhalin Island. I found it a particularly vibrant part of village life in most parts of Kamchatka, and I describe the work of the Koryak Okrug House of Culture (*okruzhnoi dom kul'tury*—ODK) in Palana elsewhere (King 2011). Here

I limit my discussion of the house of culture to a venue for native dance groups.

The house of culture is funded by the government through the department of culture. As in other administrative districts, the Koryak Okrug Department of Culture was responsible for the local art school, a regional museum, the Okrug House of Culture in Palana, and houses of culture in all of the villages. Additionally, the Okrug Department of Culture also funded the okrug's professional dance ensemble, Mengo, which specializes in stage adaptations of native dance. Thus although Palana is a small town of only four to five thousand souls, it had a professional dance ensemble, a children's art school, a natural history museum, and a vibrant arts scene centered around the activities of the Okrug House of Culture (*okruzhnoi dom kul'tury*, often referred to by its initials, ODK), and all are wholly supported by the okrug administration. The content of these cultural activities can be divided into two categories: art (unmarked) and folk/ethnic art. The first category is conceived in terms of modern world culture: oil painting, classical and popular music, contemporary performance dance—the product of professionals.[2] The second category signals indigenous cultural forms in some way and is usually referred to in Russian as *fol'klornyi* (folk), *natsional'nyi* (national/ethnic), *narodnyi* (folk/people's), or most often *mestnyi* (local/native, a usage particularly common in Kamchatka). Native art includes several activities, but craft production and dance ensembles are the most salient in public life and generate the greatest amount of discourse on traditions, creativity, and local understandings of culture. Ethnic/folk art is not limited to "primitives" or indigenes. Russians and Ukrainians certainly have folk dances, costumes, and crafts, and they too are demonstrated in Kamchatka as *fol'klornyi* or *natsional'nyi* dance. The implicit assumption is that ethnic art is connected to traditions and rooted in a collective past, whereas unmarked art is the contemporary creation of an individual genius, unchained from tradition and free to move about the globe.

Underlying all this artistic activity are some interesting notions of Culture (as a universal attribute of humanity) and cultures (specific patterns that vary). It is no coincidence that the people working in the Okrug House of Culture (officially, the House of People's Arts), which is a division of the Okrug Department of Culture, are called "culturites" (*kul'turovtsi*). Artists are specialists in Culture, and they work in a global context of cultural production, whether that be Culture as civilization, which places groups on a scale of more or less civilized, or culture as tradition, which is relatively equal from one group to another, but individuals are more versed in one culture and less in another. Culture, as a sign system, certainly moves without people necessarily moving (Appadurai 1996; Urban 2001). Although Kamchatka is on the periphery, Kamchatkans definitely participate in these trends, and people often talked about art, music, and other creative traditions within a framework of a universalist theory of Culture. However, conversations about ethnic dances and other cultural traditions reflected an implicitly anthropological notion of cultures, whereby different peoples have different cultures and one is not necessarily better than another. "We have our dances, they have theirs, and you have yours," I was often told.

These two ideas of culture work at different levels, giving rise to the contradictions of simultaneous relativism and universalism. Culture is relative at the group level—different groups have different cultures—although individuals have varying commands of particular cultures. People in Kamchatka also order different cultures into a universal scale of Culture, from primitive (e.g., Koryaks) to civilized (e.g., Americans).[3] This contradiction allows for local natives to be denied modernity in some ways of talking about native people, but it does allow them a separate place. As "primitives," they are in a position to counter and critique aspects of modernity that one may find bad or detrimental to humanity. This dual relativism and universalism in discourses about culture is related to Soviet theories of the ethnos and the dictum "national (ethnic) in form, socialist in content." So although belonging to a "primitive culture" like Koryak may relegate an individual to being primitive (in some contexts), it is also possible for individuals to convert that primitiveness to something belonging to them (i.e., it can be mobilized as cultural capital), which can be deployed in the pursuit of Culture. Yetneut, Mengo dancers, and other artists in the ODK and elsewhere are all good examples. It is important to keep in mind these two contradictory senses of the term *culture* (*kul'tura*) in order to understand Kamchatkan discourse on native dance ensembles. Grant does not distinguish them and thus conflates the Culturelessness of "primitive" Nivkhs in the context of the Soviet modernization project (teaching literacy, hygiene, mechanics) with the culturelessness of Nivkh people discontinuing traditional culture (1995:15, 158f.). In Kamchatka people would readily admit to a lack of civilization while expressing pride in primitive cultural traditions, but others would discount the need for thorough knowledge of traditions because they were playing with Culture in the civilization sense.

In 1997 the Okrug House of Culture in Palana was combined with the Okrug Center for Applied Scientific Research (*Okruzhnoi metodicheskii nauchnii tsentr*—OMNTs) and renamed the Okrug House of Folk/People's Arts (*Okruzhnoi dom narodnogo tvorchestva*), creating an official ambiguity about the kind of culture found in the institution—art *of* or *for* the people. At the time the folklorists were concerned that their scholarly efforts in documenting cultures would become diluted by, or subservient to, the artsy shows and cultural entertainment that lay at the core of the house of culture; but the director of the new organization was an eminently reasonable person, and he left people to get on with their jobs. The two organizations were combined for several reasons: they already occupied the same building, redundant administrative posts were eliminated, and personnel in the two organizations already worked with each other on folklore research, encouraged native carvers and seamstresses, and produced stage entertainment. Many of these stage productions included local native forms, but many were located within modern world culture—making use of Western rock or disco rhythms, modern dance, and Russian theater. For example, in the fall of 1997 I gave a friend who dances in Mengo some videotapes of dance that I had purchased in Seattle while renewing my visa. These included a video of Michael Flatley's *Riverdance*, which quickly made the rounds of the Palana Cultural elite. His *Lord of the Dance* performance was televised during the 1998 Oscars, which created much excitement among Palana artists. A dance concert consisting of Celtic, Spanish, and other world cultures was choreographed by Liza Yetneut in 1999 to music composed by Andrei Kosygin, son of Koryak nationalist politician and poet Vladimir Kosygin. The performance in Palana was enthusiastically received. It was a "great show" by all accounts.

Mengo

The first and only wholly professional ensemble is Mengo, named after a hero of Koryak mythology (fig. 10).[4] Mengo started in the 1960s as an informal gathering of native artists and intelligentsia in the Okrug House of Culture in Palana. The amateur group performed in Moscow in 1967 as part of a Union-wide festival marking the fiftieth anniversary of the October Revolution (Kravchenko 1995). Soon afterward

Mengo was organized as a professional ensemble under the auspices of the Okrug Department of Culture and directed by the professionally trained ballet master Alexander Gil' (1943–89; Zhornitskaia 1983:74). Originally from Ukraine, Gil' arrived in Kamchatka soon after finishing his formal training and started working in the Okrug House of Culture with notable culturites such as Vladimir Kosygin, Grigori Porotov, and others. Gil' married a native culturite, Yekaterina Urkachan, who also danced in Mengo and played an important role in its success.[5] Yekaterina Gil' had moved to the main city, Petropavlovsk-Kamchatskiy, before I arrived in 1995 and was there playing a leading role in the Kamchatkan native dance scene well into the 2000s. Several other native Kamchatkans, including Yosef Zhukov and Pyotr Yaganov, also played key roles in developing Mengo's repertoire (Kravchenko 1995). However, Gil' set his personal artistic stamp on Mengo so that more than ten years after his death, his name is still synonymous with Mengo's art and graces one of Palana's two paved streets.

Mengo has been the main cultural representative of the Koryak Autonomous Okrug for a generation. By the mid-1980s the troupe had traveled to France and Japan and made several tours across the Soviet Union (Kravchenko 1995). They were invited to Moscow for a series of performances in the parallel festivals for the 300th anniversary of Kamchatkan "union" with Russia and Moscow's 850th anniversary celebrations. In the 1990s Mengo traveled twice to Israel and Egypt to perform in world folk dance festivals as well as all over western Europe. Mengo is Soviet in various ways. As employees of the Okrug Department of Culture, Gil' and his dancers were performing official, state-approved culture, which was often taken as representative of the native cultures of Kamchatka. Dances like "Seagulls" or "Drummers" are readily identified as Nymylan or Koryak, while the dance "Little Aleut Girl" is iconic of Kamchatkan Aleuts, who are not to be confused with Alutors.

This standardization of an ethnic group by associating it with a particular dance or song is consistent with Soviet understandings of such groups (Levin 1996:93–112; Swift 1968:158–203, 241–43). Long before Gil' arrived, dance groups operating within the Soviet House of Culture organization were adapting native dance to the stage, reinforcing cultural stereotypes that are now part of the ethnographic canon in Kamchatka. Palana has native people from all over the okrug, and they have been presenting "the way we dance/sing/make hats" to ethnographers and one another for over two generations. These examples of indigenous culture have been emptied of most of the power that could have posed a threat to Soviet ideology. Before native dances were performed on stage, they were primarily performed in ritual contexts imbued with sacred power as people, animals, and spirits interacted in a sphere where everyone was a participant and there were no spectators, save for the occasional ethnographer (see Jochelson 1908:36, 68–99).[6] Emptied of powerfully sacred content (as the Soviets understood it), native Kamchatkan dances on the stage were "safe" in the Soviet context and were accordingly aestheticized by Mengo and other professionals (fig. 10).

Mengo is a big organization. Dancers do double duty in the bureaucracy, performing jobs like musical arranger, rehearsal master, and even building superintendent. In addition their staff included two secretaries, a business manager, bus driver, and of course the general manager/artistic director; in total the organization employed at least thirty people in the 1990s. They would have liked to hire more dancers to increase the size of the spectacle on stage, but financial hardship and lack of available talent limited Mengo's numbers during my trip in 1997–98. By 2001 they had recruited several young dancers

Fig. 10. Mengo perform on the small outdoor stage in June 1997. Normally they would have two or three times as many people on a much larger stage. Photo by the author.

and were pursuing an ambitious artistic agenda. Although Mengo is an "ethnic" (*natsional'nyi*) ensemble, this does not mean that all Mengo dancers are Koryak or even native to Kamchatka (*mestnye*). Many of the dancers are *priezzhie*, recruited in a nationwide professional dance market. They have the appropriate complexions and look like Koryaks on stage, but quite a few come from Sakha, Buriat, and other Siberian indigenous peoples. They studied dance in a conservatory and were either recruited by Gil' while Mengo was on tour or applied for a job with the organization, which was one of several such ensembles across the Soviet Union. I do not mean to suggest that non-native newcomers are co-opting Koryak cultural institutions and disenfranchising native people further, as Gray (2005:149) does for the Chukotkan professional ensemble Ergyron. I never heard such complaints about Mengo in Kamchatka. Indeed, as we shall see, ethnic identity of the performer is not relevant in local judgments of performances.

After Gil' died in 1986 his position was divided; Yosef Zhukov became artistic director and Valeri Belyaev (originally from the Sakha Republic, his sister an experienced lead dancer and rehearsal master for Mengo) took over the role of business manager. Unfortunately the quality of Mengo's performances declined during the mid-1990s for various reasons, not least of which was irregular funding from the government budget for culture. Late in 1997, after Mengo returned from performing in Moscow for the twin celebrations of the city's 850th anniversary and the 300th anniversary of Kamchatka's "union" with Russia, Palana was stirred by the news of an organizational shake-up in the ensemble. A long-time friend of Gil' and one-time director of the Okrug Department of Culture, Mark Niuman, was invited to head Mengo as general manager and artistic director, once again uniting the two positions in one person, as under Gil's direction. Niuman had lived in Palana a long time and was married to the star Itelmen dancer Tatiana Romanova. Himself trained as a ballet master, he was expected to invigorate the aging ensemble with new energy while bringing it back to its old roots and former glory. Niuman's first project was a special performance commemorating Gil's posthumous fifty-fifth birthday—for which he and other Mengo "old-timers" choreographed Mengo's core repertoire as Gil' had originally staged it in the 1970s and 1980s. This provided me with an excellent picture of what those dances looked like as well as a current topic of conversation and gossip, much of which centered on the scandal of Niuman's plan to move Mengo out of the Department of Culture.

My friends in the Okrug House of Culture and Teachers' College were buzzing about Niuman's efforts to "separate" Mengo from the department and to make it autonomous.

Some saw this as an attack on the new (native) director of the Department of Culture. Others saw it as an indication of future shenanigans to channel administration money away from other departments (culture, education, transportation) to Mengo. One afternoon I walked upstairs in my slippers from my Department of Culture apartment in the Mengo building and chatted with Niuman about his plans and the rumors. When I began making notes, he asked worriedly if this was going to be published. "It's for my dissertation, probably in an American scientific journal," I replied.

"Oh, that's fine," he looked relieved. As an experienced Palana politician, he had had his share of bad press in the last few years, and he was especially sensitive about the rumors of Mengo's separation: "We have not separated from anyone or anything. Mengo has become, legally and all properly, an independent legal entity (*litso*), like all normal organizations, underneath the administration. Mengo has become more independent financially, freer artistically. Mengo now has its own accounts and place in the budget, as well as its own budget." Niuman emphatically repeated several times, "We have not separated from anyone." Mengo had set itself up as an individual legal corporation, with books and accounts separate from those of the Department of Culture but still working with it and wholly funded from the KAO administrative budget, in order to increase opportunities for outside funding and commercial projects. As a "cultural organization" (Niuman's term), Mengo would always need government subsidies, as all such organizations do in the United States—as he pointed out to me; but if it was to thrive and remain financially healthy, it had to cast a wider net.[7] The economic catastrophe of post-Soviet Russia had hit Mengo as hard as anyone else. Still, in the previous five years they had managed to organize two trips to Israel and Egypt, several trips to Moscow, and also trips to

Europe. As the only professional native dance ensemble in the Koryak Autonomous Okrug, Mengo commanded prestige and wealth that no other cultural organization could, not even the Okrug Regional Museum.

As a professional group Mengo is the largest native ensemble in Kamchatka. Its artistic effect relies on the grandiose spectacle of a stage full of people. Not all its dance numbers are directly taken from indigenous culture. As mentioned, Gil' also drew upon natural phenomena like the aurora borealis and animals or used native legends as inspiration for classically choreographed European dances. However, Mengo is most famous for the native dances. These ethnic performances are the foundation for Mengo's identification as a native (natsional'nyi) ensemble. As Niuman told me:

> Earlier, under the Soviet Union, Mengo and the Chukotkan ensemble were unique as special ethnic [natsional'nye] ensembles, and we traveled everywhere, to twenty-six different countries, and that does not even count the Soviet Union. Mengo had three separate Union-wide tours. Koryaks were considered a dying people, and the ethnic politics of the time were such that it was good that they had their own ethnic ensemble. Then the people in Moscow could point to it and say, "See, the Koryak people are not dying."

Mengo represented the continuing vitality of the Koryak ethnos and, by analogy, justified the continued existence of the Koryak Autonomous Okrug through its artistic performances across the Soviet Union and the world. In the passage quoted, Niuman expressed the same rationale for developing a Koryak professional dance ensemble as the rationale I identify for government support of Koryak language education in chapter 5. I do not mean to be a cynic or a critic of Mengo's art. Their performances are beautiful and entertaining, and Niuman's statements were never echoed by others (whether indigenous or newcomer) in Palana or elsewhere in Kamchatka. Although I do not share Gray's (2005:140–42) cynical characterization of dance ensembles as empty political symbols, there is no avoiding the fact that much of Mengo's success, and certainly most of their travel abroad, is based first and foremost upon their status as an ethnic ensemble, performing Koryak and other indigenous Kamchatkan folk dances. Performing arts are quintessential cultural "forms" (although now apparently devoid of socialist content; or perhaps not), and as such they were greatly supported by the Soviet state.

After the dissolution of the Soviet Union, Mengo continued to act as an official worldwide cultural ambassador of the Koryak Okrug and the Koryak people. Judging from videotapes of foreign performances and the many invitations they continue to receive for folk festivals, cultural exchanges, and even commercial tours abroad, foreigners typically react with delight to Mengo performances, just as my wife and I did that autumn evening in 1995, and as we continue to do every time we watch them perform. As the professional ensemble of the Koryak Okrug, Mengo was taken as an official representative of Koryak culture. They perform in folk festivals and other venues in the capacity of Koryak cultural performers. However, nearly everyone *in* Mengo was never happy about their close identification with the Koryak Okrug. In 2001 they took advantage of an offer from the southern Kamchatkan city of Vilyuchinsk (across the bay from Petropavlovsk-Kamchatskiy) to move there and use that city's palace of culture, which is a larger facility and better equipped than a house of culture (see map 2). Mengo's relocation to the city of Vilyuchinsk follows a semiotic logic that places work in Culture as the dominant priority, even if local cultures inspire many of the details of their art.

In Palana during the 1990s Mengo was often criticized as being old and stale. A common complaint was that their program had not changed for a long time. When I asked my acquaintance Vanya if he were going to the special Mengo concert for the Gil' fifty-fifth birthday commemoration in February 1998, he made a face as if I had invited him to the dentist for a filling:

> They lost whatever folk content they had a long time ago, Alex, and haven't even changed their routine in fifteen years. They just sit around and think up moves that will dazzle, and they never pay any attention to the old people and how they dance. Not like Valeri [Yetneut], he has done some research, although you can argue with him, too. Masha [Vanya's wife] looks at some of the stuff he does and wonders where he got that. Mengo is a government affair, and that means right away that there is not going to be a lot of artistic creativity [tvorchestvo]. They suffer from star syndrome, you know, elites. They are far from the people [narod].

Mengo's fans (of whom there are many, myself included) would dispute Vanya's evaluation of the troupe's artistic creativity. Others were not so harsh in their criticism of Mengo but expressed similar sentiments: rehashing the same thing, far from the people, too fanciful portrayals of Koryak, Even, or Itelmen cultures. There is an irony in the critique that while Mengo is stale, unchanging in fifteen years, they have been *too* creative in inventing dances that should be Koryak, yet not creative enough because they are too far from ordinary elders living in the tundra. This logic connects Peircean icons and symbols to link up Culture (Art) with cultures (traditions). As we shall see, the two conceptualizations of culture are not as distinct as some anthropologists make them out to be. I got a rant similar to Vanya's from an Aleut man in the Petropavlovsk-

Kamchatskiy airport after I told him I was sorry that Mengo performed in Moscow but not in Petropavlovsk. He complained that Mengo had stolen "our dance" and then gotten it wrong. He did not like their Aleut Girl dance; beauty (good symbols) and authenticity (accurate icons) are intertwined in Kamchatkan discourse of dance troupes. Mengo performers themselves discount the importance of presenting real native content in their dances; iconicity of elders' dance forms was never a priority. When I talked to Mengo people, they were unanimous in the opinion that their primary goal is giving the audience a great show. When people in Mengo point out that they are the professional dance ensemble in the okrug, they emphasize that their mission is first and last artistic. Mengo performers are professional dancers and, as such, do not feel themselves bound to a tradition. They see themselves as playing with symbols and resist the social and political implications bound up with icons and indexes. The rub is that their travel to international folk dance festivals hinges on those organizations' understanding of Mengo's repertoire as being full of indexical icons to native Kamchatkan dancing.

Mengo dancers, however, have also disappointed locals in their role as professional entertainers; people in Palana and around the okrug felt that Mengo had abandoned them long before moving south. They enjoy Mengo's public performances such as those I witnessed in the Palana square during holidays like Russia Day, the KAO anniversary, and other occasions when entertainment is sponsored by the okrug administration, and they wish there were more. These outdoor performances were abbreviated and usually had smaller casts to accommodate the smaller outdoor stage (fig. 10). People across the okrug complained that Mengo put on its best shows only for foreigners. Mengo performers used to tour the okrug in small groups, giving performances in remote villages and even at reindeer herder camps. In recent years, however, such tours happened only in 1996 and 2000 as part of gubernatorial reelection campaigns, both of which failed.[8] Those exceptions aside, Mengo is rarely seen outside Palana, and infrequently even in Palana, according to local residents.

The March 1998 Gil' birthday concert produced considerable controversy in Palana when people learned that they would have to pay six dollars for a ticket, a lot of money for people who were not receiving regular wages. Mengo is a government organization, wholly dependent upon the okrug budget. Many expressed to me the opinion that this required Mengo to perform locally, like a public service equivalent to what the library or museum provides to residents. People in Mengo make the persuasive (to an American) argument that in these changing times, they cannot rely solely upon government funding, and they must try more commercial ventures. "No one goes to a performance for free in the city," was a common refrain from Mengo. Niuman gave me an explanation well adapted to post-Soviet realities but foreign to ordinary people in Palana: "People are not used to paying money for performances. Yet, if you go around to the doctor and other people, collecting *spravki* [documents], you have to pay money at every step. Can you say, "Hey I am from Mengo, it should be free"? Of course not, but Mengo is expected to work for free. Why is that?"[9] Although I did not reply to Niuman at the time, the answer is that people see Mengo as wholly supported by the government and that since it was free in the past, it should continue to be free. They have the same complaints about doctors' fees, too. Audience members complain that Mengo gets government funding for trips to Israel and Spain, but they are not willing to "pay their dues" to the people back home.[10] In the end, Mengo sold few tickets to the Gil' anniversary performance. Most audience members received free tickets by special invitation, as I did. The results were some empty seats in the small venue, a less enthusiastic audience than at other performances, and considerable resentment around town. People inside Mengo point out at every opportunity that they are the first and only *professional* dance ensemble in the Koryak Autonomous Okrug in an increasingly crowded field of native performance groups. This is a point of pride for them, but instead of being a source of local prestige, it seems to generate resentment among Palana residents, who complain about Mengo's "putting on airs" (*pretenzii*), a severe criticism in post-Soviet Russia.

One afternoon as I was watching Mengo rehearse, I asked one of the main dancers about the origin of "Rulteeny," a piece from the Chukchi myth of uniting the original men and women into one society. "Is it Koryak, Chukchi, Ukrainian?" I asked a little cheekily. He answered me:

DANCER: It's all mixed up. This is a Chukchi legend. If we want to do Ukrainian, we will do Ukrainian. [I sat there silently, not knowing where to go with that. He eventually continued:] It is a professional ensemble. You guys, in America, if you [pl.] want to do Mexican, you do Mexican.

ALEX: When I think of Mengo, I compare them to Indians or Eskimo. Eskimo in Alaska probably won't do Mexican dances, and they are probably a small group of three or four people.

DANCER: [Scoffs] A group of three or four is always easy to do. Mengo is a minimal size [twenty plus] for a professional ensemble. Over there [Russian mainland] ensembles are more like seventy people.

ALEX: You mean in the Bolshoi Theater?

DANCER: Yes, the Theater, but many ensembles there.

Since then I have learned that some of the most prominent Eskimo dance troupes in Alaska stage performances with dozens of performers on stage with no loss to the traditional quality of the dancing.[11] As professional artists, Mengo dancers argue that they are inspired by local traditions, not confined to them. Mengo's audiences in Kamchatka (and abroad) think of them as representatives of native arts, and some find them inauthentic or distant from the "real thing." When performing abroad, Mengo represents "the Koryak" or Kamchatkan native cultures. Most of their venues are international folk dance festivals, where each ensemble represents the style of dance from a particular ethnic group, from North American Indians to Balinese court dances to Texas cowboy line and square dances. Mengo's commercial tour in Germany was fostered by that country's fascination with native people of Siberia and North America. Indeed, Germans regularly constitute the largest contingent of foreign guests at the annual Itelmen festival in September.[12] These audiences are interested in the exotic art of minority indigenous peoples of the world. When asked about their interest in Kamchatka, they emphasize "tradition" and not original creativity. Several of Mengo's performances index the culture of Koryak reindeer herders through the use of props like lassos and reindeer antlers and also through the incorporation of high kicks, jumps, and other athletic stunts, which people in Kamchatka consider typical of Chavchuven dancing. Mengo's enormous success in the 1960s, leading to its professionalization in the 1970s, has made it a model ensemble for many amateur and semi-amateur ensembles, including one from a central Kamchatkan Even community described later. Valeri Yetneut was self-consciously reacting against Mengo's style and strove for a more iconic representation of these grandmothers' ways of dancing, as opposed to the "inauthentic stereotypes" he saw in Mengo's performances.

As cultural ambassadors of the KAO, Mengo are professional Koryaks first and professional artists second. This status of "professional natives" is exactly what local people deny Mengo, and Mengo dancers themselves feel in no position to claim this status locally. Indeed, they are no longer local to the Koryak Okrug since they moved to Vilyuchinsk in 2001. When I was in Palana in the summer and autumn of that year, people were sad that they had left and no longer performed in Palana at all, but it did not seem to be the kind of scandal I had expected. Perhaps the initial scandal of Mengo's 1998 separation as an independent legal entity was due to people foreseeing the dance company's departure from Koryakia, and they had become resigned to its inevitability a few years later.

Weyem

Local discourse about the low fidelity of Mengo's representations of native dance is most often in the context of comparisons with other ensembles seen as closer to native culture. Several serious amateur ensembles, or family ensembles, as they are often called, have attained a high level of success both in Kamchatka and abroad, including in Japan, Alaska, and western Europe. Weyem is such an ensemble. Named with the Koryak word for river, Weyem also performed that night in 1995 when I had my first live introduction to the great spectacle of Koryak dance on stage. Weyem was started by Valeri and Liza Yetneut, both formerly Mengo dancers. Before the Teachers' College jubilee I had interviewed both Valeri and Liza, recorded him singing with a guitar, and even attended a rehearsal before the performance (fig. 11).

Valeri Yetneut started as a dancer in Mengo, where he met his wife Liza, who had advanced training in classical choreography. He left Mengo, studied in a Kamchatkan art school for a while, and then worked with the professional ensemble Ergyron in the Chukotka Autonomous Okrug before setting up his own ensemble. Other Weyem dancers are not professionally trained, and the group is small. Dance numbers performed in the mid-1990s had between two and six performers on stage at any one time (fig. 12).

Both Mengo and Weyem adapt native dances to the stage, incorporating classical European principles of choreography and staging with some Western musical accompaniment. Both perform at Kamchatkan arts festivals, holidays, and other civic events. If Mengo dancers are professional natives as Department of Culture employees, then Weyem dancers were semiprofessionals working hard to make the big time on the world ethnic dance scene. As an outsider, I initially found performances of both to be comparable. Their differences, however, are what local people highlight in conversation about Mengo and Weyem. Yetneut emphasized to me that each of his dance pieces could readily be identified with a particular dance style of a culture: Chauwchu, Karaga Nymylan Koryaks, Penzhina Evens, Siberian Eskimo, Itelmen. In Palana circles Weyem was seen as more creatively dynamic, at least until Yetneut's death in 1997. Most important in the eyes of native people in Palana, Weyem was judged as more culturally iconic—the dances looked like dances of elders whom people knew. They said Weyem did a far better job of adapting indigenous Kamchatkan dance to the stage than did Mengo.

To the casual observer Weyem seemed much more "native" than Mengo in other ways. It did not recruit performers from across Russia but included only native Kamchatkans. The music and dance in the performances, however, did not always follow a purist ideology. Valeri Yetneut was considered a great artist in dance and music, including on the guitar. He was ambitious and had produced an entire ballet based on Vladimir Bogoraz's (1931) ethnographic novel *Vosem' plemen* (Eight tribes), a show that had played three sellout performances in Palana in the winter of 1996. By 1995 Weyem had an established repertoire of nearly twenty dances. Before Valeri's death in 1997 they had performed in Moscow, Petropavlovsk, and several towns in Alaska. I watched their performances in Kamchatka, attended rehearsals, and talked to Valeri about his choreography and performances, as I talked to Mengo people about their art.

Some dance pieces juxtapose Valeri's composed music on modern, electronic instruments with tape recordings of traditional songs. For example, the sound track changes to a tape recording of Valeri singing an Eskimo song while all six dancers perform Eskimo dance moves portraying a sea hunt, men standing and women sitting. Other pieces used recordings of elders singing. This explicit contrast of traditional performing arts with Valeri's own choreography and musical composition is also featured in Weyem's Even dance, discussed later. Yetneut's art is more than a simulacrum of traditional native culture or an adaptation of native dance to the stage. It achieves much of its great effect through a creative *juxtaposition* of native culture with a non-native art form. He seems to succeed where Mengo does not, however, by staging dance moves that he learned himself from elders in a way that local audiences find more convincing.

Like Mengo's dances, most of Weyem's dances are meant to be typical of a single cultural style. Thus Weyem and Mengo both use dances as icons of cultural groups, in a fashion influenced by Soviet anthropological ideas. Yetneut started with a typology of groups and then went out to villages and fishing and herding camps around the okrug and found dances that supposedly typified each group, much as folklorists in the 1920s went out in search of the prototypical folksongs of demarcated ethnic groups in Central Asia (Levin 1996). While Yetneut, like Gil', did adapt the dance forms he found through his ethnographic research to the stage and used his

Fig. 11. Valeri Yetneut (*left*) leads a Weyem rehearsal in 1995. Photo by the author.

own creative genius in producing the final choreography for the performances, he managed to produce representations of performances that elders and others readily identify as being "ours," especially in his dances from Chawchu, Alutor, and Even cultures. The Itelmen performance reflects more of Yetneut's creative imagination than his familiarity with cultural practices, which he claimed had long fallen into disuse.[13] Itelmen artists, led by current and former Mengo performers, started a vigorous cultural revival in the 1980s, and it sparked a new interest in abandoned dances and rituals. Yetneut extrapolated from written accounts left by early explorers and naturalists (most notably Krasheninnikov 1994) to stage these dance forms. The results were controversial. Some told me that Yetneut succeeded in reproducing dances remembered by current grandparents from their early youth. Others claimed that he made Itelmen into "Hollywood Indians," as Vanya suggested of Mengo. Many of the dance forms evoke animals like bears and various birds. Itelmen are famous for their bear hunting and bear rituals and also for eighteenth-century descriptions of their "erotic" dances, as described in the previous chapter (see also Koester 2002).

"Doing it right" was a central preoccupation of nearly everyone, and performances were often critiqued in terms of their accuracy or lack thereof in representing traditional indigenous dance forms. Frequently these conversations occurred while watching videotapes of performances at special festivals. These festivals ranged from local holiday celebrations of one kind or another in a village to district and regional competitions and special events hosted in the okrug center of Palana or the main city of Petropavlovsk-Kamchatskiy, far to the south. The most important events were in Moscow, and groups occasionally traveled abroad for international folk events or on exchange programs linking indigenous peoples of the North (particularly with Alaska, Canada, and Scandinavia). Various Kamchatkan ensembles, including Mengo and Weyem, performed in Moscow as part of the 1997 combined celebration already mentioned for the city's 850th anniversary and the 300th anniversary of the Kamchatka's unification with (conquest by) Russia. About a month later a group of people involved in the Okrug Department of Culture watched a videotape of the Moscow festival one Friday evening in my living room. An Even ensemble from central Kamchatka began their routine, and one of my guests launched into a heated critique, pointing out all the Koryak movements in what was supposedly an Even dance. She stressed that their postures were "wrong" and the leaps were "Koryakized." This led her to comment on the culturally inaccurate performances of Mengo. "Their dances look a lot like Mengo performances," she complained. When Weyem took to the stage and began dancing, my friend said that she loved their Even dance: "They dance just like our grandmothers in Ayanka, don't they, Volodya? [addressing a young man sitting near her]. I love Weyem because every time I see their Even dance, I am reminded of our grandmothers. They have all the moves, get down really low. Those grandmothers can get down really low and dance." This remark highlights the importance of the elders and perceptions of how elders dance in judging the meaning and value of a given performance. Dance ensembles that present (or are at least taken as presenting) their performances as icons of tradition are judged precisely on this basis—the degree to which the ensemble's performances resembles that of the elders, the embodiment of traditional knowledge and action. Yetneut also criticized Mengo for getting it "wrong" (lack of resemblance to elders, poor iconicity). His solution to the problem was not to turn to his own intuitions or to rely only on the wisdom of his elderly mother, widely respected for her vast knowledge of Koryak and Chukchi traditions. Instead, he got a video camera and did fieldwork, taping elders at fishing camps and at the reindeer herds in order to learn the dance forms as practiced by elders living on the land and to create a visual record for later reference. His claims to authentic representations were often validated, but even those who critiqued Yetneut did so in the same terms—do his dances resemble those done by elders, or did he "just make them up"? Most people associated with Mengo dismissed accusations of inaccurate representations as artistically irrelevant criticisms. They insisted that although Koryak traditions may have inspired some pieces, they were performing not traditional ethnic dances but contemporary art. However, those who praised Gil' and the iconicity of his choreography of native dance did so in the same terms used for judging Yetneut's and Weyem's authenticity: Gil' had visited elders at the fishing camps, observed the way they walked, moved, and danced, and reproduced those forms on the stage— "Gil' was observant; he knew how those elders walked and moved." He learned specific traditions from the authorized bearers of that knowledge—the elders. Proper icons—accurate representations of dancing—were simultaneously indexical of personal relationships with elders.

As I first got to know Valeri Yetneut, I thought he had personal, intimate connections with indigenous traditions through his mother, Aunt Masha. She personified native culture through her detailed knowledge of myths, rituals, traditional practices no longer common, and personal experiences of times gone by, which Valeri's wife Liza liked to highlight in discussions about Weyem's dances and how much more true to form they were than Mengo's. Valeri himself played down any claim to authenticity that might be attributed to his essential identity as Kamchatkan native and instead talked about his travels and experiences among native elders, whether in Chukotka or in Koryak reindeer camps. Other members of the native elite in Palana likewise ignored Yetneut's personal identity and emphasized his field research with a video camera. Later I realized that my initial impression that Yetneut's authenticity derived from his Koryak identity was not shared by most local people and was most likely a result of my own racialized assumptions about being native. In conversations, at least, people ignored Yetneut's identity and focused on his actions, particularly his ethnographic fieldwork. I had an opportunity to watch some of his video footage, and culturites watching it with me pointed out the grandpa who had fascinated Yetneut and the dance steps Yetneut had worked so hard to replicate faithfully on stage. As we were watching footage of the tundra landscape around a herd, my friend said, "Here come those two herders with their sticks." After a couple of seconds I saw a growing image of two reindeer herders walking toward the camera. One walked with his arms draped over the pole that lay across his shoulders. The second walked with his stave touching the ground, occasionally swinging it around his head. Yetneut not only took inspiration from this event he witnessed at the reindeer herd—to create his stave dance for the stage he also replicated these body postures and the gentle sideways swaying of the men as they walked. Thus the dance moves in Weyem's stage performance are iconic of herders walking the tundra and indexical of Yetneut's own experiences with herders on the tundra.

Although I do not dwell on issues of ethnochoreography, a brief detour serves to highlight the power of Weyem's dances on stage in Palana. The dance with staves is iconic of the way reindeer herders move as they walk across the humpy tundra in unhurried motions. The success of this iconicity, the verisimilitude acknowledged by the audience, is based not only on the objective features of the dance but also Yetneut's well-known ethnographic research. He was there; he videotaped elders and other herders in the tundra; therefore we can trust his representations. This and other dances serve as an index of Yetneut's presence among tradition bearers—elders and others living at a reindeer herd in the first instance and, second, living at a summer fishing camp where elders are involved in pulling salmon out of the river (or bay) with a net. A specific instance where Mengo failed to be iconic is that Mengo women dance with their long hair loose down their backs, which is not only un-native-like but is considered improper by many traditionally minded native women in Kamchatka. Native women traditionally wore their hair in long braids decorated with beads. Long, loose hair is associated with being insane or otherwise nonhuman. Also, Mengo dancers often pointed their toes in the European manner of dance, while Koryaks and other native people do not dance with pointed toes. This lack of iconicity is taken as an index for not "getting it right" more generally.

I believe that Weyem's stage performances were just as re-moved from the culture of reindeer herders as Mengo's per-formances; both took inspiration from indigenous culture to stage a Western-style performance. However, local audiences considered Weyem's performances more accurate. For them, this accuracy is not derived from the identity of the choreog-rapher. People did not emphasize Valeri's identity as Chukchi in his passport, his Chavchuven heritage, or his language skills but rather highlighted his direct access to the "real" culture through his trips to the tundra. As I pointed out in the intro-duction, native culture is represented as objectively located "out there" in the tundra, far from town. Anyone can go there and learn it, but one will not learn native culture by staying in town (King 2002a). The value of Weyem's performances, as claimed by the group and accepted by their audience, rests on Yetneut's fieldwork, his adult experiences of traveling through-out northeast Asia to watch, videotape, and learn from elders dancing. People do not explain Weyem's closeness to the real thing through Yetneut's childhood experiences or his mother's traditional knowledge but through his recent and extensive fieldwork. Implicitly, at least, this is close to the standard anthropological notion of culture as something that can be learned, something embodied in unconscious habits but not essential. It can be shared and exists primarily in the com-municative practices among individuals.

Yetneut thought of himself as an artist first and a native second. During my last conversation with him before he died, he complained bitterly about how organizers of the "Three Hundred Years of Kamchatkan Unity with Russia" festival in Petropavlovsk-Kamchatskiy (scheduled conveniently one week after the Moscow festival) shunted Weyem to a peripheral performance space with an inadequate sound system, while other ensembles, inferior in his view, were assigned the main

Fig. 12. Weyem perform in Petropavlovsk-Kamchatskiy in September 1997 at celebrations for Kamchatka's three hundred years of unity with Russia. Photo by the author.

stage. He plausibly suggested that the offense was partly motivated by the organizers' prejudice against native performers. While I cannot comment on the relative merits of the festival performances, it was clear that the Petropavlovsk-Kamchatskiy main stage was for mainstream or popular culture and Russian folk culture, while the natives were placed off to one side in a sort of "ethnic corner," relegating performers to an ethnic "ghetto" in a manner similar to what Patty Gray found in the Anadyr culture scene (2005:132–40). The situation was much different in Palana, possibly because this smaller town has long had a larger proportion of native culturites (Anadyr is nearly three times the size of Palana). One could also speculate on the different personalities of key individuals in the KAO house of culture organization versus those in Anadyr. To be sure, there were conflicts among staff, but they were never along racial or ethnic lines. Palana has plenty of racism below the surface but not in the house of culture.

With Valeri Yetneut's tragic death in September 1997 under
suspicious circumstances I lost far more than a "key informant,"
to use a crass term.[14] Although I cannot claim to have been
close to Valeri, my wife and I were in the process of becoming
friends with him and his wife Liza, and his death affected me
deeply at the time. Weyem has continued to perform under the
leadership of Vasili Barannikov, who was a founding member
of the ensemble with Valeri. When I was in Palana in 2001
they had over a dozen performers and were still performing
to enthusiastic crowds.

Keeping It Genuine: Performing Traditions

Mengo and Weyem dancers are received in native villages much
as they are received in Palana—with a mixture of admiration
and skepticism. A former Mengo dancer attending the Tymlat
Hololo was enthusiastically greeted by those already dancing
and was given the center of the room. People repeatedly commented on the beautiful quality of her dancing, which they
attributed to her Mengo experience. Back in Palana I had
an opportunity to dance with some "ordinary" Koryaks and
Weyem performers. The occasion was prompted by my Lesnaya
drum, a present from a grandmother there. An acquaintance
visiting from that village saw it leaning against the wall in my
Palana apartment and asked if he could try it out. We warmed
it up, and he began playing. This spurred everyone else in the
room to begin dancing. The Lesnaya man teased his friend in
Weyem, "You dance like a culturite"—that is, like an employee
of the Department of Culture—and not like he and others in
Lesnaya danced. In an interesting reversal, Mengo performers who saw my video recordings of the Tymlat and Lesnaya
Hololo dancing commented that the Lesnaya festival would
have been "more beautiful" if the participants had been wearing native dance parkas, which were seen in more abundance

in the Tymlat videos.[15] The criteria for visual beauty in this case were the same—performances should resemble what the elders did, but younger people nowadays are less likely to own a decorated parka. Mengo performers are sometimes seen as the paragon of native dancers, and Weyem performers can seem staged or inauthentic. I do not mean to suggest that people in small villages reverse the discursive trends on Mengo versus Weyem found in Palana, but they do provide good examples of the diversity and continuities of this discourse about genuine native dance.

Discourse in Kamchatka about native people and their lives, traditions, and ways of living and knowing uses a framework of cultures slotted into the categories of Culture. While Koryaks may be primitives, they do have "a" culture, and representations are judged as more or less authentic based upon an assessment of the degree of fit with an understanding of what the Old People know, do, and tell. Individuals gain a reputation for authentic knowledge (and thus representations) by spending time with the Old People, especially those on the periphery. Native culture is located far away from the administrative center in Palana. It is "out there" in the tundra and cannot be located in Palana, only represented there.

I am not interested in talking about the invention of Koryak traditions or deconstructing their cultural reifications. Such analysis has nothing new to offer (why rehash Hobsbawm and Ranger 1983 ad nauseam?), and it is downright harmful to people already in a vulnerable socioeconomic position (see Briggs 1996; Hanson 1991). I am delighted to report that Mengo continues to perform in such countries as Norway and Finland and that other Kamchatkan groups are presenting Koryak, Itelmen, and other dances in Germany and Alaska, for example. My point is that Kamchatkan discourses on authenticity rest upon notions of culture and identity rather different from Western commonsense notions. In the West, authenticity rests on a real and true essence that is neither a product of imitation or fakery nor invented. Walter Benjamin (1968) marks a useful starting point for understanding Western discussions of authenticity based on original and copy. His ideas on the relationship (and differences) between film and stage productions could be extended to the relationship between staged ethnic dances in Kamchatka and dancing in ritual contexts. However, this would privilege dancing in rituals as more "real" than the simulacra created by Mengo, Weyem, and other ensembles. Even if, following Benjamin, we were to privilege the simulacra, the epistemology is the same, and this is an epistemology I would rather leave behind.

Traditions are the background upon which "culture" is continuously invented every day in people's lives and in anthropologists' writings about people's lives (Sapir 1931; Wagner 1981). They are contemporary practices that are represented as being linked to the past although they are continually reinvented in the present (Handler and Linnekin 1984). In semiotic terms, a tradition derives its meaning *qua* tradition when it is understood to be an index of the past, although it may rather be a symbol without any necessary connection to historical practices. The views of tradition as historical background and tradition as contemporary symbols are contradictory only when authentic traditions require some sort of core that retains an essential integrity across time and space, whether that core is a person, a group, a thing, or a practice (e.g., Valeri Yetneut, the Koryak, a hat, or a dance; see Handler 1986). This understanding of authenticity rests upon a notion of culture as a reified, bounded, and internally homogeneous entity. Kamchatkan arguments over authentic ethnic dances are different from the Western view outlined here and part of Whorf's (1956) SAE metaphysics. Kamchatkans focus on a named style, which is learned. Culture as style does not necessarily entail an identity claim. *Koryak* or *Chauwchu* or *Even* are deployed as adjectives, not nouns. These terms refer to a way of dancing, or a way of speaking, a way of being in the world. This is an abstraction, a rarefaction of how specific people (namely, elders) act, but once the style is mastered, it remains authentic and real no matter what the context. In this way a Koryak way of dancing learned from the elders remains a real Koryak dance when it is performed on the stage for an audience, whether in Palana or in Paris. Identifying cultural traditions with the habits and styles of elders also has ideas of change and time built into it. As current elders grow older, pass away, and are replaced by different people as elders, the specific forms of traditions and the details of dances will change too. Koryak culture and examples of real Koryak dances are not naturalized, bounded objects in this discourse.

Thus it is not a contradiction to juxtapose Koryak dance moves with Western music in a single dance number. Audiences in Palana applauded this as a creative innovation. Even his critics conceded that Yetneut was talented, worked hard, and was creating something entertaining and interesting. However, when he showed a videotape of Weyem's performance to a Moscow producer who specialized in "native arts," he was criticized for "not being native enough." The Moscow producer found the use of synthesizer music inauthentic. He wanted Yetneut to create a model of traditional native dance as something totally divorced from Western influences and modern technology. Unlike audiences in Kamchatka, this Muscovite lacked the context in which to ground the indexical meaning of Yetneut's work. The brilliance of Yetneut's creativity blinded the producer to the warm glow of tradition that Kamchatkan audiences clearly perceived as a continuity in Yetneut's choreography. For the Center, natives are in the past and on the periphery and only contaminated by European cultural elements. I argue that this is a spurious understanding of culture, to which I return in the conclusion. Many Native American artists are caught in a similar catch-22 of being relegated to reproducing a dead tradition or being criticized as being insufficiently "Indian" (Penney 2004).

Like Gil', Yetneut was a great artist, and Weyem is synonymous with his name. Also like Gil', Yetneut died young, but the legacy of his art continues as the ensemble continues to perform. Unlike Gil', Yetneut was himself indigenous. His passport said "Chukchi," his mother speaks Koryak, and he grew up with Koryak reindeer herders in a small native village. From the naïve, essentialist point of view, Yetneut's accented, breathy Russian and his personal knowledge of Koryak beliefs demonstrated a direct connection to native culture that would have been impossible for a Ukrainian immigrant. In Kamchatka, however, this is a point of view that I have encountered only twice, both in unique contexts. Liza Yetneut, herself raised far from the traditional native culture of her Even ancestors, is the only person who stressed, or even mentioned, Valeri Yetneut's ethnic identity and his mother's traditional knowledge in the context of Valeri's accuracy in staging native dances and Weyem's authenticity.

The only other person in Kamchatka to make ethnic identity an issue was Mark Niuman, the current director of Mengo. He demonstrated a keen sensitivity to the politics of culture and ethnic identity during my long interview with him that day in February 1998:

> MARK: I came to Kamchatka in 1979 and married a native person. You know my wife, Tatiana Romanova, an Itelmen woman. And so I have been here ever since. But I do not think that it is proper that a Ukrainian be director of Mengo. A native should be in charge.

ALEX: Gil' was Ukrainian.

MARK: But he founded the ensemble. It was his creation. Of course he was director. What do you do? He founds an ensemble and then throw him out? Of course not. I am here to guide Mengo through this transition to greater independence and serious work.

Niuman was sensitive to possible criticism that he, a non-native immigrant newcomer, was director of the professional ethnic dance ensemble of the Koryak Autonomous Okrug, criticism that did not exist, so far as I heard from any source. I never heard anyone criticize either Gil' or Niuman for being an ethnic Ukrainian directing a native Kamchatkan dance ensemble. I discovered the many non-indigenous performers in Mengo first by accident, and then only after direct questioning on the topic. Gil's son now dances in Mengo, and I heard a couple of people make pejorative comments about that "whitey" on stage, but this referred more to appearances than to an essentialized identity. His mother is Eveny (that is, from a group with lighter complexions than other native Kamchatkans), and thus Gil's son is just as "native" as other Mengo performers, if not more so.

All the performers in Weyem are local native people. If not Koryak, they are Even or Chukchi. This contrasts with Mengo, which has many members from elsewhere in Siberia. These classically trained dancers are ethnically Sakha or Buriat and are not considered "natives" by people in Kamchatka. These identities are not salient for local Kamchatkans, however. Even though one could criticize Mengo for not being authentically Koryak because hardly any Koryaks work there, *no one says that*. I have often heard praise for and criticism of Mengo, Weyem, and other ensembles, but the ethnic identity of the performers was never an issue or even mentioned; ethnicity or race or blood quantum is irrelevant to Mengo's performative authenticity. When people evaluated a performance or an ensemble as more or less "native" or "real," their criteria were consistently based on the degree to which the performance corresponded to their own understanding of what native dances look like.

Weyem performers were not professionals, but they took their art very seriously. Yetneut devoted most of his time and energy to the group. His first priority, as in Mengo, was also a great show, but unlike in Mengo, he felt that the way to achieve the best effect was through an accurate staging of native dance forms, emphasizing the value of indexical icons over symbols—dances should be meaningful through their connections to elders and tradition and not through other conventions (i.e., fashions in modern dance). Whereas Mengo dancers were criticized by the director with words like "You're doing it wrongly; that looks bad," Yetneut's criticisms of Weyem dancers were in another vein: "That looks bad; you're not doing it like the elder (*starik*)." Mengo's aesthetic ultimately rests on basic principles of European choreography, and judgments are based on these principles. Yetneut judged his performers and his own performances by the accuracy of their reproduction of forms he learned from native elders. Unlike Mengo leaders, Yetneut (and others, including the Department of Culture person quoted on Even dancing) believed that genuine native dance is inherently beautiful and that close reproduction of these forms will guarantee a beautiful performance. Mengo performers see their art as free creativity, bound only by universal (Western) ideals of beauty. Weyem performers (and their audiences) see their art as an accurate representation of native Koryak, Eveny, Chukchi, Itelmen, and even Eskimo dances. I do not mean that people naïvely say Weyem's performances are exact duplicates of the performances Krasheninnikov or

Jochelson witnessed generations ago; people are more sophisticated than that. Nor do they say Weyem's performances are exact duplicates of the way the elders dance at home. The body positions, moves, and elements are iconic of the elders' styles of dance, or even of their walking styles, but they have been combined into a stage performance.

Ethnic dance ensembles provide some of the best opportunities for indigenous Kamchatkans to supplement their income, travel widely, and even secure a full-time job in an economic environment still suffering from the post-Soviet collapse. The commodity value of Koryak dance, or the earning potential of particular ensembles and dancers, is dependent on performances being deemed by the audience to be authentically native. Mengo and Weyem are not the only groups to have traveled abroad. Others include Lauten, El'vel', Nulgur, Lach, School Years (the children's dance troupe sponsored by the Palana music school), and the Aleut Dance group (from Commander and Nikolskoe islands), and those are just the ones of which I am aware.

4. The Culture of Schools and Museums

Most people living in Kamchatka have not lived at a herding camp, especially those in power. The views of indigenous Kamchatkans and Koryak culture typical of the scholars and travelers discussed in chapter 1 form an ethnographic canon, from which teachers, administrators, and other authoritative people in Kamchatka draw their model of Koryak culture. An intellectual legacy of the Soviet Union in Russia is the authority of canonical texts. The most sacred, of course, were those of Marx, Engels, and Lenin. The Soviet theory of culture, discussed in chapter 1, affected Kamchatkans' views of themselves. Ethnographic accounts are taught in schools and referenced in other situations as an authoritative version of what it is to be native. This official version of native culture disqualifies contemporary lives of native people from being truly "native," yet institutional and personal prejudices prevent them from being "Russian." Consequently native people in Kamchatka can find themselves in a liminal state of "not-really-native, not-Russian," which disables any social or political levers they might otherwise have. Boarding schools raise children to be ready for a modern world that turns out to have few opportunities for native people, but they find themselves judged as inauthentic natives when compared to official ethnographies.

Elites in Kamchatka are those people with some higher education and usually white-collar employment, including teachers, most administrators, museum workers, journalists, etc. The local term is *intelligent*, a member of the *intelligentsia*. These are not the disenfranchised intellectuals of Dostoyevskian fame. The reader may think of the intelligentsia as countercultural intellectuals secretly self-publishing poetry and prose critical of the Soviet regime or producing unofficial art. In Kamchatka the intelligentsia were often members of the Communist Party or the Komsomols, and all were (and are) enfranchised.[1] As part of their higher education and integration into Soviet power structures (even if at a low level), native elites express Soviet and European values more thoroughly than do nonelites (see also Bloch 2004; Gray 2005; Hirsch 2005). One of these values is a requirement that "a people" have its own scholarly community, properly certified with accepted cultural capital, such as higher degrees and membership in the Academy of Sciences. A native leader in Palana bemoaned to me more than once the total lack of native ethnographers. In such statements this person seemed to disqualify people like my friends and colleagues Viktoria Petrasheva and Valentina Dedyk, who was then finishing her doctorate (*kandidat*) in linguistics, is actively working on documenting the grammar and lexicon of Koryak, and is interested in ethnographic themes as well. I did not question this person directly, but I believe she had in mind someone modeled after Chuner Taksami. He is a famous Nivkh scholar, a member of the Russian Academy of Sciences, who has had a distinguished career in Leningrad/St. Petersburg scholarly institutions (including as director of the Peter the Great Museum of Ethnology and Anthropology during the years 1997–2001) and who has published extensively on Nivkh and other Siberian peoples. Native elites in Palana considered it a problem that "the Koryak" had no equivalent scholar (Petrasheva is Itelmen and focuses on Itelmen culture).

Looking for individuals with this kind of cultural capital in Russian society ignores native folklorists and amateur linguists found in every town and some of the small villages of the okrug, who are doing important and useful work. Aleksandra Urkachan, Ludmila Filippova, and Nina Milgichil are just three examples. Many of these people spend considerable time and resources carrying out ethnographic fieldwork, researching and documenting native culture in ways similar to the work that Soviet and Russian ethnographers have done. Laboring in obscurity are some intelligent and dedicated people, often without basic tools like a typewriter and paper, not to mention a tape recorder or camera and film. Native elites, both political activists and those of a more scholarly bent, believe that the Koryak people, or more often "indigenous people of Kamchatka," need an official organization or institute locally or "one of our own" in prestigious institutions in the Center in order to "preserve our culture" or "record our traditions."

I encountered a dramatic example of this logic of institutionalized culture in the spring of 1998, when the native-speaking Koryak linguist Valentina Dedyk was approached by the administration about the possibility of working at Herzen University in St. Petersburg as the official Koryak linguist. The Chukchi Autonomous Okrug had reportedly endowed a chair of Chukchi linguistics at Herzen, and the KAO administration was considering something similar, apparently to accrue symbolic capital with the Russian Center by supporting a chair of Koryak linguistics, a scholarly representative of the KAO, as local rumors had it. In discussions about this my friends in Palana thought such a move would demonstrate the vitality of the Koryak language and, by analogy, the Koryak ethnos and that indirectly at least, the move would support the legitimacy of the KAO as an administrative entity separate from the Kamchatka Oblast. In the end the idea was not seriously pursued by the administration on account of the cost involved.

The Soviet theory of culture (still operative in Kamchatka today)—"socialist in content, national in form"—directs native intelligentsia to non-native institutions, like schools, universities, and museums, to preserve native culture as a codified canon, instead of looking for ways to support native people and their way of life. Since cultural forms, like traditions, are to a large extent independent of the social-structural content (in Soviet terms), no contradiction is perceived between Koryak traditions and the social practices inherent in European formal education. Yet Koryak and Soviet (or Western) educational practices are often mutually incompatible. For example, for children to learn to herd reindeer takes years of dedicated work. Most individuals who study well in school and succeed in Western educational institutions have abandoned many of the Koryak daily practices that activists want to see "preserved" as Koryak traditions. However, I did meet young men and women in every village who were well educated from the Soviet school system and also had impressive skills for living on the land; combining the two ways of learning and living is possible, if difficult.

The following sections describe how people in Kamchatka talk about school experiences and relate my own experiences observing Koryak culture and language classes taught in primary schools and in the Palana Teachers' College. Russian language sources consistently portray the Soviet culture workers of the 1920s as introducing schools, literacy, and civilization to Kamchatka. However, one grandmother in Palana reminded me that literacy had a long tradition among native-born Kamchatkans. Her father was an Orthodox priest who was repressed and shot by the Soviets. She described herself as a creole and emphasized to me that Kamchatkans had a long tradition of literacy through the teaching of priests in small villages, and although the priests may not have constituted a public education system, they certainly provided schooling. Itelmens and Nymylan Koryaks living in the more southerly areas (but as far north as Lesnaya and Karaga) had long contact with reading and writing in Russian. Moreover, even if only a few individuals were literate, this did not distinguish Kamchatka from any other part of rural Russia (or much of the world) in the late nineteenth and early twentieth centuries.

The Soviets did revolutionize writing practices among Koryak, even if they did not establish the first schools. They introduced writing systems for indigenous languages, established a literature for Koryaks, and taught propaganda in Koryak through a school system. They also set about trying to get native people to act more like "civilized" people through European hygienic practices and "rationalizing" their productive activity to increase productivity and create surpluses for export out of the region. Sergei Stebnitskii started a school for Koryak children in 1927 in the northern village of Gizhiga, teaching them how to write their own language in a Latin-based script, and he later worked in a school in Karaga. Around that time, Party workers founded a *kul'tbaza* (culture base), strategically located on the Penzhina River along migration routes of several reindeer herding groups and within easy riverine access to the settled communities in that area (Gurvich and Kuzakov 1960:293ff.). These early practices of schooling and instilling Soviet values were structured by requirements to fit socialist content into Koryak forms. For example, attention to native forms included some of the early Soviet buildings, particularly a design inspired by the round form of reindeer herders' tents (yayaŋo) in an attempt to make the new Soviet spaces of schools appear friendly and familiar to locals (Antropova 1971:175; see also Khazanova 2000; Kincaid 2003). After World War II primary school became universal. I do not know a single person in Kamchatka born after 1940 who did not attend school for at least some years, and I have found them all to be literate in all senses of the term.[2]

First Day of School

The process of producing native people with advanced education and credentials often counters efforts to "preserve" indigenous culture and traditions. During a celebration of Teachers' Day at the Palana Teachers' College in 1997, two experienced teachers were asked to reminisce about their first teachers before the assembled faculty and student body (about fifty people). The first teacher to speak was a Russian *priez-zhaia* (newcomer) woman, who had lived most of her adult life in the okrug. She talked about how she and other pupils argued over whose teacher was the most beautiful, becoming teary-eyed at describing her love for her first teacher. Although she did not say so directly, this first teacher seemed to be a model for her life's career.

This reminiscence contrasted greatly with that of the second teacher, an indigenous grandmother from the southern part of the okrug. I noted down the second reminiscence in detail because I recognized it as a familiar story told to me by many indigenous Kamchatkans born before 1960. She highlighted the fact that on the first day of school she did not know a word of Russian:

> The children all called the teacher Fyodor. It was a small village and everyone knew each other this way, and they didn't even know his patronymic. I said to him, "Fyodor, I am not going to study because I don't know a word of Russian. How am I going to study in Russian at school?" He started school in Russian, and the children didn't understand a word. Then

he started again by giving the children the Russian word for "mother." *Lasx*—mother, *lasx*—mother. He repeated what it is in Itelmen and then again in Russian, and that was how we started learning Russian.

Learning the forms of Russian/Soviet social hierarchies was (and continues to be) an integral part of initial school experiences for children. Twice this teacher repeated that they did not know how to address their teacher properly, but by the end of the year they were addressing him correctly, Fyodor Innokentievich. This memory documents a Kamchatkan child's cultural movement from indigenous culture and society, where elders and kinsmen are addressed by their given name in the local language (Itelmen), into European Soviet culture and society, where hierarchies are salient in banal everyday speech.[3] Her first teacher brought her into Russian language and culture and taught her the proper respect for social hierarchies in Russian society. The use of Russian instead of Itelmen takes the young person out of local and familiar contexts and embeds her in a wider field of power and meaning. The Russian use of patronymics when addressing elders or other esteemed individuals is only part of this new way of speaking. The Soviets understood the power of the Russian language as an index of the state and a new Soviet modernity for non-Russian peoples. The transformation of Itelmen- and Koryak-speaking children into Russian-speaking, Soviet women and men involved more than just a shift of subjects from one semiotic field of signs to another. It also changed the nature of those two different sign systems (cultures). A century ago Koryak language and culture in Kamchatkan villages was unmarked, nothing special, just part of everyday life. Russian language and Russian practices were marked as aspects of the ruling elite, techniques of the colonial masters collecting taxes and maintaining order. After three generations of schooling in the Soviet and post-Soviet

Fig. 13. All across Russia the school year begins on September 1, and this included the small κ–3 school in Paren' in 1998. Children line up with flowers to present to their teacher, while parents, assorted villagers, and the ethnographer applaud. Photo by the author.

systems, Russian has become the unmarked, "default" culture, the normal way of operating in Kamchatka (fig. 13). Speaking in Koryak, herding reindeer, drying salmon, honoring local spirits, and a million other things previously considered perfectly ordinary in Kamchatka have become "marked" as traditional activities in contemporary towns and villages.

In a conversation I had with two native people, a folklorist and a teacher, both actively working "to preserve our traditions," the central paradox confronting native elites was nicely expressed by the teacher: "It's too bad that they didn't have writing earlier. Then they could have written all those legends down. Now they have disappeared into the past as elders have left." The folklorist responded with regret that she did not start serious work recording indigenous traditions right when *perestroika* started (about eight years before she took up folklore), recording legends from all of the elders who have since died. Native culture needs to be "preserved" only because people are taking up other practices more in tune with Soviet/European values, including going to school and learning to write in Russian. However, no one ever proposed that children leave school to learn native ways of living as a viable strategy for personal success. Even reindeer herders—who often pointed out that their profession is difficult to master and takes years of training "from when they are so high [hand at waist]," according to one retired herder—preferred that their children went to school and studied European subjects. Leaving school early and moving to the reindeer herd or living on the land most of the time was described only as an option for those who failed at school.

Many accounts of native people's introduction to school were less pleasant than the one presented earlier. I have recorded quite a few "first day at school" stories by native people in Kamchatka. All were spontaneously volunteered in a context of talking about school in general or studying or childhood. Although many people volunteered such stories, I could not figure out how to elicit them, and so they came to me only as "notes in bottles." A native man who has been very successful in Soviet and Russian society, including having obtained advanced degrees, volunteered his first experience at school over a cup of tea in the office:

> When I was nine or ten, my father sent me to school. It was November. They had already been studying lessons for three months. My father did not know. He was illiterate [*negramot-nyi*], so I showed up in a [reindeer skin] parka in November. I sat in class, and I didn't know any Russian. It was very hard. The teacher held up a card and asked what the name of that letter was. I didn't know, but someone nearby told me it was

"mama." I said "mama" and there was a lot of laughter at me for that.

"Mama" or "mother" in Koryak is *əlla*, thus the Russian *mama* consisted of nonsense syllables to the small boy speaking only Koryak. I asked if it was difficult in school, and he repeated that it was "very hard." I asked if the teacher was strict, and he answered after a pause, "Well, yes. She was a good teacher, a really good teacher. She was good-hearted, a good-hearted person. I have a cousin, older, who studied in school for seven years, but he could not move past the first grade, so finally his father told him to come back to the herd and work. He has been at the herd ever since." The narrator is one of a class of native people who now move with great facility between two cultures. My friend who earlier lamented the lack of native ethnographers was thinking that one of this class should have striven for the highest levels of European cultural achievement, which would somehow contribute to the "preservation" of native culture. Ironically, the child who could not succeed at school, who failed miserably, is now one of the grandparents who are the last generation steeped in native "traditions."

These two accounts are generally positive in their evaluation of the teacher. I recorded a total of seventeen accounts of early school years by native people of all ages, and such positive evaluations make up only one third of the total. Four other accounts do not provide a judgment one way or another on the experience, making the "not bad" accounts about 60 percent of the total. The other 40 percent are negative, some dramatically so. One young man told me his father had been forced to kneel on rock salt in the corner for speaking "two words" in Koryak. A native *intelligent* (educated professional) told me of being captured from the tundra and brought forcibly to town, where she was scrubbed clean and her long braids were cut off, her hair shorn outside the schoolhouse in view of other students. This was an inauspicious introduction to school for someone who would become a teacher (and an excellent one) herself! Elders talked about running away from school back home, only to be brought back to school by force, often with the aid of older students. These personal stories are similar to the personal narratives documented about Native American boarding schools in the nineteenth century (Coleman 1993). It is ironic that just as the United States was phasing out a system of harshly assimilative boarding schools in the Indian education system, the Soviet Union was in the process of setting up precisely that, while also being influenced by American pedagogues like John Dewey (Bloch 2004:100). Petra Rethmann (1995:48) notes that she also "heard of several attempts by pupils to break out and run away," presumably because their experience was unbearable. Like other people native to the subarctic, native Kamchatkans did not beat or even scold their children. Discipline was more subtle and indirect. The imposition of the disciplinary regime of school, or even more dramatically, the boarding school, was no doubt a "hell" (as one man told me) for young children accustomed to what they perceived as total freedom of movement and action. The Merriam Report made similar indictments of American Indian boarding schools in 1928, leading to a call for reforms in disciplinary procedures to reduce (among other things) the incidences of children running away from the schools (Szasz 1999:18–28; see also Coleman 1993).

Growing up in Boarding Schools

Kamchatkan boarding schools (*internat* in Russian) significantly ruptured the transmission of traditional native culture, but we should not think of this as if the *internat* were a football player intercepting the pass of a ball (called Koryak culture) between a parent and her child. Rather, they replaced the traditional Koryak context of growing up with a Russianized Soviet context. Children lived nine months away from their parents, often a long journey away. However, even native children living in a rayon center were required to reside in the boarding school, away from their parents except for a few hours each week. This experience is certainly largely responsible for a significant rupture in Koryak culture, which is experienced as a "loss" of native traditions by the people concerned (both children and parents). The losses were opportunities missed: children were unable to eat Koryak food, wear Koryak clothes, and speak in Koryak, all of which they found familiar and comforting. The schools were also responsible for providing a different set of opportunities for those same children, many of whom are the native elite of the current generation, who bristle at others' criticism of the boarding school system (see also Bloch 2004; Liarskaia 2004). One woman with a good job in the local administration told me that she felt her success in life was due to the boarding school:

> The school in [my village] went only to the 4th grade, and after that we went to the internat in [the rayon center]. Now the internat is for not-normal children [pointing at her temple], but then it was for everyone. Later my mom bragged to others that her daughter turned out the best of all, and she raised me. I told her, "You did not raise me at all. You were drunk all the time. The internat raised me." I am what I am thanks to them.

These days native children who cannot perform well in the normal village school, often boys, are sent to the boarding school in the rayon center to study. However, this person's assessment that boarding schools today are only for slow or mentally disabled children is unfair. Teachers in two different native villages told me common stories about bright children who at the time (1997–98) were happy to be in the boarding school and safe from homes troubled by poverty and alcoholism. It is true, then, that the children in Kamchatkan boarding schools these days are more likely to suffer from serious social or psychological problems than those in mainstream schools; but more important, simply closing the internats will not add to "cultural revival" efforts and may worsen a bad social situation.

Still, ordinary schools in the okrug can be harsh in their treatment of native children to this day. A native activist in a rayon center complained about Russian racism toward Koryaks: "[My friend's daughter] is in elementary school and the teacher hassles her for being Koryak, not dressing right, smelling bad." The poorest residents of the okrug are native, and many of these people do not have indoor plumbing. Many can no longer afford the cost of going weekly to the public bath, let alone buying new school clothes for their children every fall.

I do not mean to paint the Soviet school system as a villain, destroying Koryak culture, although some in the native elite in Palana do just that: "We grew up in the internat and now we cannot sew, or do anything that our parents could do. We aren't natives, and we aren't Russians. We can't do anything now," echoing Nivkh complaints of culturelessness (Grant 1995:15, 158ff.). However, in less reflexive moments, the same people can demonstrate considerable knowledge of Koryak traditions as well as adroitness with Russian culture (civilization). A common complaint was that the boarding school taught dependency by providing everything for the students without requiring anything in return; they were housed, clothed, fed, all for free, and as adults these people expect the government to continue providing for them; they do not know how to act independently and take care of themselves. Sometimes the same people making these kinds of criticisms of the boarding school system told me in another context that their current success in life is due to the education they received in the boarding school. Such ambivalent attitudes reflect the complexity of life choices presented to indigenous Kamchatkans, common to native people across Siberia (Bloch 2004; Gray 2005). As I made clear in chapter 2, participating in Koryak culture, such as speaking, dancing, fishing, and sewing—following the elders—is more than just a nostalgic hobby for Koryaks. These activities feed their souls, but equally important to their souls are things like a university education or a good job. Many Koryaks want to see their children equally at home in Koryak culture—speaking the language, capable of living on the land, being flexible and self-sufficient, while also at home in the "modern" world—speaking Russian and/or English, Japanese, educated to high Russian standards, and capable of securing a good job, whether that be as a teacher, business entrepreneur, administrator, mechanic, or pilot. Koryak parents would agree with Luther Standing Bear's 1933 call for young Indians to be "doubly educated" so that they may learn "to appreciate both their traditional life and modern life" (Reyhner and Eder 2004:325).

Since the early years of Soviet power, leaders have expressed the need for "native cadres" like the ideal indigenous ethnographer discussed earlier. Tatiana Petrovna Lukashkina, who passed away at an advanced age in 1998, was part of the first generation of native cadres trained at the special Leningrad Institute of the North.[4] She was usually identified as Itelmen (especially in the last years of her life, when she was participating in the Itelmen national revival), although she reportedly spoke Koryak better than Itelmen, and she is a hero of the Koryak Okrug. Tatiana Petrovna was legendary for her transformation from an ignorant, provincial (and primitive) native to an ideal, modern Soviet citizen, a teacher and role model for native girls and young women. She met Lenin's wife Nadezhda Krupskaya, which was often pointed out to me as an index of her substantial Soviet cultural capital and another reason (among many) for the high esteem in which she was held. She worked as an elementary school teacher and was active in establishing and directing children's dance ensembles, pursuing the Soviet program of "socialist in content, national in form." Tatiana Petrovna represents the solution to the paradox (unseen by most native elite) that I discuss here. Tatiana Petrovna was successful in school and attained advanced education in the Center. She returned to Kamchatka and taught school to generations of native Soviet children, the ideal way of transforming them from primitives to modern citizens, according to Soviet authorities themselves, and she participated in the encouragement of "native culture" within the confines of an encompassing Soviet (European) culture and society (i.e., ethnic sprinkles). Her picture is on the wall of the Koryak Okrug Regional Museum in Palana with other legendary figures of the native elite, some of whom have Palana streets named after them.

Just as in the 1930s, Kamchatkan elites are still clamoring for the development of "native cadres." This was a major concern of an impromptu gathering of native *intelligenty* in Palana, organized by the Koryak politician, poet, and former deputy to the Supreme Soviet, Vladimir Kosygin. It was also a major issue at the Third Congress of the Koryak Okrug branch of the national indigenous association RAIPON a few weeks later. Speaker after speaker bemoaned the lack of trained professionals in the okrug, including a dearth of lawyers, doctors, accountants, teachers, and others. The solution proposed was the same as that proposed since the beginning of the Soviet Union three generations earlier: send the brightest native students to the Center for free higher education and require them to return to Kamchatka and work in their specialty.

Palana Peduchilishche—The Teachers' College

Sending youth to St. Petersburg, or even Khabarovsk, for higher education is expensive and often traumatic for the student. A localized institution for basic teacher training is the pedagogical *uchilishche*, an institution set up in the early years of the Koryak National Okrug. An *uchilishche* provides specialized education intermediate between a high school and a university or institute, conferring a certificate analogous to "A-levels" or a *gymnasium*.[5] Students who have completed the ninth grade enter a four-year program, after which they are certified for a specific profession (primary school teacher, nurse practitioner, mechanic) depending on the kind of *uchilishche*, or they may continue advanced studies at a university, leading to a *diplom* (diploma for a full course of undergraduate university education). After World War II the original okrug *peduchilishche*, or Teachers' College, in Tigil was closed and students were sent to Petropavlovsk-Kamchatskiy. As the Koryak Autonomous Okrug moved to establish itself as a separate administrative territory of the Russian Federation, independent of Kamchatka Oblast, the administration supported an initiative by local teachers to set up the Palana Teachers' College (*peduchilishche*) in 1990 (fig. 14). The Teachers' College confers certificates in two specialties—preschool and elementary education. Every year a few of its graduates go on to university education, at least one to Herzen Pedagogical University, specializing in languages and the humanities, which qualifies a person to work in preschool, primary or secondary education, the Palana Teachers' College, government administration, or other white-collar positions.

The curriculum in the Palana Teachers' College reflects its ethnic (*natsional'nyi*) status as an institution of the Koryak Autonomous Okrug. Standard Koryak, Even, and Itelmen languages are taught, in addition to other school subjects like Russian language and literature, geometry, mathematics, and English. A class in "regional studies" follows a natural history approach to studying Kamchatka, including flora, fauna, and local history. A separate class is devoted to native history and culture. There are also classes in pedagogy and teaching practicals.

For the first seven or eight years of the college's existence the class on Koryak history and culture was taught by a Russian *priezzhaia*, who had been the director of the local souvenir factory until it closed due to unprofitability.[6] In the Teachers' College she also taught ethnic decorative arts (i.e., beadwork and sewing of reindeer skin) and a teaching practicum in traditional culture. Aside from only one or two of my friends, I never heard anyone seriously dispute this Russian woman's ability to teach a class in Koryak culture. This reflects a pervasive logic in the KAO that disconnects essentialized ethnic identity from authorized knowledge.

This is a logic common to many spheres in Kamchatka, and it also allowed incomer administrators to represent indigenous interests without coming under attack. Natives who do attack such non-natives are often pejoratively labeled "nationalists." The presumption is that knowledge, whether linguistic competence or culture more generally, can be learned by anyone and thus, unlike what is commonly supposed in North America, one does not need to be essentially indigenous "by blood" in order to be an authority on indigenous traditions or even

Fig. 14. The Palana Teachers' College was converted from an apartment building. Photo by the author.

to represent indigenous political interests. The secession of the KAO from Kamchatka Oblast to independent status as a "subject of the Russian Federation" was not engineered or even primarily stimulated by native politicians and activists, as some descriptions have it (Krupnik 1995). KAO independence politics were led mostly by former Communist apparatchiks; I could find no political movement based on Koryak culture when I was looking very hard for one in 1995, and I have kept my eyes open thereafter.

The Koryak culture class taught by the Russian in the Teachers' College relied heavily upon the text of Antropova (1971), and like that book it emphasized things (typically called material culture) over other aspects of Koryak culture. However, other teachers, many of whom were native, conducted classes in village primary schools in a similar manner. The specific topics covered traditional clothing, sleds, fishing and marine hunting, mostly emphasizing the tools used and their construction. The teacher emphasized the adaptive nature of Koryak clothing, how it developed to preserve body heat by using only materials found in Kamchatka. I attended Koryak culture classes in the spring of 1997, during the early part of my research, and I was surprised at the emphasis on material culture. The Russian teacher in Palana used what I eventually learned were standard tropes; for example, on the motivation behind traditional clothing decoration by native women: "They looked around at the world around them and saw mountains, rivers, and so forth. They decorated their clothes taking inspiration from their soul, every woman just for herself." She emphasized to the students the comprehensiveness of the text (Antropova 1971): "Everything is well described in there." During a segment on fishing the teacher explained in detail how traditional fish nets were set up and let some fish go by: "The more fish that get past the nets, the more will return the following year, a law of nature." A discussion of Koryak culture, referred to in the text as "pre-revolutionary" (i.e., before 1917), was portrayed in a romantic, noble savage manner, people in tune with the rhythms of nature and oppressed by the tsar. Seven years after the end of the Soviet Union, the Soviet understanding of culture remained vigorous in Palana and around the okrug. I chatted with the teacher after that first class I witnessed. I explained my interest in Koryak culture and its role in the okrug. This prompted a short lecture on Koryak headgear. Hats were a sign of regional variation and cultural differentiation; every Koryak group made them differently, and Evens were even more different. I took notes, hoping to gather more information to help me sort out the differences to which she only alluded. "These subjects weren't taught at all before the Peduchilishche, and now there is even a school in Manily teaching Koryak culture in the first grade," she told me.

At the time I thought this situation was due to personal patronage. The director of the souvenir factory had the right connections to trade that experience with native culture into a position teaching it at the new Teachers' College. That would follow the Soviet logic of "socialist in content (homogeneous, accessible to all), and national in form (Koryak culture)." While this may have been the case to some extent, her years of experience in the souvenir factory were also taken to validate her knowledge of native sewing. In the course of the following year and a half I found the same themes of material culture, Koryak harmony with nature, primitive mapping of the visible world onto decorative arts, and clothing as an index of local culture expressed by many kinds of people all over the okrug: teachers, hospital attendants, merchants, reindeer herders, and government administrators, both *priezzhie* and *mestnye*. The fact that every group has its own style of hat, marking particular cultural differences while still being unifiedly Koryak as opposed to Even, which has a distinct style all its own, was repeated to me several times. On the other hand, I found all the various hat styles attributed to Koryaks and Chukchi in any village anywhere in the okrug. Just as a baseball cap, knit wool hat, and cowboy hat can be stereotyped as geographically distributed in North America, various styles of native hats are thought to index a geographical distribution of cultural styles. However, in both cases, these stereotypes quickly fail upon close examination.

The people using hat form (style) as a metonym for a culture or as an index of a cultural style, whether native or non-native, were more connected to the state and formal education than other native people: teachers, folklorists, educated professionals. Such reification of culture from experiences and ways of acting in the world to specific things follows a pattern of greater experience with academic education and Soviet anthropology and is associated with a more "museumified" model of culture discussed later. The people who talked about hats being appropriate for different seasons, one more comfortable in the rain than another, or prettier than another, were much more likely to be the kind of natives herding deer, spending time at the fishing camp, and having knowledge of traditional culture learned from elders.

Since autumn 1998 the Koryak history and culture class has been taught by two different native women, who combine personal knowledge of indigenous traditions with the cultural capital of a university degree in native studies. I asked my friends in the Teachers' College about this change, wondering if the change to native teachers was an exception to the logic just outlined. I learned that the two native teachers were preferred not because of their *identity* but because of their *experiences*. They could teach native culture classes in a more engaging way due to their personal experiences. Personal identities were not foregrounded, following the same pattern I found in talk about dance. Thus although culture or tradition may be easily reified in Kamchatka, it is rarely racialized, despite such a predilection latent in state policy and international indigenous political movements.

Making Things, Learning Tradition

The okrug center Palana has the highest concentration of native activists, from leaders of the okrug RAIPON to would-be grassroots organizers and teachers dedicating their lives to teaching native culture to children, although such people can be found in small villages like Khayryuzovo, Tilichiki, and Paren'. Nadezhda Kaizerovna Khelol is one such grandmother working in the Palana orphanage, formerly an internat. She has set up a family museum and a small workshop where she teaches young girls sewing and beadwork, simultaneously teaching them about Koryak traditions and inculcating a sense of personal pride in their heritage. Like the Teachers' College teacher earlier described, Khelol started her teaching of Koryak decorative traditions as an employee of the souvenir factory, and after it closed she continued teaching "ethnic arts" (*prikladnoe iskusstvo*, literally "applied arts") to children at the Palana school and then later at her own space in the orphanage building.

Khelol clearly articulated a practice-based understanding of teaching and learning culture and language: "It really hurts me that they have closed all the ethnic (*natsional'nye*) industries. I don't just teach sewing and national arts, but also working in the national (*natsional'nyi*) language. That's the most important thing, not to lose your native language (*rodnoi iazyk*)." I noticed that Khelol tacked between sentences in Koryak and sentences in Russian when instructing the primary-school-aged girls in technique or evaluating their progress. As many other activist-teachers, she highly values "our own" language, but most of her instruction to the girls was in Russian. Passing on native traditions for Khelol, as for most other teachers, is about controlling a specific skill set in material culture, most often manifested for girls through decorative beadwork. This follows the logic that the Soviets encouraged in the elaboration of ethnic "forms" that decorate socialist content (European socioeconomic organization). Thus while Khelol's pupils engage in learning Koryak culture in a manner that contrasts greatly with the instruction in schools, the fundamental assumptions behind both remain similar: cultural differences are symbols that can be learned, whether through instruction or experience. One's native culture or native language is not necessarily an essential part of a native body.

A third former souvenir factory worker was teaching similar classes in Lesnaya, a small native village not far from Palana. She was teaching sewing and beadwork to young native girls in an after-school program funded by the okrug Department of

Culture through the auspices of the okrug art school. She also made a direct connection between supporting Koryak culture and schooling: "I moved here six years ago, after the souvenir factory closed. One must support our culture. It would be a shame if it disappeared into the past. I was born and raised in [a now closed village]. They don't even have power there. I went to school [in this village] until the fourth grade, and then I lived in the internat in Palana. Papa would get me in the spring on a sled." The teacher showed me samples of her pupils' work, and a great deal of it was very skilled. The girls in the class, like those in Palana with Khelol, seemed to take their work seriously and were hard at it, even in the cold and poorly lit village school building. Like Khelol, this teacher considered native language education an important part of her work. She opened her class by announcing that today they were going to make a "sun," saying the Koryak (Nymylan) word *titken*, which she wrote on the board and had them repeat, emphasizing the importance of learning "their ethnic language" (*svoi natsional'nyi iazyk*). A "sun" is a disc of beads sewn in geometrical patterns of contrasting colors with a trim of reindeer fur around the edges, like rays of sunlight. A "moon" is similar to a sun without the reindeer fur border. When several girls had nearly completed with their suns, the teacher said, "*Yagelegin*, how would that be in Russian?" One girl blurted out, "Sun!" and the teacher forcefully corrected her with, "Moon! Moon! . . . Finish a sun and begin a moon. *Yagelegin, titken*, you need to know your own native language well [*svoi rodnoi iazyk*]." As I show in the following chapter, these attempts at teaching Koryak language to children in a classroom are futile. Although they had been making these decorations for several months and could do it well, they still had not connected the foreign Koryak words to the different decorative elements.[7]

I had several conversations with this teacher, and on another day she talked about the ethnic identity of clothing, repeating what I had been told in Palana, that the variations in clothing styles index differences among groups all classed as "Koryak." Hats are always prominently singled out for their geographical variation, indicating different ethnic groups:

TEACHER: Our clothing is highly variable. Even Lesnaya clothing differs greatly from that in Palana. And ornamentation varies. We have Lesnaya ornamentation, and in Palana, it is totally different. We have Kamenskoe clothing, Olyutorskiy, Karaginskiy, Palanskiy, Lesnovskiy. And they in general decorate their own clothing differently. And they have their own ornamentation. So, each has their own style.

ALEX: How is Palana different from Lesnaya?

TEACHER: From Palanskiy? Well, Palanskiy clothing, for example, *malakhai* [Russian word for native hats] are sewn completely differently. They also decorate parkas in their own manner, with their own ornamentation, malakhai also. You simply need to show some examples, and we don't have any here. . . . Our clothing is very different, even parkas; parkas look totally different. They look different. But you probably already know this yourself.

ALEX: I can tell a difference [lying], but I can't describe it.

TEACHER: I don't know why they are different.

ALEX: Fashion?

TEACHER: [laughing] Yes.

After some thought the teacher added that hats also vary with the seasons, winter hats being the warmest and summer hats most often being sewn out of skins made water-repellent by smoke, but her teaching is not about the use-value of such items or the way of life associated with them. Her teaching was primarily about continuing Koryak artistic/decorative traditions: "My task is to instill the desire to make art (*tvorchestvo*) in the children, working with materials. Working with materials is very satisfying—right girls?—and practical. . . . This kind of labor education enables the development of Art in children. And this is a great collective of friends." Following a Soviet logic of culture, where ethnic forms amount to little more than decoration, the best manifestation of tradition is in the decorative arts. The girls' success in sewing and failure in speaking highlight the differences between enskillment and instruction (Ingold 2000). They learn to sew through doing it but are expected simply to memorize words without constant practice and reinforcement.

I did not connect all three of these teachers back to the Palana souvenir factory until after returning to the United States and analyzing my data. The common philosophy underpinning their various teaching techniques is born out of their shared experience of working for several years at the factory, where women sewed trinkets and clothing accessories as commodity production, and they all taught children in special extra-curricular classes on sewing and making beaded decorations. Even though their explicit goals may have been very different, from the persecuted nationalist to the apparatchik, their portrayal of Koryak culture was similar in its emphasis on material culture and using non-native institutions for transmitting native culture to younger generations. Their implicit model of culture, which I argue comes from some standard Soviet models such as those used by Bromley, Antropova, Gurvich, and others, is open to the same critique that Handler and Linnekin level at the way culture is used by nationalist movements generally: "They find it difficult, if not impossible, to describe the group-based differences of individuals in precise terms—how Quebecois differ from Americans, from French, from Eskimos" (Handler and

Linnekin 1984:278). Thus, whether culture is commodified or museumified, the reifying logic is the same.

In Kamchatka the Soviet ideology of "socialist in content, national in form" also results in a detachment of personal identity from claims to authorized knowledge or authentic representations. Since according to this ideology the ethnic "forms" are (mostly) independent of the fundamental socioeconomic structures, they can be lifted out of their original context and put into a box without any loss in their "authenticity" or value to the people connected to these forms. A Koryak hat sewn by a Russian in a Palana factory is no less "really" Koryak than one sewn by a grandmother in a fishing camp far from town and Western influences. This Soviet construction of authenticity, already presented in the context of dancing, would be rejected by a nationalist discourse, one that essentializes ethnic art by making an inherent connection to the ethnicity of the artist. Ethnic art galleries in Seattle, for instance, require that their art be produced by Indians if it is to be considered "Indian art." According to at least one Seattle gallery manager, the identity of the artist is the primary factor in pricing an object—not the objective qualities of the piece, as seems to be the case in Kamchatka. This Soviet logic of the institutionalization (putting into a box) of indigenous culture makes seamless the movement from the souvenir factory to the classroom as sites of cultural production. However, such after school classes for girls to develop decorative sewing skills can also be part of a larger set of practices of personal empowerment, building skills and pride in self, community, and one's cultural identification.

The Ethnographic Canon and Canonized Ethnographers
The regional studies teacher at the Palana Teachers' College invited me to attend sessions of her class where she wanted to focus on the early scientific ethnographers who had studied

Kamchatka, especially Bogoras and Jochelson. According to the teacher, these were people the students should know, those who had studied Kamchatka, its land and people, language, culture, and folklore, because they produced the first modern, scientific descriptions of native peoples of the area: Chukchi, Koryaks, Evens, Itelmens, Yakuts, and Eskimos. Jochelson began the serious study of the Yakut people (now called Sakha) and studied Chavchuvens. Bogoras studied Evens and Kamchadals. The teacher explained in her class lecture that the two ethnographers were members of the group People's Will and were first sent to the northeast in exile: "But such educated people do not stop working. They continued their work [and by analogy so should the students in these economically difficult times]. They were like the Decembrists. They collected information over several years."[8]

The village of Paren' received special mention in her lecture. This village was described as having big, complex problems that began long ago. The administration has wanted to close the village, but native people consider it their home and do not want to leave. The teacher described a program she had seen on local television some years before, emphasizing that it had been scary to watch how bad life was there. People in Palana and other parts of the okrug often named Paren' as the most remote and isolated village, and thus the most native. Several people in Palana encouraged me to go there to learn Koryak culture.

I take no credit for the thorough and impassioned lectures this teacher gave on Jochelson and Bogoras; my involvement in Kamchatka, presence in the class, and provision of props were merely a stimulus. She passed around photographs from the American Museum of Natural History taken by Jochelson, which Valentina Dedyk had brought back from our trip to New York in 1996. Everyone was amazed at the great quality, studying the photos closely and murmuring that they looked as if they had been taken yesterday.[9] The students were fascinated by the scenes of Koryaks inside semi-subterranean houses from a century ago. The teacher explained that the goal of the expedition had been to find the common roots of the cultures in Kamchatka, Chukotka, and Alaska. She showed the Russian-language edition of the *Crossroads Alaska* catalog (a spin-off of the *Crossroads of Continents* exhibit; see Shossonne 1996) and brought up Raven mythology and other commonalties: "The Bering land bridge connected the continents together. Be sure to read Valentina Romanovna's article that she wrote about herself [in the *Crossroads* catalog]."[10] Igor Krupnik asked Valentina Romanovna Dedyk to write the entry for Koryaks in the Russian translation of the *Crossroads Alaska* exhibit catalog, to replace the somewhat bland one he had written for the original English language version. Though the exhibition had aimed to emphasize personal stories and testimonials of native people on both sides of the Bering Strait, there had not been time or resources to secure the texts for the Koryak and other Siberian cultures (and necessary translations into English) for the original English edition. Dedyk's (1996) article tacks between the two trends I have been discussing throughout this book. On the one hand, she assumes Koryaks and proceeds to describe them, which was her charge from the editor, but she nevertheless weaves in a personal account of *being* an indigenous Kamchatkan in contemporary Russia, which falls between Koryak and Chukchi.

To return to the Teachers' College lecture on ethnography and ethnographers, the regional studies teacher next held up a book of cultural leaders in Kamchatka, mentioning that some had died from excessive drinking, and launched into her passionate conclusion. She lamented one talented man, Lazarev, who did many great things but was ruined by vodka. Whereas the class on Koryak history and culture presented fishing tools and sleds for their own sake, the session on ethnographers in regional studies had a larger goal of personal empowerment and self-fulfillment:

> So why do you need this? You will be teachers, propagandists in the future. The scariest thing is nationalism. You don't need to take this information and turn it into some kind of nationalism. It is impossible to keep "a people" [*narod*] pure anyway. There is love. We should know each other and understand each other. That is why you should know about these people and about yourselves. Valentina Romanovna is an example, herself a Chukchi woman. She knows the Koryak language beautifully and has two Koryak children.

My colleague Valentina Romanovna Dedyk usually identifies herself as Chukchi, as it is listed in her official identification. There are various legends about wars between Chukchi and Koryaks as groups of the former were moving south into Koryak territory, which continued up to the imposition of Soviet power in the 1920s.[11] The reference to her Koryak children is due to her Palana Koryak husband, who likes to joke that family squabbles are interethnic warfare. While "national" can be glossed as "ethnic," it can equally be glossed as "racial," and the accusation of "nationalism" in Kamchatka is often used much as the charge of "racism" is used in the United States or Britain. When I asked about this meaning directly, people almost always denied that Russia had racism. That was only in America and the West; old propaganda dies hard.[12]

Although the Koryak culture class and the regional studies session covering ethnography seemed dramatically different in presentation and content, they shared a common subtext that native culture and traditions are learned from books and taught in school. However, this teacher emphasizes a relational approach to understanding people's lives. Instead of moving to groups, she quickly latches onto a person—a particular individual whose own life belies the single ethnic categories dominant in official ways of talking about culture and ethnicity. Other teachers in the Teachers' College did exhort their students to talk to their grandparents and to do folklore research during summer breaks back home in their small native villages, but that kind of discourse was not nearly as pervasive in the schools and museums I visited in outlying villages all over the okrug. Perhaps village schools may change as Palana Teachers' College graduates take up more posts. In the school-museum model of culture I saw in the 1990s, native language and culture are codified into a set of static, official texts best learned through a European style of reading, memorizing, and reciting. Native culture in this model is not a worldview or a strategy for living—not genuine, to adapt Sapir's trope. It is not a general set of symbols orienting the self or structuring principles organizing personal action, nor is it contingent or shifting. The regional studies teacher's use of Dedyk as an example of interethnic harmony is interesting because Dedyk does not consistently identify herself as Chukchi. Sometimes she calls herself a Koryak, especially in her role as Koryak language teacher and native-speaking linguist. When the regional studies teacher spoke of "love" and specific people, she came closest to speaking of living in a way similar to Sapir's trope of a "genuine" culture, but when she spoke of culture in the abstract, it was bounded and discrete.

The following winter I witnessed a scene that struck me as strange at first, but I later realized it follows this Soviet logic of culture as documented folklore. I had been invited to a small village to attend an annual thanksgiving ritual (Hololo) for successful hunting of seal, bear, and wild sheep. Also invited was Liza, a Koryak school teacher and folklorist from the southern part of the okrug, and we visited the local preschool, school, and internat together between the festivals. When I asked her what kind of work she was collecting, Liza answered that she was collecting descriptions of festivals and elders' memories: "*Mestnye* people did not have writing. Knowledge was transferred orally, and it is lodged in the brains of elders." She did not have a tape recorder but was adept at rapidly taking detailed notes while recording oral histories from any elder native who would answer her questions. During our visit to the kindergarten and internat she played Koryak games or activities with Koryak themes that she used in her school back at home. The village teachers were happy for the change in pace and so were the children. They enjoyed playing at being a reindeer sled team, building a "yurt" (as they called the yayaŋa), and other things. Liza organized a game with the children playing at being grandfathers. Several children proudly told us what their grandfathers hunted.[13] "My grandfather killed two big deer this year." "My grandfather killed rabbits," and so on. The last game acted out a short poem about the wealth of Kamchatka: fish, animals, deer, *yagel* (reindeer moss). When my folklorist colleague held up a picture of a reindeer yearling without antlers, one girl called it a horse, which provoked stifled giggles from the teachers sitting in the corner. Liza then shifted to Kamchatka's different culture groups, but the children seemed to think Itelmen was a kind of berry. She asked the children who they thought they were, and they answered, "People!" (*liudi*).[14] She then asked, "What ethnicity [*natsional'nost'*]?" They did not understand the question, so she told them "Koryak," and then Liza said that Kamchatka also has Eveny. Cultural or ethnic identity is not something that these children are learning at their mothers' breasts. They do not encounter it in everyday life in the village. It is most salient in Soviet institutions, including government administrations, schools, and universities, or the ethnographic interview.

After more games in the internat, Liza asked the children (aged six to nine years) some questions as a form of propaganda to get them to stay in school, following the same philosophy as the regional studies teacher in Palana: "Are you going to study? Will you finish school and the institute? Study your region? Of course you will, need to tell your own children about it, grandchildren." I was struck by the irony of a folk-lorist telling children to work hard and stay in school so that they could study their native culture. There was no mention of the elders, respecting grandparents, or listening to them to learn the old ways, methods that she herself used to gain the knowledge she was teaching in school, although her reason for *visiting* in that village was to learn from the elders herself. This speech followed the Soviet logic of cultural reification, in which culture is an object of research and scientific study, although her actions took her to talk to grandparents for insight into local tradition. It is then preserved in museums, books, and institutions like folklore ensembles. Although her exhortation to the children reflected her own life (obtaining an education, which she then used to document the traditions of her ancestors), it was also marked by an absence of justifying formal education for a good job. There are not any jobs to be had in that village or most of the rest of Kamchatka, and as a native activist, she is not about to encourage the children to move to where the opportunities are—in the local city of Petropavlovsk-Kamchatskiy or farther afield in Moscow or St. Petersburg.

For Liza and others there does not seem to be a contradiction between preserving native culture and emphasizing the value of non-native institutions, like schools, that actively work to prevent the transfer of traditional knowledge from older to younger generations of native people in Kamchatka and across Russia. Native culture is defined as history and thus more a subject for academic study and museum display than a way of life for young and old together. The irony is that Koryak culture has not been consigned to the dustbin of history; it is not located only in museums, where it is preserved *in vitro*, but is found all over Kamchatka *in vivo* as part of everyday life. You just have to hang out with the right people, who are not necessarily elders and not limited to isolated herding camps in the tundra, although such people and places are good points to start one's inquiry.

The day after my visit to the internat with Liza I was making some notes in the early hours of the morning during the course of the Hololo ritual. It was about 2:00 a.m., and most of the adults were in varying stages of intoxication and no longer interesting to talk to. At this point half a dozen children, aged eight to fourteen, encircled my position and bombarded me with questions from what was my name to what was I doing to what was my favorite rock band. I suspected that they had not talked to an American before, since I had been told I was the first Russian-speaking American to visit that village. I chatted with them, also asking about their perceptions of the rituals and attitudes toward hunting.[15] My folklorist colleague Liza and a native activist from the rayon center came over, thinking to "rescue me," but I assured them I was fine. Every conversation has the potential to generate more data for the ethnographer. Later Liza commented to our hostess, "Those children sure know a lot. An eight-year-old knows all the fine details of ritual and tradition that I am trying to learn." Our hostess answered, "Yes, they're great kids. Of course, they live with their parents. We *internatsi* don't know anything, but they live it." At the level of unselfconscious discourse, the level of subtext, native elites understand and readily acknowledge the contradiction between Soviet schools and preserving native culture, but even the most ardent "nationalists," who are devoting their lives to supporting Koryak culture, prefer to send their children to school to receive a good education in order to succeed in wider society, not to the reindeer herd to learn the ways of their grandparents. I also prefer to send my children to school and encourage them to study books. This preference for the culture of schooling is predicated on an Arnoldian or "civilizational" approach to culture, where people have more or less culture. The more cultured individuals are those with schooling and the full attributes of modern civilization. "Primitive" Koryaks (a term not always used pejoratively in Kamchatka) have less civilization, but they also have a different culture, and thus gaining more civilization results in a "loss" of primitive culture. The Soviets set up such a symbolic move from primitive culture to modern socialist civilization as an unmitigated good thing, but nowadays people are not so sure. However, they remain frustrated in their attempts to revalue symbols of Koryak culture as being of equal or greater worth than symbols of Russian culture (civilization).

Things in Museums

The model of culture operative in Kamchatkan schools and other public venues is a museumified one—practices are represented chiefly through artifacts, preferably old, and on display in glass cases although not commodified, since they are not meant for exchange. The Koryak Autonomous Okrug boasts a large number of museums of two kinds: independent regional studies museums supported by the local administration and one-room natural history displays in the local school. The most established museum in the okrug is the Koryak Okrug Regional Museum in Palana, and there are relatively new, small museums in Ossora and Tilichiki. The Palana high school and many schools across the okrug, including those in some of the smallest villages, also have similarly styled museums representing the diversity of the region following a natural history approach—separate displays on the geology, flora, fauna, and ethnology of the area, whether that be the entire okrug or just a small area around a village. All these museums primarily serve an educational function, although the Palana museum has some scholarly resources and a growing collection of paintings and sculpture by local artists. Museums play a similar role in the consciousness of people in Kamchatka as they do in the United States. Museums are repositories for history, preserving the past and safeguarding it for future generations.[16]

Palana's Okrug Museum suffered from chronic bureaucratic neglect and a lack of continuity in directorship or staff in the 1990s.[17] My wife Christina worked in the museum for six months in the first half of 1998, and I was a regular feature there, working in the museum library, talking to the staff about native material culture, just having tea and chatting, and attending the museum's public events, including two art exhibitions and a photographic exhibit of Palana. Most of the display space was devoted to native Kamchatkan cultures, including a highly prized diorama envied by the oblast museum in Petropavlovsk-Kamchatskiy (figs. 15, 16). It was the work of a *priezzhie* artist couple, Alexander Pirozhenko and Viktoria Krupina. The diorama of a Koryak fishing camp on the Okhotsk shore has people dressed as one would see them in the latter part of the twentieth century, and one can actually recognize individuals from the neighboring village of Lesnaya in the faces of the four-inch figurines. It is a portrayal of contemporary native life in the mid-1980s, when it was made, and not an imagined, romanticized past.[18]

Tours of the ethnographic exhibits were not so contemporary

Fig. 15. The main exhibition room of ethnographic artifacts in the Koryak Okrug Regional Museum includes things donated and made on commission. Photo by the author.

Fig. 16. The museum's diorama in the main ethnographic hall is famous for its contemporary depiction of life at a Lesnaya fishing camp. Faces of known individuals are recognizable. Photo by the author.

in their orientation. The tour guide often spoke in the past tense in describing the other ethnographic exhibits, which include sleds, boats, tools, clothing, and other items documented by ethnographers like Jochelson and Antropova; these items are portrayed as part of a dead culture preserved under glass. In 1997 the staff member in charge of leading tours was a Russian *priezzhaia*, and she spent considerable time studying books in the museum library in order to understand the context of the items on display. One day she was talking about several items as I was photographing them, and the museum librarian came into the room, shortly followed by the director. These two individuals were Koryak, and they answered my questions about the uses and meanings of particular things in terms of what their parents and grandparents had told them. Whether gained from studying ethnographic accounts or from childhood recollections, the descriptions of practices associated with the ethnographic items in the museum were marked in the past tense. Whether learned from a book, a class, or while growing up by *performing* those practices, the culture seemed to be dead.

The director of the local museum in Ossora learned her Koryak traditions from her mother and her older siblings. She does not have any higher degrees, however, so she enrolled in a long-distance course on ethnography based in an institute in Petropavlovsk-Kamchatskiy. Although she already had considerable knowledge of Koryak customs, beliefs, and techniques of craft production, she did not control the appropriate vocabulary indexing specialized, professional knowledge of the subject. Instead of taking classes in management, accounting, and other skills for directing an institution like a museum, she was studying ethnography in order to approximate more closely the ideal of Chuner Taksami, the native ethnographer.

The director of the local museum in Tilichiki, also a Koryak and knowledgeable of that culture, has a higher degree but in business administration, and she complained that she was not taken seriously by government administrators because she did not have an ethnography or museum degree. Thus while I initially thought her education would be adaptable to overseeing the financial and administrative needs of a museum, she found it worthless in the eyes of her superiors. She described to me her work in the school and in the kindergarten with native children, especially teaching native language, which was important to her since she spoke the local dialect of Alutor while the school teaches official Chavchuven Koryak. The Tilichiki museum director explained to me how she tried to speak to children in Koryak when working in the museum. Her museum tour was remarkably engaged with Koryak culture in the present tense, even as it referenced the elders. We were standing in front of the rock collection, which one finds in every museum, but instead of the usual geological explanations, I got Koryak ones. She told us that there are legends associated with many of the rocks, summarized two or three stories, and talked about the importance of sacred rocks in general. She explained that most of her work in the museum consists of storytelling and includes a mix of Russian and Alutor languages, which the children enjoy, but she gets no support from the administration, not even the ethnic Koryak officials. The museum can barely afford its monthly phone bill, let alone the salary of the director and one staff member. Not only does the museum not have a sorely needed typewriter— she cannot even borrow one from another part of the local Department of Culture bureaucracy in order to type up her extensive materials on Koryak folklore.

At first glance the Ossora and Tilichiki museums, founded in the 1990s, resemble a nationalist project of glorifying tradition, homogenizing diverse cultural practices into a single ethnic group. Their directors have good nationalist credentials through personal identity as Koryak and traditional knowledge embodied in command of the language, rituals, or beliefs. However, these two museum directors find such nationalist validations of their cultural capital to be of little worth, even among "fellow" natives. The post-Soviet administrations still require the universal (Western) validation of cultural capital through certificates, conferred in Western institutions of higher education (see Bourdieu 1984). "Nationalist" cultural capital is recognized only after it has been converted into institutionalized cultural capital, thus de-nationalizing or de-essentializing the cultural capital in question (knowledge of Koryak traditions, material production, language). This makes it impossible for nationalist discourses, following patterns described by Handler (1988), McDonald (1989), and others to have any power in Kamchatka.

Native Craft into Art

Female material production was traditionally dominated by skin preparation, sewing clothing, and clothing decoration and is still important to those who live on the land today (Rethmann 2001:133–54). Preparing skins started with the death of the animal. Male craft production was and is dominated by carving in various materials (wood, bone, ivory). Traditional male inclinations toward carving were explained as individual artistic responses to necessary craft production: "a man has to carve a piece for a reindeer or dog harness; he makes a knife handle, and then decorates it; a herder sitting alone with the deer takes out his knife and carves a figurine out of a stick for his amusement or a gift to his children." While I stayed with a reindeer herd in Middle Pakhachi, the herder Slava, whom we met in chapter 1, used an ax to rough out a rifle stock from a birch log. He had carved one the previous fall but had broken it just behind the trigger when he smacked a dog attacking a deer during the corral. "The dog is still whole, but the rifle broke," he explained flatly. He cut a four-foot log about six inches in diameter with a saw, and all the other work was with an ax or knife until he finished it with a rounded chisel. He had it done in about a week, working on it during free time in camp.

This gendered division of material production continues in the production of ethnic commodities. Gender is marked in all Russian nouns, and in Kamchatka the feminine version of "master [artist]"—*masteritsa*—refers to a native grandmother sewing artworks, which can be as simple as a beaded pendant trimmed in fur (a sun) to something more practical, like beautifully decorated reindeer-skin boots or hats, or something as breathtaking as a large wall hanging (*kover*—carpet in Russian).[19] Wall hangings are sewn in a quiltlike manner in either rectangles or circles and usually display a combination of geometrical and representational patterns (people and animals). These wall hangings are not only displayed in local museums as works of art but have traveled to Japan, Western Europe, and Canada as well. Marina Pritchina and Alexandra Popova, two grandmothers from Karaginskiy Rayon, are famous across the okrug for their work and for their world travels resulting from the wide appreciation of their masterful pieces.

Men's carvings include wooden masks and figurines, bone or walrus ivory pendants engraved with themes from the natural and mythological worlds, and antler or ivory carvings, from a finely detailed reindeer team pulling a sled to simple figurines for a keychain or knickknack. Representative artists include Tolya Solodyakov and Valeri Brechalov in Palana and Yegor Chechulin from Il'pyr. The sale of native commodities occurs all over the okrug, but Palana and Ossora have the most active markets with better access to foreign visitors and a local population with more regular cash than in other parts of the okrug. They also have better communication to Petropavlovsk-Kamchatskiy, the main city and port in Kamchatka. Native crafts in Palana are most often found in two places: in the House of Culture and in a gift shop that includes all manner of souvenirs, jewelry, and other luxury items. Irrespective of ethnicity, all kinds of people can be seen walking the streets in Palana wearing carved ivory earrings or beaded pendants. Native commodities are also found in many apartments around town. Native crafts are often bought as a gift for a local friend or a visiting guest. For example, artist Tolya Solodyakov considered the local police to be important customers. A VIP of some sort from Moscow was coming, and the police department wanted to give him a local gift. They did not have all the money Solodyakov wanted, but he told me, "You don't want to lose a good customer, so I gave them a deal that time."

Sasha Antonov is another carver famous for his Koryak masks. He had a workshop in Palana, which employed Solodyakov, Brechalov, and others, but in 1999 he moved to Petropavlovsk-Kamchatskiy for better employment opportunities for his wife as well as better access to foreign markets. Galina Peskavets is another artist living in Petropavlovsk, sewing items mainly for the visiting tourist market. In 1997 she produced a lavishly decorated Itelmen dance parka on commission for a dealer in Seattle, worth thousands of dollars. While Antonov and Peskavets produce authentic native art for sale, neither is native. They both came to Kamchatka as adults and have made it their home. Their claims to authenticity come from the usual sources, producing cultural items appropriately iconic of what current elders/grandparents have or similar to items documented in trusted scholarly publications. When people in Palana or Petropavlovsk compare the work of Antonov with that of Solodyakov, for example, or

Peskavets's native sewing with a native grandmother's, their race or ethnicity is not discussed; only the objective traits of the product itself are at issue.

While carved masks and sewn pendants are appreciated for an objective beauty that transcends cultural particularities, they are relegated to the folk-culture status of "craft" by both ordinary Kamchatkans and cultural elites. They are not considered high art, like an oil painting or a sculpture of perhaps one-half meter or more in wood or clay. Even the breathtaking *kover* (wall hanging) of a native master like Pritchina or Popova is not fully high art when on display in the Petropavlovsk-Kamchatskiy museum, as attested by the fact that the artists were not individually identified, as they were for every oil painting, regardless of the painting's artistic merit. Instead, a *kover* was identified as "Koryak" or "Even" or "Itelmen." In Palana the distinction between folk and high art is clearly demarcated by venue. While older things belong in the museum, new items of folk art are more often found in exhibitions in the House of Culture than in the Koryak Okrug Regional Museum. High art is displayed in Palana's Okrug Regional Museum, upstairs from the ethnographic exhibits. The upstairs walls of the museum in 1997–98 were dominated by oil or watercolor paintings, and thus the sculptures displayed must also be high art. These sculptures also tend to be in the Western tradition of representational art (busts, animals) and much larger than native carvings. Artists famous in Palana include Alexander Pirozhenko and his widow Valentina Krupina, Valentin Severin, Vladimir Lazarev, Kirill Kilpalin, and Vadim Sanakoev. Half of these people are indigenous, and all typically paint Kamchatkan themes, often landscapes or scenes from native life, whether in traditional form (people in deerskin parkas), or in more contemporary garb (rubber boots, cloth jackets). When folk art makes its way into the

Koryak Okrug Regional Museum in Palana, it is added to the ethnographic collection.

Clearly there is a hierarchy separating the "high" culture of Western art, which was mostly located in the upstairs rooms, from the "folk" or "low" culture of Koryak art, which occupied the ground floor of the museum. This hierarchy followed commonsense assumptions about what art is in Kamchatka and other parts of the world; foremost, it is not utilitarian, and its production requires specialized training or apprenticeship (Price 1989). Western/world culture is also ranked hierarchically above indigenous/local culture. The painter or sculptor working in a Western tradition is referred to as an "artist" (Russian—*khudozhnik*), while the native seamstress or carver is referred to as "master [artisan/craftsman]" (Russian—*master*). In either case the identity of the artist is not the issue. People with Koryak, Russian, Even, Ukrainian, and Itelmen stamped in their passports are classed as an "artist" or a "master" only because of the commodity they produce and nothing else. The fact that Severin, Lazarev, and Kilpalin were *mestnye* (natives) while Krupina and Sanakoev are *priezzhie* (newcomers) is never considered in local evaluations of their art. This is very different from the situation in North America, where objectively similar abstract paintings are classed as "Inuit" or "modern" art by virtue of the race/ethnicity of the artist and not solely in terms of the formal qualities of the work in question.

Whereas identity politics in North America often produce claims to the effect that artists must have a certain blood quantum or other essential identifying attributes in order to produce authentically native representations or art, people in Kamchatka have requirements like professional anthropologists: knowledge or skills obtained through practice and/or by careful and focused fieldwork. Despite every individual having a passport stamped with one (and only one) ethnicity, people in Kamchatka do not subscribe to such an essentializing discourse. Instead they implicitly have a relational, practice theory of culture. A culture, or at least a specific segment of it, can be learned through study and practice, just as one can learn to repair a truck, sew, or speak a foreign language. People in Kamchatka do not confuse ethnic labels with real life.

For professional anthropologists, however, the purpose of fieldwork is different from what it is for local Kamchatkans, who assumed my field research is dedicated to preserving tradition, learning vanishing forms, or salvaging their culture before it disappears. Anthropologists usually do not study dances in order to stage them, and linguists do not study languages simply in order to speak them. Locals were initially amazed by my ability to speak some Koryak but often later disappointed with my limited competence in the language. They were also often confused at my interest in talking to children and young adults.

It is interesting to note that female former artist-employees of the souvenir factory have gone into teaching, while male artists who are attempting to make a living through the production of native decorative art for sale are individuals with an aptitude and interest in the activity and little or no formal training, let alone certification. This reflects a typical gender difference in post-Soviet career opportunities. Women in Kamchatka are more likely than men to have earned degrees of one kind or another, which can be parlayed into white-collar employment, while men were engaged in production jobs that did not certify them with transferable skills, such as for teaching or office work. These women from the souvenir factory had access to jobs in an institution denied those without certification. However, the woman working in the Lesnaya school quit a few months after I interviewed her because she had not received her salary for several months, and she found life back in Palana easier. Carvers like Brechalov, Solodyakov, and Chechulin, in contrast, were optimistic that their profitable sales would improve over time. It is difficult to attribute this difference to gender alone, however, because there are many examples of women who derive significant income and fame from private art production and sale, such as Pritchina and Popova.[20]

Soviet schools were very good at providing a baseline education in literature, math, and sciences far superior to that in most American schools, especially when comparing rural areas in Siberia with similar rural areas in North America. I was often astounded by how well read reindeer herders and other ordinary people were. They knew Pushkin, Tolstoy, and other literary classics and also discussed books they were currently reading, evaluating the relative merits of authors' prose style as well as the plots of various adventure novels. People with only a high school education also frequently demonstrated a good command of biology, geometry, and other school subjects that could become relevant in conversations while living on the land, herding deer or drying fish.

School classes and museum tours devoted to national/ethnic culture and history are where young Koryak children are supposed to learn about their traditions and their own culture. Few organized programs bring children together with elders to learn about their traditions by doing, even though many of these traditions provide the best avenue for meeting current and future nutritional needs, not to mention a foundation for a solid sense of self-worth, neither of which seems to be provided to many native children by schools in Kamchatka. Thus symbols are powerful guides to how people live their lives and bring up their children. When beliefs or practices are marked by symbols of tradition or of Koryak culture, then those practices are relegated to history or folklore. Their implicit worth is graded below practices marked as modern. Speaking Koryak is one such practice that is particularly salient here. As I show in the next chapter, these Soviet legacies for thinking about culture and language are powerful in shaping efforts in language revival and many people's reactions to these programs.

5. "This Is Not My Language!"

Koryak Language in Schools

A way of speaking is one of the most salient markers of self and other present in everyday life. The way one speaks indexes not only ethnicity and social identity but the entire being of the speaker and the array of real and possible relationships among speaker and audience (Hanks 1996; Silverstein 2004). This linguistic anthropological insight into the indexical power of language was implicit in the discussions I had with elders and others in small, mostly native villages in Kamchatka, nearly all of which have some Koryak language teaching in the local school. Indigenous language revival programs are directed by educated specialists working in the administrative center of Palana. Several times in Kamchatka I heard stories about elders complaining that the Koryak language children were learning in school was not "their" language. Kamchatkans would often volunteer the importance of speaking "one's own native language" (*svoi rodnoi iazyk*) and the need to teach it to children who are growing up speaking Russian. Many people, if not all, were supportive of the idea of teaching Koryak in schools, but most of these people were critical of the implementation. Koryak varies considerably in phonology (accent) and vocabulary from one speech community to the next, and this variation has proven troublesome for language revitalization efforts, which have been relying on an approach to language that seeks to promulgate a single standard way of speaking through newspapers, textbooks, and materials for schools.

In describing a language it is possible to achieve a degree of precision such that every person can be said to be speaking a unique language, or indeed the same person in different cases can speak different languages, but it is more useful to generalize somewhat and gloss over some of the minute variations in sound quality, word use, and sentence construction in order to describe the linguistic habits of a group—a speech community (Sapir 1949 [1933]). I follow Dell Hymes's ethnography of speaking approach, which focuses on these habits, and a speech community is simply the product of habitual speech or common ways of speaking.[1] The term *dialect* is conventionally used to describe variants of a language that are supposedly mutually intelligible. In Kamchatka, Koryak is often described by linguists and language program specialists as having nine dialects, although one could argue for more or fewer. When grandparents in Tymlat or Middle Pakhachi complain that the school teaches children some kind of Koryak that is "not my language," they give voice to a set of dialect categories emphasizing difference over continuity. I found that standard Koryak as taught in schools (specialists call it Chavchuven or Chavchuven Koryak), emerges from a view of language glossing over variations in ways of speaking that ordinary speakers consider to be linguistically and socially meaningful differences.

Koryak is endangered, which means that people are shifting to speaking Russian (Kibrik 1991; Krauss 1997; Vakhtin 1994, 2001a). Koryak language revival programs work to halt or reverse this shift away from using Koryak. I have found that these revival efforts in Kamchatka betray what Handler

(1988) has identified as a nationalist reification of culture: a single cultural group should have a single language. As I discuss later, the earliest explorers equated a single distinct language with a single distinct social and cultural group. This idea continued through the Soviet theory of *etnos*, which persists in organizing official programs like Koryak language teaching in schools. To speak like "one of us" is to be one of "us." This identification is so strong all across Siberia and Russia that linguists and anthropologists have long noticed the term "native language" (*rodnoi iazyk*) in questionnaires most often understood by respondents to mean the individual's heritage language (e.g., Koryak, Eveny) and not necessarily the language the individual grew up speaking as a first language or the dominant language in that person's linguistic repertoire (see Vakhtin 2001a:77f.). I found most people in Kamchatka talking about the importance of learning *svoi (rodnoi) iazyk*; they did not mean their "native language" (as linguists understand that term in English), but the language of their parents or grandparents, or "heritage language," as anthropologists would put it. In practice, then, there is a great tension between the standard Koryak found in schools and the Koryak spoken by the elders, the (great-)grandparents. A focus on the way of speaking of the school children's grandparents would privilege practices based on speech communities instead of privileging elite notions of what the indigenous language is; that is, the notions of specialists and officials.

The concept of a speech community was initially formulated by William Labov (1966, 1972) and John Gumperz (1965; see also Gumperz and Blom 1972). Definitions vary, and some include a sharing of communicative norms as well as sharing a common code (language in the narrowest sense of grammar and dictionary). I follow Duranti's characterization of a speech community as "the product of the communicative activities engaged in by a given group of people" (1997:82). This ground-up approach avoids falling into traps of nationalist thinking or presupposing a language (or culture) and then describing it. It is collective and relational, focusing on the *activities among* people, whether they be grouped by residence in a village, as specialists in a single occupation, or by other relevant criteria. A single village of just a few hundred people, like Middle Pakhachi or Paren', includes people speaking different variants of Russian and variants of Koryak.

I use the term "variant" self-consciously to avoid assertions regarding the prestige, level of institutionalization, or degree of difference among codes. Dialects are commonly thought of as unofficial (sometimes disparaged as "substandard") variants of a language or, more precisely, of the official codified and institutionalized dialect of a language. Common parlance in English and Russian places speakers of a dialect in an inferior position to speakers of a "proper" language. However, in linguistics the terms *language* and *dialect* can be used to make some interesting generalizations expressly for comparative research and typological investigations. Linguists working on comparative-historical problems, for example, speak of mother, daughter, and sister languages to describe relationships among speech varieties that have changed over time.[2] Problems most frequently arise when ideas or hypotheses developed by historical linguists in careful argumentation are bandied about without appropriate qualification. In this way heuristic typologies or interesting conjectures for possible lines of research can seem to become hard facts describing a black and white world. I believe such a misunderstanding of heuristic categories has contributed to the official erasure of variation and difference and imposition of a single standard Koryak, which key language specialists see as having the weight of historical precedent behind it.

Languages, Dialects, and Speakers

The first careful description of indigenous Kamchatkans included an interesting description of the variety of languages. Krasheninnikov identified three Kamchatkan peoples (*narody*) speaking three languages: Kamchadals (Itelmens), Koryaks, and Kuriles, the last of whom resided on the islands of that name (1972:195). He also distinguished herders from settled Koryaks, based on their economy, which paralleled a linguistic difference: "The reindeer Koriaks even have great difficulty in understanding the settled Koriaks, and especially those who border on the Kamchadals, because they have borrowed many words from them" (Krasheninnikov 1972:195). Further into the book he refined his taxonomy of languages and dialects:

> The main difference between this nation and the Kamchadals is in their language, which according to Steller, has three dialects. The first, which can be considered the principal language, is that spoken by the settled Koriaks who live on the Sea of Okhotsk and by the reindeer Koriaks. Another dialect is used by the Oliutors; the Russians refer to this as the second sea Koriak language. It is much harsher than the first. The third dialect is that of the Chukchi; its delivery is freer and softer, and it is spoken in a rather sibilant manner. Other than this, there is such a great similarity between their words and idioms that these three peoples can easily understand each other.
>
> However, if the Oliutors are considered to have a separate dialect, there are as many dialects as there are ostrogs [forts/villages], since there is much variation in dialect between one ostrog and another. The farther north one goes, the more Koriak words one hears, but in the south there are more Kamchadal words. (Krasheninnikov 1972:294)

Krasheninnikov may have started with the categories Kamchadal, Koryak, and Chukchi, which he most likely learned from Russian Cossacks residing in the area, and did his best to fill in those categories with linguistic description. His description, however, is more sophisticated than a categorical separation into three "peoples," subdivided into dialects or subgroups. The first careful investigation of the native languages of northeast Asia presents evidence of a plethora of language communities, which may be arranged on a continuum based on mutual intelligibility (not to be confused with geographical distance but related). From this point of view, people from speech communities who easily understand one another should be placed close together on the continuum. People in communities that have difficulty understanding people speaking other variants of Koryak are placed farther apart on this analytic continuum. Krasheninnikov could not even draw a line between speech communities using Itelmen and those using Koryak, two languages supposedly very different from each other.[3] This suggests that Bogoras, for example, who studied Koryak before studying Itelmen, may have discounted words he already understood as "Koryak" in an attempt to get at a "pure" Itelmen language. It is interesting to note that Georg Steller describes exactly that kind of continuum of Koryak and Itelmen: "The closer one gets to the Tigil River, the more the language deviates from that around Bolsheretsk [far to the south] and is gradually mixed in with the Koryak language so that many Itelmen words have Koryak endings and Koryak words have Itelmen endings" (Steller 2003:5). This single sentence describes a sociolinguistic landscape of much greater variety than can be found in the writings of today. Unfortunately, neither Steller or Krasheninnikov thought it important to expand upon the variety of practices among Koryaks, and they stick to three basic categories of natives: Chukchi, Koryaks, Itelmens.

Jochelson described the linguistic diversity among Koryaks in more detail than Krasheninnikov. Following Bogoras, Jochelson (1908) divides the Koryak into four main dialects: Northern Kamchatka, Reindeer and Kamenskoe-Paren' Koryak, Alutor, and Kerek (cf. Bogoras 1922). He qualifies this typology with the note that "every group of Reindeer Koryak, and almost every village of Maritime people, have their own provincialisms, with a few insignificant phonetic and lexical peculiarities" (1908:429). Dialectical differences are marked in phonology, vocabulary, and sometimes grammatical morphology. Jochelson's distinctions are an attempt to typologize a continuum of variation into a larger set of groups, but it is fundamentally the same sort of typology as that of Krasheninnikov.

The indigenous languages of Chukotka and Kamchatka, aside from Eveny (a Tungusic language), can be grouped into a small language family commonly called Chukotko-Kamchatkan (Fortescue 2005; Bobaljik 2007). Chukotko-Kamchatkan is divided into northern (Chukotian) and southern (Kamchatkan) subgroups (see fig. 17).[4] Most authoritative accounts divide Chukotian into four languages: Chukchi, Koryak, Kerek, and Alutor. Kamchatkan consists of Itelmen languages, two of which are long extinct. Turning our attention to the northern branch, Chukchi and Koryak have long been identified as separate languages, based on phonological, morphological, syntactic, and discursive differences. Bogoras (1922) acknowledged important distinctions between two groups of Koryak speakers (now called Koryak and Alutor), and even further lexical differences, but did not see them as significant enough to warrant classification as different languages. Kerek and Alutor were previously thought of as dialects of Koryak, but they are now classed as separate languages from Koryak proper. Alutor is sometimes referred to as "Nymylan" (from *nəmnəm*, Koryak for village, settlement), but in Russian-language publications and in Kamchatka, the name Alutor refers to the variant of

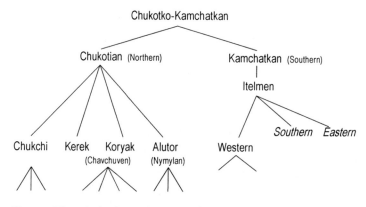

Fig. 17. Historical relationships among Kamchatkan languages.

Nymylan originating in the Pacific coast villages from Tymlat in the south to Vyvenka in the north, while Okhotsk coast villages were grouped into four or five subgroups of Nymylan. The language spoken by reindeer herders was selected as the official version of Koryak, based on their relatively large population. This language and the people who speak it are also often referred to in Russian as Chavchuven (from *čawčivaw*—Koryak for rich person/rich in reindeer), although Chawchu is also heard in Koryakia.

Koryak and other Chukotko-Kamchatkan languages are often described as belonging to a larger group: Paleoasiatic or, as it is often called in English, Paleosiberian, a language family that began as heuristic speculation and was reified into an entity presupposing real linguistic relationships among the languages grouped under the term. Paleosiberian or Paleoasiatic was first suggested in the middle of the nineteenth century by L. I. Schrenk as a hypothetical language family of what now appear to be isolated languages (Ket, Yukaghir, Nivkh, Koryak, etc.), which are supposedly the last vestiges of a once large set of ancient Siberian languages displaced by incoming languages of other stocks, (i.e., Turkic, Tungusic, Samoyedic;

Fortescue 1998:5; Kreinovich 1934:3–4). This idea was picked up by no less an intellect than Roman Jakobson, who had the linguistic genius to think big while keeping in mind the individual details. Jakobson noticed interesting similarities among these languages in terms of their sound and morphological systems, which warranted discussion with the appropriate caveats: "If nothing warrants our assuming a genealogical relationship between the Luorawetlan [Chukchi] family, the Yukaghir family, the Gilyak [Nivkh] and the Yeniseian [Ket] family, one gets nevertheless a glimpse of the affinity of all these languages owing to ancient geographical proximity" (Jakobson 1942:604; see also Austerlitz 1977). There is no linguistic evidence linking isolates such as Ket (spoken in central Siberia) and Nivkh (spoken on and near Sakhalin Island) with Koryak and Chukchi. While Kreinovich, Jakobson, Austerlitz, and other careful scholars always kept this in mind, the repeated use of the term Paleosiberian in publications, especially in the titles of books discussing Siberian linguistic problems, has reified the hypothetical congeries into a language family (e.g., Jakobson et al. 1957; Iailetkan 1980:4). One should also keep in mind that geographical proximity can play a role in languages coming to resemble one another through borrowing (convergence); words, sounds, and even grammatical categories can all be borrowed (Thomason 2001:60–94).

There are other precedents for heuristic groups such as Paleoasiatic. Edward Sapir and Leonard Bloomfield took the comparative methods of historical reconstruction, so successfully used in the study of Indo-European, and applied them to little-documented languages such as those of Native North Americans, with particular success in historical reconstruction of Athapaskan and Algonquian languages (see Sapir 1933). The languages that make up each of these two families are closely related, and there was little contention from other linguists.

More provocative groupings suggested by Sapir, such as Na-Dene and Penutian, remain controversial. In this same vein, all indigenous Siberian languages have been grouped into one of three large "families": Uralic, Altaic, and Paleosiberian/Paleoasiatic. Uralic includes Hungarian, Finnish, Khanty, and other languages in an Ugric subgroup and Nenets, Selkup, and other languages in a Samoyedic subgroup (Campbell 2004:188–92). Altaic is an attempt to connect such widely distributed families as Mongolian, Turkic, Tungusic, and Manchu with Korean and Japanese into a large "superfamily." Although there is strong evidence for historical connections among at least some of these groups, Altaic as a whole is generally not accepted by linguists as a convincing grouping (Campbell 2004:345, 352).[5]

Grouping linguistic isolates into the Paleoasiatic "family" fits with the Soviet obsession with groups and nations, as outlined in chapter 1. The only thing shared by all these languages is that their speakers were all classed by the Soviets as the most primitive nomads, and their language is not obviously related to Uralic or Altaic. Such a grouping follows the same logic as that which promotes a unitary Koryak language. Making generalizations about a single Koryak language can be useful in the appropriate context, while enumerating the different variants of Koryak described by linguists can be useful in other contexts. Problems arise, however, when either perspective becomes a rigid standpoint from which to characterize an objective view of the world and other positions as simply "wrong" on all counts. As will become clear, the greatest problems arise when overgeneralizations drive policy decisions.

Official Koryak

The so-called Koryak language in northern Kamchatka is a chimerical beast, difficult to pin down and describe succinctly. There are no systematic studies of mutual intelligibility among variants based on comprehension tests, but I found that spoken Koryak varies considerably from one region to another, in some cases even between nearby towns. For example, Vasili Borisovich and Nina Nikolaevna Milgichil both speak Nymylan Koryak of the Okhotsk Sea coast. However, Vasili grew up in Paren' and speaks that variant, while Nina grew up in the now closed village of Mikino (located on the north coast of Penzhina Bay, to the west of Manily). In conversations with me they confirmed that these two varieties are similar and mutually intelligible. However, when it came to transcribing wax cylinder recordings from 1901, they both quickly identified which recordings were by Paren' speakers and which by Mikino (Waikeno) speakers. Nina Nikolaevna found it difficult to understand several passages of the Paren' recordings that her husband was able to recognize and vice versa.

This kind of variability, for the most part, is erased in official descriptions of Koryak, especially those coming from the okrug capital of Palana. Linguistic studies and textbooks of Koryak emphasized a single official language in the twentieth century, but most native people emphasized the plurality of linguistic practices. Native intelligentsia insisted that I learn official Koryak, while in small peripheral villages, pointing out to the American ethnographer unique features of the local language seemed to be a favorite conversational topic. Greater attention to describing Alutor (still often called Koryak) and other dialects of Koryak may lead to still greater recognition of the diversity of languages spoken by native Kamchatkans.[6] Variants of Koryak are usually described as being associated with a particular village or place. However, indigenous Kamchatkans are highly mobile, like many other people around the world, and any single village has speakers of different varieties, some with profound lexical and phonological differences from one another. One key feature distinguishing nearly all variants of Koryak (and Chukchi variants, too) is the form of the glide sound [y] in standard Koryak. This sound varies dramatically from one variant to another, spanning a continuum from [t], [s], [z], and [dz] to [r] in Chukchi, functioning as a shibboleth, an index of larger dialectical differences. This pattern of phonological variation makes it difficult for speakers of unofficial varieties to read standard Koryak, which is written following Russian spelling rules (King 2005). I rarely (if ever) heard anyone complaining about the way other people spoke their language, but most people did complain about the form of Koryak taught in village schools. I think this may be due in no small part to the fact that official Koryak—called *palanskii koriak* (Palana Koryak) by most nonelites—seems to suffer from a lack of native speakers.

A Bible translation project yielded my first clue that the principal linguist training teachers and broadcasters for the okrug, and the managing editor of most projects in Koryak, was using a model of the language that did not correspond to that of any speech community aside from the coterie of professionals she was instrumental in training. In the spring of 1997 a team of Bible translators arrived in Palana to check the accuracy of a Koryak translation from Russian of the Gospel of Mark. A British couple with a Moscow translator had a near-final draft that had been translated by Alevtina Zhukova. They asked a Koryak radio announcer to read the text aloud as they recorded her. Then they asked a series of questions to determine her understanding of the text. Native speakers who were not literate in Koryak then listened to the tape of her reading. The tests found that Zhukova's translation was grammatically adequate but discursively incomprehensible. She had not marked topics appropriately, and listeners or readers easily confused various actors in the stories. One of the testers told me of his dissatisfaction with Zhukova's work and her approach to the project, and I was reminded of Whorf's comment about his own problems learning to *use* grammatical Hopi appropriately (1956:138). The expression of meaning—in other words, speaking—is more than just putting subjects and verbs together into grammatically correct strings. My friend Valentina acted as official host to the team in her capacity as Koryak language teacher in the Teachers' College and resident Koryak linguist. Valentina defended Zhukova, her teacher, explaining that they were only working with a rough draft.

Later, around the kitchen table with Valentina and her husband, I got the whole story. Valentina had done the first round of translating, using a copy of the Bible in Russian as a source. She explained that this was horribly difficult work. The Russian-language Bible she was given to use is even more archaic in its language than the King James version is to a modern American. She did the translation as a favor to her advisor, who supported the project not on religious but on geopolitical grounds. Zhukova's argument was that by making such a classic text as the New Testament available in Koryak, the language could be better preserved, and its present plight of near extinction would gain a higher global profile. Valentina was not very sympathetic to this argument, but when one's dissertation supervisor asks for a favor, it is better to comply. Valentina had spent some days on the translation and produced something that she believed was in a language that "the grandmothers" would understand, as she put it. Then she handed over her manuscript to Zhukova, who took it and edited it heavily. The translation testers were frustrated that Valentina had done this because they suspected that Valentina's original translation was much more comprehensible, and Valentina was frustrated with herself for not keeping a copy, but she had had no access to a photocopier at the time.

Koryak-speaking elite in Palana typically repeat the history of the codification of official Koryak as a natural result of the economic salience of reindeer herders and their languages. They explain that Chavchuven, the Russian term for Koryak reindeer herders' language, was spoken all over Kamchatka because reindeer herders speaking the language moved across large territories in search of optimal pasturage. Town-dwelling maritime hunters, Eveny reindeer herders, and Itelmen (farther south) traded with Chavchuven Koryaks and with one another through the idiom of the dominant group: Chavchuven. Two of Bogoras's students, Georgi Korsakov and Sergei Stebnitskii, were the first Soviet linguists to study indigenous Kamchatkan languages systematically, and they referred to the Koryak language as Nymylan following contemporary fashions (Korsakov 1940, 1952; Korsakov and Stebnitskii 1939; Stebnitskii 1934, 1937). This was confusing because they were focusing on a Chawchu variant of Koryak, spoken by reindeer herders, whereas Nymylans are maritime town dwellers. The postwar years saw further codification of an official or standard Koryak language, now referred to as Chavchuven (*chavchuvenskii iazyk*) to distinguish it from Nymylan or Alutor dialects (Zhukova 1968a, 1968b, 1972). From the late 1940s until the early 1980s, however, linguistic work slowed and publishing became much less frequent, as the Party followed a policy of assimilation to Russian language and culture (Vakhtin 2005). Native language education in Kamchatkan schools was eliminated. Native-speaking Koryak children were required to learn Russian, and using their native language was punished, sometimes harshly, as described in the previous chapter. Nearly all children of reindeer herders and most others were forced to live in boarding schools where they were required to speak Russian at all times. This active repression of indigenous languages continued until the 1980s, when restrictions on the expressions and publishing of non-Russian cultures and languages were eased considerably, although by then the less populous languages like Koryak and Itelmen were already endangered and undergoing significant shift. During the era of *glasnost'* Koryaks were again going to Leningrad to study linguistics and native-language pedagogy.

The late 1980s and early 1990s saw the publication of a comprehensive grammar and textbook for Koryak language teachers and a Koryak-Russian/Russian-Koryak student's dictionary. Staff at the Institute for Teacher Development, in collaboration with St. Petersburg and Moscow scholars, have authored a series of textbooks for preschool through fourth grade. These textbooks assume that Koryak is alive and well, and that children are coming to school with a native command of spoken Koryak, denying the sociolinguistic reality that children speaking Russian as their first language need to learn the language of their elders through a second-language-acquisition strategy.

Anyone familiar with the Soviet Union will see its legacy in a practice of top-down, centralized language policy, even for something as local as indigenous language revival in small, isolated villages. During the heyday of Soviet power, education policy was dictated from Moscow, ensuring a uniform curriculum from earliest preschool through postgraduate education (Grenoble 2003). Already by 1990 native language advocates had established the Teachers' College and the okrug Institute for Teacher Development, both of which focused considerable resources on native language education. The independence of the Koryak Okrug from Kamchatka Oblast implicitly required the existence of a Koryak ethnos. Thus the official native language, Koryak, must be codified and promulgated in the appropriate official channels, such as radio, TV, and print. The educational institutions of the entire okrug should also reflect the uniform existence of the Koryak nation, although some diversity in the okrug was acknowledged: the Itelmen in the south, the Even in the north, and Nymylan Koryaks have their differences from Chavchuven Koryaks. But policies ignored differences among populations classed as Koryak.

Publishing Textbooks

In the early years of the Soviet Union, primary schooling using local languages was common in Kamchatka, as in other parts of Siberia. As stories in the previous chapter illustrated, none of the native children spoke a word of Russian. The very first Soviet teachers in Kamchatka, like Stebnitskii and Vdovin, initially worked with translators in the classroom, but they worked hard to learn local languages and were quickly teaching children in their own language (Bartels and Bartels 1995:37–38; Stebnitskii 1931:48ff., 1932). Stebnitskii's translation projects with vanguard Koryak communists like Koryak author Ketsai Kekketyn had the goal of bringing the Soviet message directly to the native people of Kamchatka through the establishment of a Koryak literature (e.g., Kekketyn and Stebnitskii 1938). This included the usual political ideology of the importance of the local soviet, the pernicious qualities of shamans, and the virtues of hard work in the collective fishing brigade or reindeer herding collective. The goal of native language publications and bilingual education was to bring a primitive people into the modern world as quickly as possible through the communication of socialist content in the form of Koryak language.

One of the earliest textbooks in Koryak is *Jissa-Kalikal* (Red Book), which Stebnitskii wrote with the assistance of Evytkan from Apuka and Kachiqelaivin from Kamen, near modern-day Manily, using Latin letters (Stebnickijnak with Ev't'kanak and Qacg'lajv'nak 1932). In figure 18 we see how the first few

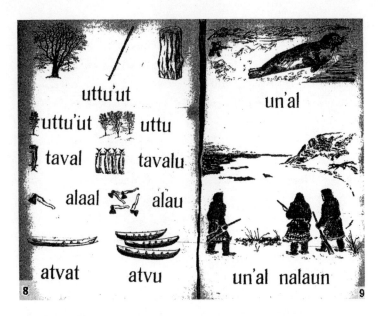

Fig. 18. Pages from *Jissa-Kalikal* (Stebnickijnak with Ev't'kanak and Qacg'lajv'nak 1932). Page 8 reads: "Wood. Wood, woods. Dried (salmon) fillet, dried fillets. Ax, axes. Boat, boats. Page 9 reads: "Seal. They spotted a ring seal."

pages introduce writing through the juxtaposition of text with pictures familiar to everyday life, such as wood, dried fish fillets, axes, boats, and a ring seal, and page nine ends with the simple sentence: "They spotted a ring seal." Pages 22–23 have simple questions and answers connected to specific scenes (see fig. 19).[7] *Jojoŋa* is the inner sleeping tent, where men rest and eat during the day. Note the word *tumgu* in the last two lines on page 22. Meaning "friends," it was seized upon by the Soviets to translate their keyword *tovarishchi*—comrades. Page 23 takes a swipe at shamans: "A shaman jumps around with a drum. . . . Earlier sly shamans deceived us. Earlier we were in the dark and listened to shamans. Down with shamans!" Later pages discuss cooperatives and collective herding and

Jojoŋa.

Ta'aj ojamtavьl'o jojok valajkь? Ta'aj qlavulu tu ta'aj ŋavьtqatu?
Qlavulu vagallajkь gakojŋa.
Jaqlajkь qlavulu?
Ŋavьtqatu kokajvьlajkь.
Ŋavьtqatu kumŋalaj:–Tok, tumgu qьqojat'ololatьk!
Ток, tumgu, qьqojat'ololatьk!

22

Aŋaŋьl'an.

Aŋaŋьl'an ɡajajaja tgajtьjkьn.
Aŋaŋьl'an kьt'ajŋajkьn.
Jaqalqal tgajtьjkьn? jaqalqal ajŋajkьn?—alvajtьŋ!
Ajŋon tamjuŋ-aŋaŋьl'a natamjuŋvolamьk.
Ajŋon muju nьlajtьmuju aŋaŋьl'an mьtvalomьn.
Alvaŋ aŋaŋьl'o!

23

Fig. 19. Pages from *Jissa-Kalikal* (Stebnickijnak 1932). Page 22 reads: "Inner sleeping tent. How many people are in the inner sleeping tent? How many men and how many women? What are the men doing? The women are cooking. The women call out, 'Hey, friends [comrades] eat some reindeer! Hey, friends, eat reindeer!'" Page 23 reads: "Shaman. The shaman jumps around with a drum. The shaman is shouting. Why is he jumping? Why is he shouting? For nothing. Earlier sly shamans deceived us. Earlier we were in the dark and listened to shamans. Down with shamans!"

fishing enterprises in local terms as well as decidedly nonlocal topics of heavy industry and capitalism, large cities, and political figures like Stalin, Molotov, and Kalinin.

The Cyrillic Koryak books from the late 1930s and 1940s look very similar, the main difference being more inclusion of celebratory material about Stalin and fewer entertaining tales that children would enjoy reading, most likely the result of official rebukes by ideological watchdogs (Grant 1995:99).[8] Looking at the cover of *Kaleyəlŋəyon* (Reading Book), co-authored by Kekketyn and Stebnitskii (1938), we see three boys on a beach and a good example of early Soviet Orientalism (fig. 20). Published in 1938 (just two years after Kekketyn published a primary school reader using the Latin orthography), the boys in their reindeer-skin clothes are already anachronistic. Photos from this period I have seen in the Palana Regional Museum show that most people were wearing a mix of homemade clothes and manufactured clothing, especially in summer. Indeed, a drawing on page 18 of *Jissa-Kalikal* bears a striking resemblance to a 1901 photograph by Vladimir Jochelson of the village of Itkana and may have been copied from it. I do not mean to criticize Stebnitskii or other authors, as they most likely had little control over the illustrations, but all these textbooks from the 1930s and 1940s are remarkable in the juxtaposition of traditionally garbed native Siberians with modern national leaders, factory workers, and other scenes of Russians operating machines. The semiotic operation contrasts Koryak people and Koryak culture with a Russian European industrial modernity, implicitly locating Kamchatkans in a primitive past, but there are multiple, complex meanings at work in these books. While speaking Koryak is an implicit index of being primitive, these books also suggest that this is not necessarily the case; one can use Koryak to describe modern technology and international politics, as in *Kaleyəlŋəyon* (fig. 20). Assuming that Koryak people and culture belong to a primitive past is common in the Center, as we saw in the Muscovite producer's critique of Yetneut and Weyem in chapter 3. The theme of Koryaks as primitives is also blatant in the November–December 1994 issue of *Passport to the New World*, a magazine marketing Russian opportunities to sundry foreigners on Aeroflot flights and in Russian hotels. This issue featured the investment and tourism potential of the okrug, describing Koryaks as a "primitive tribe" (Pakhomov 1994:36).

ХЭЧЧАЙ КЭККЭТЫН
ТО С. Н. СТЕБНИЦКИЙ

КАЛЭЙЫЛН'ЫЁН

УЧПЕДГИЗ · 1938

Fig. 20. The cover of *Kaleyəlŋəyon* (Reading Book; Kekketyn and Stebnitskii 1938). The volcano and city across the bay in the background are reminiscent of Petropavlovsk-Kamchatskiy—a city several hundred miles to the south of where most Koryak speakers lived at the time.

куэу мынэнгэвэлан оптынвык. Гы-
нин вэтатгыйн'ын школак.
То яхам колхоз-майн'ычъа гэнн'и-
вылин Йытэк яйгочавн'ынвын' шко-
лан'.

Нымэлъэу илгытэви.

Акко, Ёлтыгыйн'ын лыхвэгин'кин.
Ынан уйн'э-йын аявака урвах. Ынно
уйн'э агаймматка илгытэвык.
— Ток Ёлтыгыйн'ын, мынилгытэ-
вылхив, — ивнин Хэчъанак.
Ёлтыгыйн'ын елхиви элгытавъяян'.
Намалкэйтыван.

— Ан'айхыко! Нэеллывэтгым гай-
мат! — гайхыахалин'ава иви Ёлтыгыйн'ын виньвэ.
— Акко, элвыкэ уечем!
Ынно малкит ковъен'тон.
Тыттэл нымэлъэу нилгытэвын.
Акко, Ёлтыгыйн'ын тэхын мийкут-
вий. Ынно витку-ат нымэлъэу илгытэви. Нэйылын туюрвах.
— Акко, вотхо хоныпын' тыян'-
вон' илгытэвык элгытавъяк! — иви Ёлтыгыйн'ын н'ытома.

Выввэлъаткогыйн'ын.

(Мамаканэн панэнлтвын.)

Титэ гыммо майн'анма Эпухвэе-
мык, тайн'анма н'анко аняввэ коччон'-
волан'. Мую еппа вэтаньмэч энъэл-
кэ, ятан мытковвэлъаткон'волан', гым-
нин н'авъелъалн'ытомгын Эйн'эвн'э-
выт, Эвн'ыто то Йыэйн'эв.
Хэймэн' майн'ыхайыкмин'у хоянь-
н'ыволан' оечвылъэтын', яхам нако-

12   13

Fig. 21. Pages from *Kaleyəlŋəyon* (Kekketyn and Stebnitskii 1938).
The story beginning on page 12 is titled "Well washed," and reads:
"Huh, Yotəgəŋən is dirty. He does not wear a shirt. He does not
want to wash. 'Well Yotəgəŋən, we will wash you up,' said Hech-a.
Yotəgəŋən went into the bathhouse. They undressed him. 'Nasty!
They will probably bake me!' Yotəgəŋən cried out fearfully. 'Eh? Even
hotter then!' He struggled to breathe. They washed him up very well.
So then Yotəgəŋən felt better. He got well washed for the first time.
They gave him a new shirt. 'Hmm, now I will always wash in the
bathhouse!' said Yotəgəŋən as he went out."

The boys indicate the target audience for the book in figure
20, and notice that the youngest boy is the one instructing
others who appear to be older boys. This also reflects a typical early Soviet ideology of youth, progress, and overturning
the received wisdom of the elders in favor of the New Way.
Inside the book are pictures of Lenin, Stalin, and Moscow.
The text explains the Revolution and the leaders of the young
country. One page explains what airplanes are and how they

fly, emphasizing the good things they bring to local people, such as mail. On pages 12–13 pupils read the vignette "Well washed" (see fig. 21) The Koryak boy Yotəgəŋən is dirty, does not wash, and does not have a proper shirt. He gets help washing and ends up agreeing to wash regularly.

As Bruce Grant (1995:85) and Patty Gray (2005:91) have noted, Russian patterns of washing and cleanliness, which required the liberal application of water and soap to floors, clothing, and naked bodies, was a key part of Sovietization. In chapter 4 I related the traumatic first day of school of one seven-year-old girl, literally captured from her home in the tundra in about 1970, when she was publicly scrubbed and shorn of her traditional long braids. I found that native Kamchatkans remain sensitive to these kinds of indignities. In 1998 I purchased several copies of the newly delivered translation of Jochelson (Iokhel'son 1997) and gave them to people and village libraries as I traveled north through Tilichiki, Manily, and Paren'. While flipping through the pages and reading various sections on Koryak social organization and material culture, nearly all readers stopped at page 26 when their eyes fell on the subheading "Cleanliness" (*chistota*) in large, bold type. There Jochelson describes in two paragraphs how Koryaks do not wash, their cooking pots are full of reindeer hair from their clothes, they eat putrid food, and in spring they eat the larvae of flies implanted in the sides of deer (see Jochelson 1908:416).[9] I read the original English account (marked with a much smaller, less noticeable subheading) as the ethnographer's complaint about the months of discomfort he endured in an alien culture. My Koryak acquaintances reacted to Jochelson with stories about textbooks that said similar things and with experiences of racist condescension from Russian authorities.

Despite the good intentions of some dedicated individuals, standard Koryak language has emerged from a matrix of Soviet assimilative education, deprecating Koryak values and traditions and replacing them with Russian customs (see also Gray 2005:106ff. for the Chukchi experience in Chukotka). This is a legacy that may be insurmountable as current language revival activists struggle to produce relevant and engaging teaching materials. Although never articulated directly by people in Kamchatka, it is clear that standard Koryak and Koryak instruction serve as an index for Soviet education in general. While I found that nearly everyone in Kamchatka values positively formal schooling and education, people also have ambivalent memories of unpleasant experiences of their own education. By the 1950s bilingual education was replaced by a systematic oppression of Koryak-speaking children. Speaking Koryak was harshly and systematically punished, and a Russian-only environment was strictly enforced in the schools. A Koryak language teacher told me a typical story:

> When I started first grade we spoke freely in our language. We spoke poorly in Russian and it was difficult. They punished and scolded us in school for speaking in our own language. Our teacher was strict and not nice. One day a friend and I were put in the corner just for conversing in our own language. He scolded us, saying we should never speak in Koryak, but only in Russian. I was a child, and I couldn't understand why it was a crime to speak in my language.

I heard similar stories, including one man telling me of his father being forced to kneel on rock salt in the corner for the same offense a generation earlier than the woman quoted. There are many such stories from Native American experiences in boarding schools, including having one's mouth washed out with soap for speaking in an Indian language and not English (Child 1998:28).[10] Punishments exacted on natives in Kamchatka for speaking Koryak were similar to punishments of misbehavior from disrespect to fighting. The

American punishment is more directly connected to language, making Native American languages analogous to vulgar or obscene English words. These practices were effective; every person I encountered in Kamchatka born after 1945 has native or near-native fluency in Russian.

Coincident with repressing spoken indigenous language in Kamchatka, scholarly research on Koryak was crippled in Moscow and Leningrad. For example, when Alevtina Zhukova published her Russian-Koryak dictionary (1967), she was denied permission to publish the Koryak-Russian half. The logic may have been that it was most important to make a show of supporting those interested in learning Koryak, or perhaps a Soviet bureaucrat thought half a dictionary was plenty enough money spent on an indigenous Siberian language. Her former students told me other stories of Zhukova's work being watered down or refused publication by authorities who did not want to expend resources on primitive Siberian languages.

The currently used alphabet book is designed for seven-year-old children in the first grade (Zhukova et al. 1991). It is typical of the textbooks used in Koryak language classes in the 1990s and similar to the Chukchi text discussed by Gray (2005:106–07).[11] It opens with scenes of children arriving for the first day of school. The first twenty-seven pages are all pictures, providing the teacher with scenes for engaging students in typical what-question language activities. Strangely, some scenes include airports, garden plots, and home appliances, for which Koryak has no vocabulary. Letters are introduced on page 28 and whole words on page 33. By page 93 students are supposedly reading short texts on books, Lenin, Gagarin, Palana, Soviet holidays, and Koryak tales. At least half of the book focuses on situations like those pictured in figure 22, where boys in a boarding school are dressing and washing (note the cleanliness theme again), and many of the featured

Fig. 22. Pages from *Bukvar' dlia pervogo klassa koriakskikh shkol* (Zhukova et al. 1991). Pages 10–11 of the Koryak alphabet book provide scenes to provoke words with key letters. Other pages show children playing with manufactured toys, in a sandbox, putting on generic winter fur clothes, vacuuming the house, harvesting potatoes, and at the airport as well as at the reindeer herd and the fishing camp.

items, like clocks and tooth paste, require Russian loan words. Subsequent textbooks continue the structure of teaching native-speaking Koryak children how to write and formalize their language. Unfortunately, no children are learning to speak Koryak as their native language. Ninety-nine percent of first grade children speak Russian as their first language.[12] These textbooks do not accommodate this linguistic reality, that Koryak has undergone significant shift, and language and education efforts must be from a second language acquisition perspective.

Textbooks published after glasnost have a much higher incidence of unassimilated loan words from Russian than those published before the war. Substantial sections in every book are devoted to semantic areas with which Koryak cannot cope, mostly mechanized technology and nontraditional activities like newspaper publishing, farming, and mechanics. Russian words for car, ship, and soldier, for example, are borrowed straight into Koryak without accommodation to Koryak phonology. Words like *avtomobil'*, *korabl'*, and *soldat* contain sounds that do not exist in any Koryak variant, most notably voiced stops—[b], [d], and [g]. These words remain Russian, and their function is to assure that children are familiar with and respect a Western ideology of scientific progress and industrialization. These books were authored in the 1980s when the Soviet Union was still viable, and educational policies were set in Moscow and directed by pedagogic centers under the close control of the Party. The books explicitly index Russian language with modernity as Koryak slips away into non-use.

I want to emphasize that I do not mean to criticize the individual *people* involved with native language research and education in Palana, many of whom are my friends. They number about a dozen souls and are sincere in their desire to prevent their language from dying out. They are working in unheated offices and at low salaries to develop Koryak language materials. Curriculum specialists in Palana are not allowed to make necessary trips to villages in order to collaborate more closely with local communities. The political and bureaucratic structures, and some of the top bureaucrats managing them in the Palana administration, are the culprits hamstringing Koryak language revival teaching.

Official Languages and Variation

This divergence between the official, codified version of the language and actual use of the native language in any given speech community is not limited to Koryak. The Soviet linguist

Petr Skorik has constructed a similar sort of official Chukchi, which in several ways is even more divergent from spoken Chukchi than official Koryak is from its "vernacular." Chukchi distinguishes the gender of a speaker through phonological differences, which speakers recognize as "talking like a man" or "talking like a woman" (Dunn 2000b). Men's speech was selected for the official version, and this results in women radio and TV announcers "talking like men," producing cognitive dissonance among the Chukchi audience (Gray 2005:108). Just as Zhukova has corrected native Koryak speakers for "incorrect" usage, I was told that Skorik had even failed native Chukchi speakers in written Chukchi language exams, because dialectical differences in lexicon made words unrecognizable, and phonological differences made reading and writing the language difficult for Chukchi speaking nonstandard dialects (see also Dunn 1999:10, 19–20; 2000b: 395–96). This seriously undercuts long-standing assertions by Soviet linguists about the uniformity of Chukchi as opposed to the variability of Koryak dialects.[13]

The Koryak speech community in Palana is especially complex. The area is traditionally home to two speech communities: maritime hunters living on the coast speaking a localized dialect of Nymylan and reindeer herders roving the interior speaking Chawchu. After the Soviets established the town in its current place on the Palana River eight kilometers from the Okhotsk coast and made it the capital of the Koryak Okrug, speakers of other dialects moved there. Most of these people attained university education, often in Leningrad or Moscow, and they often work in okrug radio and television, the newspaper, the Teachers' College, or in the Institute for Teacher Development (many work at more than one of these organizations simultaneously, and they all know one another). These people come from all over the okrug. Many are from reindeer-herding backgrounds and so should command official Koryak. In fact, there is considerable variation between speech communities even among reindeer herders.

Although native intelligentsia in the okrug capital of Palana themselves collectively represent this linguistic diversity, they participate in the project of reproducing the imagined unity of the "Koryak language" (*koriakskii iazyk*) mostly because this system has become the status quo. Critiques of methods, writing systems, or other standards of Koryak language education are seen as refusals to build on past progress and thus as intrinsically regressive. These well-intentioned people are also caught between their desire to implement an effective language revitalization program and the bureaucratic structures of the Koryak Autonomous Okrug administration. More than one person has confided to me that individuals have been told not to shake up the system if they want to keep a job in the department of education. The scholars employed in the okrug Institute for Teacher Development and the Teachers' College, for example, are tasked with developing teaching materials, mostly textbooks, for the recognized indigenous languages of Kamchatka—Eveny, Itelmen, and Koryak. Chukchi speakers in Koryakia are ignored because the Chukotka Autonomous Okrug should be looking after "their" language. More important, nonstandard variants like that spoken in Middle Pakhachi, Lesnaya, or Paren' are not accommodated because catering to every single speech community is seen as impractical. The education system is designed for delivery to large populations, where the standardization of materials can yield economies of scale, but in the case of an endangered language of small communities, it is penny wise and pound foolish. The small amount saved by not serving each separate speech community is at the cost of rendering nearly all of the materials useless at the point of delivery—classrooms in specific communities (cf. Hinton and Hale 2001).

Smart people developing Koryak language curriculum and publishing are caught in a political and symbolic system that leaves them little room for innovation. Their work is guided by Soviet definitions of modernism and rationality. From the most erudite levels of philosophy and science to the most banal conversations on the factory floor or farmyard, Soviet life was dominated by an ideology of progress, which has ironically resulted in conservatism and lack of innovation among native-language activists, and even when activists do try to innovate, they are usually blocked by even more conservative managers from above. Although communism itself has been discredited, people in Kamchatka think of their education and training as advanced, better than what was available in the past. This is certainly true; I was often impressed at how well educated the people living in small rural villages were. Soviet ways of thinking are premised on linear development, and "reversals" in scholarly or social progress challenge not only linear development but also the sense of self-worth of the people who participated in that development.[14] Speaking and writing in a particular manner are bound up with powerful emotions. Language indexes not only social power and ethnic identity; it also serves as an index of personal being. Unfortunately, Koryak language programs in schools have not been able to connect learning and using Koryak language with positive emotions or a sense of empowerment.[15]

Nearly every school in the okrug with an appreciable number of Koryak children has had some kind of Koryak-language instruction for ten years now. The results of these massive investments in personnel and educational resources have been dismal. During twenty months of fieldwork covering a representative sample of the region, I found no children learning Koryak, and perhaps one or two children under ten years of age who could understand more than twenty words, which they never use actively unless under duress in the classroom (cf. Krauss 1997; Vakhtin 1998, 2001a). A second grade class I observed in a coastal native village was typical: the teacher tried to review kin terms and other nouns associated with family life (tea, cup, spoon, etc.), but the children did not know the material. Since the children were not native speakers, as the textbook assumed them to be, the lesson was primarily an exercise in translation and vocabulary testing. On a note supporting Rudolf Steiner's pedagogy, the children seemed to have the most fun, and were the most fluent in Koryak, during a short exercise break. They moved and touched body parts like head, arm, leg, foot, and said those words as they performed the action. Otherwise, it was clear that the children did not command any resources for generating Koryak sentences at any active level. Children whose first language is Russian cannot be expected to learn such a different language as Koryak sitting at desks.

According to specialists and administrators in Palana, native language education is going as planned and achieving results in small native villages in the northern part of the region, like Middle Pakhachi. However, talking to parents and teachers in Middle Pakhachi and observing children produces a different picture. Many parents see the cultural revival movement as a step backward: "They want us to move back to the tundra and raise our children out on the tundra, in a yayaŋa. But it is too late; our roots have already been cut off. Children aren't willingly going to leave these warm houses for the tundra." Like many other native people, this mother feels herself pulled in two opposite directions by cultures she thinks of as contradictory: speaking Koryak indexes tradition and the local landscape and is associated with the past, while speaking Russian indexes modernity and connections to the wider world. She wants her children to participate in a modernity she identifies with Russian culture, especially in material and social terms. From this point of view, her children are not about to live as she did as a child, as her parents did when they were young, but that is what she understands as one of the goals of the cultural revival advocated by native activists, most of whom live in Palana or in rayon centers. In a different context, she worries about the reindeer herd and who will look after it when all of her children are adults. Soviet ideology, much like the ideologies of Protestant missionaries and American government administrators in the United States, pitted indigenous traditions as counter to "modern" customs. This dichotomy of tradition and modernity was key to the Soviet project, especially among indigenous Siberians. Many anthropologists working in Siberia have shown how effective the Soviet state was at inculcating in people a fundamental ambivalence toward traditions and ideas of the traditional, although this sometimes has the effect of making tradition a realm in which one can resist state projects (Balzer 1999; Bloch 2004; Grant 1995; Gray 2005; Ssorin-Chaikov 2003). Thus traditional ways of speaking (in Koryak) can be used to resist the perceived state program of Koryak language standardization. I believe that parents found a state-sponsored project to promulgate official traditional language galling because the state and the traditional are more commonly seen as mutually exclusive symbolic categories.

Koryak-speaking parents believe that their language has not adapted to everyday situations encountered in town with machinery and European furniture. Koryak language teaching in the school is often viewed as a waste of time and money that would be better spent on teaching more marketable skills:

"It is pointless. The train has already left, Alex. The young people do not understand the language any more; our sixteen-year-old can't understand her grandmother. Anyway, we encourage her to study in school, learn English, and get into the Teachers' College in Palana." Koryak language skills will apparently not help a child in the world economy, but English and a college degree will. After three generations of Soviet ideology—evaluating Koryak language and culture negatively as "primitive" or "backward," while lauding Russian and other European languages as modern and international—it is no surprise that native people in Kamchatka frequently do not see Koryak language revival as "progress," as something valuable or even coeval with modernity.

Koryak language teachers in villages like Middle Pakhachi, Lesnaya, and Paren' have no delusions about their job. However, they tell me that young students are initially interested in learning the language and enjoy it. But students and teachers quickly become frustrated at the lack of materials, despite the okrug's commitment of considerable resources. The first teaching plan for native language and culture was based on a program developed in the Sakha Republic. As one village teacher explained to me, "Palana gave us a copy, and said, 'use this as a base to work from.' It was totally inappropriate. If we were the egoistic nationalists that the Yakut are, then maybe we could have made it work." Palana sees its efforts as the promulgation of a national language—fundamentally the same program as in Sakha-Yakutia, except on a smaller scale.[16] Local people recognize the imposition of a standard language as a nationalist project and reject it, not wanting to be associated with the negative connotations of ethnic nationalism. Clearly the state has no business in organizing traditional ways of being, from the perspective of indigenous Kamchatkans. This resonates with the Soviet logic of tradition and modernity presented by Grant (1995) in his book on Nivkhs' "century of perestroikas."

Village teachers believe that a Sakha-style nationalist program is inappropriate to the Koryak situation for several reasons. Foremost among these is that official Koryak is not suitable to the local community, even though people in villages like Middle Pakhachi and Achayvayam speak a variant close to official Koryak. Several Palana bureaucrat-scholars see Yakut policies as a good model to follow in their attempt to achieve the goals of okrug-wide uniformity in native language instruction, as is clear from Middle Pakhachi teachers' stories about Palana specialists visiting their village:

> [An Institute specialist] told me she wanted to eliminate dialects. They chose the Palana dialect because it is convenient and what they speak. In 1993 they arrived and watched Tanya teach Koryak. She presented the dialect in Palana. The textbook is all written in standard Koryak, so there is no getting around it, but Tanya pointed out how their grandmothers and parents spoke the language, and that she also spoke that way. [The specialist] was very critical, yelling that she should in no case teach any dialects, but only the standard.

In a similar incident another textbook author from the Institute in Palana stated that their goal was to eliminate the dialects and "build a new language out of nothing." He said, "We will make a new nation out of this one." Local teachers complained to me that it was clear that he was not interested in the needs and desires of Middle Pakhachi Koryak speakers. These two visits by the Institute for Teacher Development were focused on enforcing the official language, which is implicitly connected to the nationalist program of Koryak political (administrative) autonomy. As in other villages, official Koryak is a foreign imposition on children through the educational system. Elders in Middle Pakhachi reject the language children are learning as not a real language, and children quickly lose interest or respect for the activity.

The two Institute employees mentioned had moved to other jobs by 1999, but current indigenous language pedagogues remained handicapped by the legacy of those same policies. I should point out that neither of these two specialists speaks what *linguists* would call Palana Koryak, which is grouped with Nymylan/Alutor. The first grew up speaking Chavchuven among reindeer herders living far south of Middle Pakhachi. The second is a native speaker of Anapka Alutor, and he was criticized by others for mixing Alutor words with Chavchuven words in his texts for teaching official Koryak, commonly called Palana Koryak or Palana language. In Kamchatkan villages, the term *Palana language* refers to this kind of language found in books but devoid of a speech community aside from a small group of professionals developing textbooks in the 1980s and 1990s.

Even though Alutor/Nymylan is thought of as a separate language from official Koryak/Chavchuven, there have not been coherent education programs developed for Alutor. The absurdity of such policies was made dramatically clear to me in Tymlat, where people speak Alutor (usually called Nymylan by Tymlat villagers). The school has a native language teacher, originally from another part of Kamchatka, who is fluent in standard Koryak and teaches that in the classroom. This is not an accident. The woman teaching Koryak lessons in the preschool is also a Chavchuven speaker, as was the previous Koryak language teacher in the elementary school. The preschool teacher and the former elementary Koryak teacher commented that Nymylan and Chavchuven are not mutually intelligible: "It took me a long time to learn Nymylan, and even now I barely understand it." They told me that the two of them plus the current Koryak teacher are the only three Chavchuven speakers in the whole village. This did not invalidate their efforts at teaching "national" language (*natsional'nyi iazyk*, as it is typically called). Rather, it meant they were the only people in the village qualified to teach Koryak. This is true if "Koryak" refers only to the official Chavchuven dialect, but the heritage language, the language needing revival efforts in this village, is Alutor.[17]

This "school Koryak" is rejected wholesale by the adult community, who complain that it is not their language. Children interact with this language only in school, and they learn only a few dozen words. Classroom observation and discussions with parents and students lead me to conclude that such Koryak instruction only hurts any individual attempts at cultivating native language skills among children in this and other villages.

My last example is set in the village of Paren' on the north coast of the Okhotsk Sea, on Penzhina Bay. Here the teacher takes materials sent from Palana and translates them into Paren' Koryak and does not use any printed materials in the classroom (fig. 23). All instruction is oral or dependent on the blackboard, with students copying lessons into their notebooks. The teacher uses games a lot in Koryak language instruction. "I speak in native language [*v rodnom iazyke*] and they understand," the teacher told me. This small village of 250 people cannot support a full school, and after the third grade children are sent across the bay to a boarding school in Manily, the main village of the rayon. There students were often marked down for using the language they had been taught, the language of their grandparents. Finally, the village teacher met with the boarding school officials, and it was decided that students speaking Paren' would not be marked down for using those forms, but instruction is still in standard Chavchuven,

Fig. 23. Nadezhda Mikhailovna Plepova teaches Koryak language lessons as well as everything else to six pupils working at four different grade levels in Paren' (the sixth child is outside the frame). Photo by the author.

a language poorly known by the children's grandparents and considered foreign in their home village. People in Palana encouraged me to go to Paren' because its isolation should have preserved "real traditions" and native language better than in more accessible villages. More than once I heard Paren' characterized as Kamchatkan Kamchatka; that is, the edge of the edge. I was surprised, then, to discover that the Paren' language was closer to extinction, with fewer, older speakers than in most other villages. This was contrary to what I had been led to believe from discussions with native elites in Palana. It also points up the fallacy that geographic isolation always means conservative traditionalism.

This small Nymylan village with a half-dozen pupils from kindergarten through third grade has a full complement of textbooks and Koryak readers in excellent condition. The books are in great condition because they are never used. As the teacher explained, "They are not the way we speak here. I can't use them." In this remote village I saw for the first time a Koryak reader about Lenin's childhood (Ul'ianova 1989). It was translated from the Russian by a Koryak speaker under Alevtina Zhukova's supervision, with the Russian text as an appendix. It looks like an expensive book with a nice binding, heavy paper, and quality text and graphics. I have seen only twelve copies of the printing of eight hundred, and all of those were unused in Paren'.

Upriver from Paren', across the political boundary in Magadan Oblast, is the small village of Upper Paren', populated mostly by reindeer-herding Koryaks speaking Chavchuven Koryak. In Upper Paren' children attend the local village school, and they spend summers at the reindeer herd, where the language spoken is mostly Koryak. However, in Magadan Oblast there are no Koryak language programs in schools. Some parents lamented to me that it would be better if their village were inside the okrug boundaries, so that their children would get Koryak language instruction in school. While the Nymylan speakers inside the okrug in Paren' are sent useless materials in Chavchuven Koryak, speakers of that language just across the border are denied those same materials, which they would find helpful. Okrug Koryak education policies do not allow the provision of materials for speakers of non-standard dialects of Koryak, even though they are readily acknowledged as separate languages by scholars and the community of education professionals in Palana. Hence the Paren' teacher struggles to translate the Palana-made materials into the local language and pleads with grandparents to use the language more in everyday life. Some do. While chatting with one grandmother in Paren', I asked if she speaks Koryak to her grandchildren. "Yes, but it is pointless. They translate into Russian. Their parents can't speak Koryak. They can understand it, but they don't speak it. The Koryak language in the school is no good. You speak to the kids and they don't understand." I asked her to elaborate, and she said, "They don't memorize the words." One should not overestimate the incredible work and effort required for native speakers of Russian to gain an active command of Koryak, structured so differently from Russian or other European languages. I certainly find Koryak very difficult to learn, especially when most fluent speakers would rather chat with me in Russian than coach me through some crippled bits of Koryak just to help me with a language lesson. Language teaching is also very hard work for the fluent speakers who already have a myriad of other more pressing daily problems to solve.

There is nothing inherent in Koryak preventing it from adapting to nontraditional semantic areas like flying in airplanes, repairing snowmobiles, or reading books. However, speakers of the language have not been given the opportunity to adapt foreign words to Koryak phonology and morphology or to coin new words out of portions of existing Koryak words. Soviet linguists attempted to impose Russian words upon Koryak by codifying them in dictionaries and school textbooks. Koryak speakers understand that these words remain Russian, and I have found that code switching from Koryak into Russian is most often associated with a topical shift to Western technologies. However, I was present during at least one conversation entirely in Koryak where a man in his late forties was explaining to his older brother (perhaps in his early fifties) how his outboard boat engine had broken and how he repaired it. He used Russian words for the engine parts, but their phonology was greatly shifted into Koryak patterns. My research reveals that indigenous Kamchatkan languages are primarily used for conversation among elders or in their presence, which agrees with observations reported by Nikolai Vakhtin (2001a:168–70). Soviet ideologies of modernity and development have shaped language policies in Koryakia and across Siberia. The "modern development" of small, indigenous Siberian languages like Koryak has been seen as resting on the same sociolinguistic and political principles as the standardization of Russian and universal literacy in that language (Gurvich 1987; Zhukova 2001). It is ironic to read about the "opportunity for development" of Koryak "in the modern age" through schooling, recording folklore, and use in print and broadcast media (Zhukova 2001:59), when Sovietization and its aftermath have caused a dramatic reduction in the real use of Koryak as a way of speaking in everyday life. A century ago, before there was a USSR or writing in Koryak, the language (in all its varieties, including those no longer spoken) was commonly spoken by people of all ages in areas across northern Kamchatka, aside from the occasional conversation with a Russian administrator (or ethnographer), when a translator would be needed. By the end of the twentieth century, it is difficult to quantify the use of different varieties of Koryak. For Karaga or Paren' dialects, use is quickly approaching zero. For most other variants, it is very small, as my investigations seemed to show that Koryak dialects were used primarily for conversations among elders or in the presence of elders.

Koryak language education in the Koryak Autonomous Okrug suffers from a common plight—a lack of communication and coordination between target communities, on the one hand, and activists and organizers on the other. The predominance of a singular, official version of Koryak over the needs of local communities represents the power and success of Soviet theories of culture and language in influencing policy and even ordinary citizens' ways of thinking about how people speak and use language. People in Russia believe that a way of speaking, a language, marks a particular culture or ethnic group in a one-to-one correspondence. The legacy of Soviet nationalities policy and the nation-state logic implicitly behind the Koryak Autonomous Okrug encouraged thinking and policies that bolstered the unity of the "Koryak People" and denied or glossed over variation. The Soviet educational system played a major role in shifting people from speaking Koryak, Alutor, and other native languages to speaking Russian. Now that native languages are endangered in Kamchatka, the post-Soviet educational system is imposing another uniform language in schools, this time perversely referred to as "their own" (*svoi*) or "native" (*rodnoi*) language. Native language instruction was a key function of the Koryak Okrug as an incipient nation state and not simply a means to declared ends—survival of native languages in northeast Asia.

Conclusion

Koryak Culture and the Future of Tradition

Human beings inhabit a meaningful world. The patterns and organization of these meanings, many of which are unconscious or implicit, are what culture is all about. It continues to be a keyword that never seems to be out of fashion. Culture, variously termed, is at the middle of large clashes ("civilizations"), is often under threat ("our way of life"), the frequent focus of revitalization efforts ("our traditions"), and constantly debated ("morals, morality") in many places around the globe. People labeled "indigenous" in one way or another find themselves at the center of these debates about civilization, tradition, and morality. Indigenous Siberians are an excellent example in this regard, and I found people in Kamchatka talking a lot about culture and "our traditions" (sometimes contrasted with "their traditions").

Boasian anthropology produced a double-edged discourse on culture and culture theory that emerged from long, sustained conversations with Native Americans and other "indigenous peoples." Boasians both developed a theory of what culture is in the abstract and what particular cultures look like as historically emergent systems of thought and action. At the same time they were often using examples learned from field-work to critique their own culture and were participating in a political discussion aimed at improving "American culture" more generally. Boasian culture theory was certainly not homogeneous, as one can see in the critiques by Sapir (1917) and Goldenweiser (1917) of Kroeber's fondness for ideas of the superorganic. Still, we can see a general recognition that anthropology and its scientific work was also inherently political (Stocking 1992:92–113). The term *fourth world* is now commonly used to describe the similar socioeconomic position of indigenous communities in places like northern Canada, the Brazilian Amazon, Highland New Guinea, and Kamchatka. The postcolonial legacies of these communities reveal common patterns of economic and political domination coupled with representations of culturally exotic others. My ideas about an anthropological theory of culture and tradition are profoundly shaped by many long conversations with people in Kamchatka. The political power of this culture theory should not be underestimated. A sense of the value of traditions and a sense of self embedded in participation in "a culture" is a key part of fourth world political maneuvers both in local communities and in wider, global venues (Sahlins 2005). The stakes are high, often life or death. As I conclude my arguments on the intellectual value of a Boasian semiotics to understand Kamchatkan discourse on indigenous culture and tradition, it is important to keep in mind some of the specific people who contributed to my understanding.

My wife, Christina, and I returned to Middle Pakhachi in September 2001. I gave people copies of pictures she and I had taken, collected more information on those photos, and followed up on various questions relating to myth, ritual, and religion. One afternoon during tea, we watched part of a videotape I had made at the corral. As we watched herders lasso their deer on TV, Tanya, the elder sister of my friend Valentina (Valya) Dedyk, commented: "That's history now,

Alex. We do not have our own deer like we used to. The herd got so small, they had to unite with the private herd of Achayvayam. We hope that they will be able to build it up, but it's doubtful." The people I lived with at the Middle Pakhachi private herd had gone their separate ways. The herder Slava had left herding to feed his young family through hunting and fishing. Volokha and Rita had gone with the last Pakhachi deer to join the Achayvayam herd. Tanya's daughter Oksana had developed tuberculosis and was in the hospital in the district center of Tilichiki. Her son-in-law had lost himself in a bottle, and already in 2001 her two young grandchildren, Yurik and Yulia, were calling their grandparents "Mama" and "Papa." The general mood in Middle Pakhachi had grown only grimmer since 1998, and I did not have the heart to ask about identity, herding, and religion. I could not think of a way to bring up Slava's great line, "without deer there is no culture, nothing," without making it seem as if I were rubbing their noses in the loss. Certainly they were still people, after all, but they seemed more desperate than when I left in 1998. Traditions provide capable people with the flexibility and fortitude to shift to alternate forms of making a living, of course. While hunting seals, fishing for salmon, and hunting other animals may not be as prestigious or preferred for the reindeer man, those practices are as much part of a genuine culture in Kamchatka as herding deer. Indeed, it was clear to me that even though he was no longer herding deer, Slava was no less Chukchi as he fed his family with seal, salmon, and other tundra food.

In a January 2002 letter Tanya wrote that her daughter Oksana had succumbed to tuberculosis and died. A couple of years after that Valya visited me in Aberdeen to work on Koryak linguistics (see Dedyk 2006), and I learned that Tanya herself had died of TB, which is ravaging much of Russia as a whole. About two or three years after that, one of Tanya's teenaged sons also died of the disease. Tuberculosis is a disease of poverty and poor nutrition, and most people in Russia are poor. Koryaks are fourth world, some of the poorest of the poor. Canadian Inuit are likewise fourth world in their similar rates of sickness and death due to TB, the incidence of which is over one hundred times higher among them than in the general Canadian population.[1] Valya and her family are now caring for several relatives' children in Palana, which follows a common pattern of adoption in the Arctic. Through regular correspondence with Valya and other friends in Kamchatka, it seems that 2001 may have been the economic nadir. Certainly wages have become more regular since then. During these kinds of crises, recourse to traditional practices of living on the land (e.g., hunting and fishing) and the ability to activate latent traditional kin networks are critical to survival itself, let alone thriving. While life in Kamchatka has been hard after the end of the Soviet communism, it has always been hard, except perhaps for what can now be seen as an usually prosperous period from the 1970s to the mid-1980s.[2]

The 2006 consolidation of the Koryak Autonomous Okrug with Kamchatka Oblast into Kamchatka Krai followed the program of Vladimir Putin to consolidate the okrugs (all associated with indigenous Siberian minorities) with their neighbors in order to reduce the eighty-nine administrative subjects of the Russian Federation to a more streamlined structure. However, it was also an expression of the dissatisfaction of okrug residents with the administrative apparatus in Palana. It will be interesting to see how this change in administrative structure affects programs specially designed for indigenous Siberian communities. The four rayons of the okrug, together with Bystrinskiy Rayon (just south of Tigilskiy Rayon) may still be classed as "ethnic" (*natsional'nyi*), which would still provide for special language and culture programs in schools and other venues. The dissolution of the okrug, however, may actually help to break down the logic of standardization and homogenization of indigenous Kamchatkan ways of speaking and being in the world. This would be a good thing, for people in Kamchatka recognize the personal and moral strengths of diverse traditions and the multiple possibilities for innovation and play with Koryak culture.

Discourse on living with Koryak traditions is most likely to present a reified and compartmentalized view of culture when traditions are discussed explicitly. Robert Brightman (2006) identifies similar trends among American Indians' ideas about their own cultures in a discussion of Indian "ethno-anthropology," following Folgelson's (1974) coinage. Brightman's wide-ranging discussion points out that many Native Americans shared with anthropologists ideas of culture as something that could be "lost" or was "dying," especially in the early and middle twentieth century. In particular, Indian "biculturalism" is predicated on a concept that white culture remains other, not part of "Indian culture": "Indians and many anthropologists have converged in defining 'Indian culture' as an endangered and diminishing stock of 'traditional' elements that are rapidly losing ground to white influences. Indians were losing 'their' Indian culture and were acquiring 'our' white culture—which could not, however, be simultaneously ours *and* theirs at the same time" (Brightman 2006:380). This explicit discourse of cultural compartmentalism denies the lived realities of Indians and Koryaks incorporating practices like speaking a European language or using a television into a coherent indigenous culture that we can call Koryak or Cree, for example. Robin Ridington (2002) points out that Indians do not stop being Indian when they eat pizza, despite legal rulings to the contrary. This view of tradition and culture sees traditions as discrete elements that can be lost or stolen, a view most dramatically presented to me by the distinguished anthropologist Chuner Taksami, whom I discussed in chapter 4.

A Native Ethnographer on Classic Ethnographies

In June of 1998 Chuner Taksami arrived in Palana with nine hundred copies of the Russian translation of Jochelson's (1997) volume on the material culture and social organization of the Koryak. Jochelson had produced in the 1920s a Russian translation of his English book (1908), but it was not published before he emigrated to the United States in 1927, after which he became *persona non grata* and his work was branded "bourgeois." The manuscript had lain unpublished in the archive of the Museum of Anthropology and Ethnography in Leningrad for nearly seventy years before the Koryak Autonomous Okrug Department of Culture sponsored its publication as part of a larger program to publish old manuscripts that address the traditional cultures of the native peoples of the okrug. The Jochelson manuscript was the first to be published, partly because it required so little editorial preparation before going to press. It was also based on research conducted a generation before Soviet ethnographers like Orlova and Stebnitskii arrived in the 1920s; after Jochelson the next two manuscripts published in the series were Orlova (1999) and Stebnitskii (2000).[3]

The official presentation ceremony was in the theater of the okrug duma building, where many performances are held. Introduced by the head of the okrug Department of Culture, Chuner Taksami emphasized the need to preserve culture and traditions. "Publishing this book allows adults and children to learn those things. We published the book, and people say now that we are finished, it's preserved. No, things have changed a lot since then. There is still a lot of work to do." This seems to suggest that Koryak culture is an open-ended process that can undergo significant transformations and still remain a subject of ethnographic research. Other comments indicated a more material concern with native culture. Taksami's comment that "foreign colleagues, Americans, Japanese" now come and collect material was followed by a short tirade against an American family he had visited in Alaska not long before. They had bought up huge quantities of traditional artifacts in Chukotka in a matter of weeks. Thus he connected foreign linguists and ethnographers collecting materials on native language and traditions with foreign art dealers buying old and valuable items at very low prices and selling them abroad at a profit. Representatives of organizations in Palana then got up and spoke in a Soviet-style parade of dignitaries, obligatory at such events. Some thanked Taksami and others responsible for the publication of the book, while others simply promoted their own cause or organization (native language education, opening closed native villages). The first person to speak following Taksami was an official representative of the KAO branch of RAIPON, who said, "Our children are waiting for this book," reflecting the ideology of learning traditional native culture from a book in school instead of practicing it as a way of life. Others also acknowledged the importance of this book for the children.

Taksami's reification of Koryak folklore into things that can be carried off like parkas and clothing follows from a Soviet understanding of culture common among Kamchatkan educated elites. We can compare his call to protect Koryak culture from folkloric looters with his Soviet declaration of the value of sharing cultural heritage three decades earlier: that practical and useful elements of Nivkh culture had "become the property of all the peoples with whom the Nivkhi live and work," as was good and proper in modern socialist society (Taksami 1967:201).[4] Whether in socialist or capitalist property regimes, cultural property remains a reification that disconnects knowledge from people's lives. This is easy to do if one's focus is the stuff of life, whether that be stories, dances, or hats and sleds, instead of a focus on lives as lived (Handler 2003).

While Taksami may describe Koryak culture as changed and insist that there is still much work to be done in recording and analyzing it, many people in Kamchatka (native or not) believe that Koryak culture is mostly "lost" or "in the past." Thus reading a book like Jochelson's is the *only* way to study Koryak culture. This model of culture is sometimes used locally, however, as part of a program of engagement and empowerment of young people and tradition. On my last day in Palana in September of 1998, I was the main event at a conference organized by Valentina Dedyk under the auspices of the Teachers' College. She and some of her students gave presentations on ethnographers who had worked in Kamchatka, including Krasheninnikov, Dittmar, Stebnitskii, and others. At Dedyk's request I talked briefly about the Jesup expedition, highlighting the participation of Dina Brodsky (Jochelson's wife) and Sofia Bogoras. My mostly female audience at the Teachers' College was very interested in the invisible but important contributions of Jochelson's and Bogoras's wives. The audience, mostly Peduchilishche students but also including House of Culture artists and folklorists, seemed most interested in my presentation on contemporary Koryak culture in the okrug. I narrated several brief video clips touching on a geographically and thematically broad range of native practices I had encountered during my peregrinations about the okrug: the spring corral in Middle Pakhachi, a Hololo ritual in Tymlat, a Paren' blacksmith producing one of the famous Paren' knives, and scenes of fishing along rivers or the seashore. Scenes of native life far away from the center of Palana were the most exciting for my audience, the most authoritatively "Koryak."

After the presentation I was interviewed by reporters for both the okrug newspaper and the okrug radio station. The radio reporter, a young woman in her late twenties or early thirties, is one of three Koryak-speaking staff at the TV and radio station. She asked me to comment on changes in Koryak culture from Jochelson to the present. This was certainly not an invitation to a sound bite. I did not record the exact wording of her question, but I did note down that she phrased the question in terms of "losing traditions." I tried to explain that I thought this was a misconception. Cultures change, they always have, and they will continue to do so. Koryak culture undoubtedly changed before contact with Russians, and now it is changing in different ways. This is not necessarily a "loss." My goal was to validate contemporary Koryak people's lives and identities as *Koryak* and not as "assimilated" or "debilitated." The reporter was surprised by my response. She saw the discontinuation of practices as described by Jochelson as a loss, and this was clearly a bad thing.

This characterization of contemporary Koryak culture as less than what it used to be makes contemporary Koryak people less native but, unfortunately for them, not more "Russian" or "modern" or whatever one would oppose to "Koryak" or "indigenous Kamchatkan." Bruce Grant (1995) found that such a discourse of cultural loss dominated discussions about Nivkhs and Nivkh traditions on Sakhalin Island in the early 1990s. There Nivkh traditions could be likened to a battered old car, traded in for a shiny new one (socialism) that turned out to be a lemon (Grant 1995:16). I found such talk common in the more urban social spaces of Palana and among educated professionals. The emphasis on material culture denies authenticity to natives who do not live in a skin tent, speak their heritage language, travel on a sled, and fish with traps like their (great-) grandparents (cf. Brightman 2006; Ridington 2002).

Attempts at nationalist discourses that require an essentially biological identity as "Koryak" for legitimate or authentic representations of Koryak culture are short-circuited by the Soviet system of cultural capital, which requires paper certificates behind any authority. During my going-away party at the Teachers' College after the conference, I was asked to demonstrate my Koryak language ability, and I obliged by running through my repertoire of the few sentences I had memorized. After shouts of approval by the indigenous women present at my linguistic performance, one teacher joked, "We will have to write up and stamp an official certificate of Koryak language ability before you leave! You are a nobody without paper here [in Russia] (*ty nikto bez bumagi zdes'*)." She was only half-joking. In the Soviet Union and now the Russian Federation, you were and are nobody without paper. This is the common quality connecting the teachers who used to work in the souvenir factory, native language teachers, and the principal artists in native dance ensembles. In the modern world people must be certified as authoritative or authentic, and heritage must be official to be valued.

This book is not an attempt to unpack the details of the forms and meanings of Koryak culture as presented to me by the elders. Instead of an analysis of reindeer herding practices or hunting rituals and their implicit cosmology and other aspects of contemporary life, I analyze the representations of tradition and traditional culture that underpin all kinds of talk about language, culture, and tradition. I became fascinated by the fact that many ordinary people talked about Koryak culture in terms that implicitly followed a sophisticated anthropological understanding. These unreflective models of indigenous culture contrasted with more articulated notions. Talk about native culture, such as that from Taksami and my journalist interviewer, were more likely to reify culture into the kind of stereotype so often the subject of criticism by those who think the culture concept untenable. I find the culture concept unavoidable. I think anthropologists have two choices: (1) present a dynamic theory of culture connected to the way people live their lives or (2) bury their heads in the sand and let sociologists, political scientists, or (worse still) politicians define culture for us. I am going with the first choice.

In much of the debate and angst over representations, power, inscription, and the like over the last two decades, the main goal of anthropology—learning something new about people, about humanity—gets lost. Getting on with anthropology does not mean ignoring the valid critiques of textual strategies of authorizing texts and masking power relations (Metcalf 2002). While I have power in Kamchatka, in terms of indefatigable good health, adequate clothing and equipment, and tremendous mobility, I was also at the mercy of "the natives." Any success of this text comes from my relationships with people in Kamchatka, many of whom are serious intellectuals and are therefore identified by name in the preceding pages. My ethnographic portrayals are not strategies of having the last word but attempts at fulfilling promises I have made to many people: getting it right and representing their lives as lived, their real humanity, to the broader world.

Crowell (2004) makes the important point that anthropologists' power of representation implies a certain responsibility to be fair as well as truthful, and to be supportive of struggling communities as well as honest. While highlighting the political economy of cultural production may be an interesting anthropological analysis, such a move cannot escape its own political agenda, even if unintentional. To call the dance traditions I describe "invented traditions" misses the point of what people in Kamchatka are doing. Edward Sapir points out in his discussion of custom that it can be easy to demonstrate shallower histories for various traditions than the ancient origins that are imputed to them; for example, "Much of the ritualism of the modern Scottish clans is secondarily rather than lineally conservative," which is to say, the history of tartans and other Scottish clan traditions is not as deep as its advocates make it out to be (1931:371). However, one cannot ignore the politics of scholarship, and one has to question the motivations behind the rigorous debunking of Scottish traditions at the hands of the celebrated historian Hugh Trevor-Roper (1983), particularly as his timing was coincident with the beginnings of an eventually successful political movement for Scottish devolution. Thus I wonder at the continued popularity of Hobsbawm and Ranger (1983) among anthropologists who do not intend to deconstruct or discredit the cultural revival movements of the people they are describing. As Sahlins (1999:403–4) points out, "invention of tradition" analyses amount to little more than Malinowskian debunking of charter myths (see also Brightman 2006:381–86; Jolly 1992; Toren 1988). I do not share Rogister and Vergati's (2004) enthusiasm for taking the Hobsbawm and Ranger treatment to places around the globe.[5] Tradition is better thought of as the ground upon which people innovate figures (Wagner 1981). It is the semiotic milieu into which a person is socialized, and the age of traditional practices/beliefs/things is not as important as their general acceptance as traditional by the community in question.

Dancing

Sophisticates may snigger at the assorted ethnic dance ensembles performing Siberian dances as inauthentic simulacra of long-repressed sacred rituals. Authenticity, as typically understood in the West or even as commonly used among anthropologists, is an obsession of museum curators. It is tied to Western ideas of identity and the individual, to the notion that a singular, unique essence inheres in every performance, event, or person, unchanging through time (Taylor 1992; Trilling 1974). For example, Benjamin (1968) values the copy made by the cinematographer over the original event of the play or action filmed, but he nevertheless holds the distinction between original and copy to be important. A better model of culture and performance understands that whether it is a recording or a live performance, every instance is both a copy and an original. The distinction between original and copy also reveals our obsession with origins, how it "really happened," and is key to distinguishing myth from history. Distinguishing the real from the fake or imitation is not necessarily a spurious activity. In this sense I find judgments of the genuineness of a given performance, artifact, or even personal identity to be very interesting. They remain, however, what Boas called "secondary explanations" and belong to our data, not to our anthropological analysis of them (1911:63–69). We need to be continually on our guard against imposing our own categories of judgment upon those used by other people. Good anthropology is properly concerned with meaningful distinctions operative locally, and not with attempts at sorting a global inventory of traits and artifacts by a universal typology.[6] I agree that nearly every group of people has criteria by which people distinguish real from fake (e.g., true friend, valid claims, real wealth, effective authority), but the criteria can be different from one place to another (see Kaneff and King 2004).

Comments by people from all walks of life in Koryakia comparing Mengo and Weyem make clear that local evaluations of beauty are bound up with local ideas of authenticity. Mengo incorporated Koryak and other native Kamchatkan cultural motifs as decoration for a Soviet (European/Western) art form: the grand stage spectacle. Mengo was typical of such Soviet ethnic dance ensembles. Gil' took native motifs and incorporated them into a total narrative. Kicks, body moves, and drumbeats are integrated into a unified whole, which is structured by basic Western principles of good choreography. Yetneut's presentations were characterized by a juxtaposition of native and Western elements. A Western musical composition on a synthesizer was followed by a tape recording of an Even grandmother singing solo. Gil' incorporated native motifs learned in the field, preserving the effect of "Koryak dance" while modifying the specific forms to suit the choreographic needs of the moment. In contrast, Yetneut took great, even obsessive pains to replicate dance steps and body postures as he learned them in the field from the grandfathers (the reindeer herders, the quintessential natives) without changing or accommodating them to a unified whole. Yetneut's form is the content. It is not a layering of native "decoration" upon content of Western provenance. Yetneut said he left Mengo in part because Mengo did not dance like "real" Chauwchus. He was spurred to found Weyem because of a desire to stage an authentic representation of the way of dancing he remembered from his Manily home. In a conversation with me, Yetneut said he felt his research was validated by a laudatory telephone call he received from a Manily Chauwchu grandfather after Weyem was broadcast on local television there. Yetneut was not a boastful person, but when he did boast of his success, it was about the validation of his authenticity by the elders, directly from their mouths.

I want to emphasize the similarities between the art of Yetneut and of Gil'. Palana audiences readily identified Weyem's "Pokamchaw" dance as representative of Karaga, the Chauwchu dance as representative of Koryak reindeer herders, and so on. In this sense Yetneut followed the Soviet pattern of assuming the existence of culture groups and then set out to describe their choreographic styles. If one were instead to investigate the multiplicity of ethnochoreography in northeast Asia, I suspect that one could map a continuity of difference and similarity for dance forms similar to how various ways of speaking Koryak and Chukchi languages merge, blend, and overlap. If one were to plot choreographic styles on a map, however, it is highly doubtful that they would correspond to linguistic groupings or primary economic strategies or hat styles. More important, such an undertaking rests on a spurious model of culture. A spurious culture is one where forms are fetishized for form's sake and where the creativity of a person is repressed by dogma. "It is . . . a spiritual hybrid of contradictory patches, of watertight compartments of consciousness that avoid participation in a harmonious synthesis" (Sapir 1949 [1924]:315). This is something that I believe both Yetneut and Gil' successfully avoided. Their art shares a modern celebration of a harmonious synthesis and blending that ultimately rejects purist approaches to dance (i.e., purists' ideologies of cultural heritage). "Tradition" that has been immutably frozen and kept pure from outside contamination is thus part of a spurious understanding of culture. This is the idea of culture and tradition operative in the comments of the Moscow film producer who criticized Yetneut's performances for not being "native" enough. That is a version of tradition devitalized by the "dry rot of social habit" and not invigorated by creative minds (Sapir 1949 [1924]:315). The culture in Koryakia that I have been describing here, the culture where value and authority rests on the fidelity of a performance and not the identity of the performer, is a genuine one, but Koryakia is a small part of the world and not at all dominant. Soviet culture was spurious (as is that of post-Soviet descendants) precisely because it required watertight compartments of consciousness. This is similar to ideologies of biculturalism in North America, which Brightman (2006) rightly points out is a ludicrous caricature of how people actually live in a (largely unconscious) synthetic mode of cultural blending.

Ideas of cultural purity or compartmentalization remain common across the world, but when I ask, "Is this an authentic Koryak dance?" I am interested in what Koryaks and other local Kamchatkans have to say. Although it is interesting, I have not done research on how their European, American, and Asian audiences answer this question (save for those Europeans residing in Kamchatka). Thus I have been interested in authenticity as a culturally relative category to get at how a particular group of people identify something as being "done properly" rather than "improperly" or "wrongly." Local discourse about the traditional authenticity of particular performances or the ensembles more generally can be found in other parts of the former Soviet Union (Doi 2001:102ff.) and in other parts of the world (Bigenho 2002:12ff.). My Kamchatkan case material strikes me as unique, however, in the criteria used to validate the authenticity of dances—the moral relations of dancers to elders and the manner in which dancers learned how to dance, not the knowledge or the performances necessarily in of themselves. In chapters 2 and 3 I suggest that a semiotics of dance helps us unpack the complex meanings and values attached to dances, cultures, and knowledge. Native people in northern Kamchatka locate the value and morality of a performance in the sense that "one is what one does." This idea disconnects the performance from an essential, fixed identity of the performer and highlights the importance of the total context in order to understand the meaning and value of the performance. Anyone who masters the forms attributed to elders— the original keepers of traditional culture—is considered to control the associated patterns of native culture, whether they be dances, carvings, language, rituals, or economic practices. In this context it is not so strange for non-natives to produce "authentic" representations of native traditional culture or to represent the "real" political interests of disenfranchised native people. Bigenho (2002:14) found a similar case in Bolivia, where non-Indians could perform authentic indigenous music. Claims about a real Koryak hat, a properly Koryak dance, or real Koryak language are not necessarily simple descriptions of the objective features of the thing in question. In Kamchatka they imply claims of power to define authorized knowledge and authorized representations (signs) of culture. These representations are not mechanical replications, but reproductions, just as people themselves are reproductions (reproduced).

Although strikingly different in appearance at first blush, both Mengo and Weyem performances are hybrid mixtures that work as integrated wholes, and both are very much at home in the modern circulation of world art. The "harmonious synthesis" of Sapir's genuine culture is achieved by the audience, which understands the playful creativity achieved through moving in two cultural styles at the same time. Such movement is unavoidable in Kamchatka. It is spurious to pretend that reindeer herders do not use rifles and snowmobiles or that Koryak dancers cannot hear prerecorded music. When I call Soviet and post-Soviet culture spurious, I do not mean that it is fake—all cultures are real/genuine (see Handler 2003)—but that it cultivates a certain deviousness. A devious ideology champions a diversity of cultural forms but only if those forms are gutted of most of their meaning and power. I believe Sapir was decrying what he saw as a similar trend in the ideology of multiculturalism in America. The surprising thing about Kamchatka is how little purist ideology I heard. The journalist, some teachers, newcomers, and a few political activists expressed purist ideology in critical remarks, but native people living in small villages did not seem much bothered by implications of contamination in and of itself. They were more concerned with a proper funeral, sincere respect to spirits, or effective fishing—a concern with doing it "right" was not a concern with reproducing a static tradition. Ann McElroy (2008) has found a similar pattern among Inuit in Canada, and Brightman (2006:386) points out that dynamic and synthetic models of culture are most likely to emerge in discourse that does not include terms such as *tradition* or *culture*. That has certainly been my experience listening to the discourse of native Kamchatkans.

Native cultures are in the background of nearly everything the okrug House of Culture does, but most of the artists in Palana are interested in transcending the local and engaging in the global exchange of performance, creativity, and beauty. All the world is indeed a stage. Dance ensembles in Kamchatka are interesting because they provide a single focus for examining both Soviet and post-Soviet cultural configurations as well as a discourse through which native culture is described and defined, both consciously and unconsciously. Native people in northern Kamchatka value performances that can be characterized as "indexical-iconic" figures (Silverstein 2004, 2006). Resembling the speech and actions of elders is iconic, and these performances also index broader social relationships. This evaluation disconnects the ethnic identity of the performer from the performance. Again, someone who masters the forms attributed to elders—the keepers of traditional culture—controls the associated patterns of native culture, whether they be dancing, speaking, or doing something else. I argue that the authenticity or validity of a performance as judged by local Kamchatkan audiences is not based on any essential identity of the performer but on the qualities of the performance, making it possible for non-natives to produce "authentic" representations of native traditional culture. Judgments and other discourse about Mengo and Weyem illustrate how the ethnic identity of individuals is not addressed in evaluations of authentic manifestations of culture.

The understanding of "real" native culture as I have discussed in chapters 3 and 4 makes representations of culture alienable from personal identities, which is quite different from many situations among Native North Americans. As previously mentioned, Palana is not a place where authentic native culture happens, according to the way people in Kamchatka (both native and non-native) think. For them urban life and indigenous Kamchatkan culture are in separate, mutually exclusive spaces. Palana is inherently a European cultural space, and native culture can only be represented there. These implicit understandings provide a context in which European immigrants can claim to represent not only indigenous culture but also the political interests of disenfranchised native people. Just as Gil' could arrive in Kamchatka, research indigenous dance by visiting elders, and then stage Koryak dances, non-native politicians can learn indigenous political interests by spending time with indigenous people and represent those interests in their name. In both cases the representations are open to attack not on the grounds of essentialized identities but only in terms of the fidelity of the representation. It is ironic that Kamchatkans' rather anthropological understanding of culture and performance, avoiding essentializing pitfalls, opens symbols of native culture to control by immigrants, who may or may not have native interests at heart. Unlike the public performances of dance ensembles, the representations deployed in politics are often difficult to scrutinize. Native Kamchatkans seem to ignore or actively dismiss the politically powerful discourses of reified and essentialized cultural identity just as much as most of them dislike hearing standard Koryak. I have found that only a few politicians make use of the objectifying and essentializing discourse on culture that dominates the "cultural property" and "heritage" activities so common among indigenes of North America, Australia, and around the world (Errington 1998; Handler 2003; Kaneff and King 2004; Morphy 1995; Wright 1998). Doing so may help native Kamchatkans to profit better from their dances, hats, and other culture traits, for which other people are often willing to pay handsomely.

Dancing in Kamchatka concerns more than cultural continuity or self-fulfillment. David Koester points out that dance troupes are connected to cultural revival movements or ethnic politics in the minds of many Kamchatkans (2005:651). The Soviets, as we have seen, supported ethnic dance ensembles as a genre of politically safe cultural expression that could accommodate the ideology of "national in form, socialist in content." I have suggested, however, that folk-dance ensembles and performances address other political agendas besides the obvious politics of ethnic nationalism. While I have discussed only four dance ensembles in detail, there are scores of dance ensembles up and down the peninsula dedicated to performing indigenous dances. These groups often travel locally, and many are invited to international events, usually as representatives of native Kamchatka or Siberia.

If one were so inclined, it would not be difficult to pick apart the choreography of probably all of these ensembles as being distant from the "authentic" traditional dances of elders recorded on videotape or documented in detailed written descriptions from times past. Such a deconstruction would be poor scholarship on several accounts, however. First, setting up the "traditional" as an authentic standard, against which all deviations are judged, assumes a spurious model of tradition that is static, unchanging, and not transferable to contemporary situations. Second, it perpetuates a modernist hierarchy whereby Western-educated scholars decree what is genuine tradition through codification and inscription into authoritative knowledge (an ethnographic canon). This is a simple trap to fall into, especially in Siberia. I found myself placed on such a pedestal in Palana on more than one occasion, sometimes by journalists and on other occasions by culturites or other professionals. Despite my attempts to answer questions about Koryak traditions (often those connected to the spirits) in terms of "what the grandmothers in village X told me," I found others deferring to my words as authoritative when I would rather they had deferred to their own experiences and their own relationships with elders. Kamchatkans are just as modern as anyone, and in the modern market of ideas, voices validated by institutional affiliation (a university) and cultural capital (higher degrees) are attended to more closely than other voices (Bourdieu 1991; Fabian 1983; Hymes 1996). Third, and no less important, deconstructing Kamchatkan dance ensembles or any other possibly "nationalist" groups is just as much a political activity as a scholarly one. Of course all scholarship is political; we cannot recuse ourselves from political debates and entanglements. To pretend to be able to is disingenuous. At the end of the day we can only ask: "Who benefits and who suffers from the fallout of what we write?" and be prepared to make friends and enemies accordingly.[7]

Speaking

Soviet ethnography has established a theory of culture in Kamchatka that equates language (in the narrow sense of grammar and vocabulary) and culture in a one-to-one correspondence. People in Kamchatka, from the highly educated elite to ordinary native people living in small villages, are familiar with this theory of culture and accept it as natural, a simple description of the way the world works. The Koryak Autonomous Okrug had a titular nationality in the Koryak, and official policies supported the unitary view of the titular nationality through a native language education policy that homogenized a continuum of difference into a single standard, following the logic of a "nationalizing state" (Brubaker 1996). The only ideological alternative, as local officials and activists see it, is a plethora of languages, each indexing one of a large number of separate ethnic groups, which would undercut the imagined integrity of the Koryak ethnos. You are what you speak, or as Michael Silverstein puts it, "You are what you say about what you eat" (2004:644). A way of speaking both represents and significantly constitutes a way of being. Although there are many empirical examples in the ethnographic record where ethnic groups and language groups do not overlap in a one-to-one correspondence (Sapir 1921; Hymes 1968; Dorian 1999), modern states are quick to institutionalize ethnic groups as a legitimate form of political affiliation. The Soviet Union was no different in this regard, as we see in the administrative organization following codified "national languages" as expressions of the rights of these groups to their cultures, while policies of symbolic and overt repression of indigenous language use played a significant role in shifting people's primary modes of linguistic expression from various indigenous languages to speaking Russian (see also Grenoble 2003).

Laada Bilaniuk's (2005) ethnography of Ukrainian linguistic practices and ideologies demonstrates the pervasiveness of Soviet language policies. One would assume that the experiences of a European population, numbering in the millions and speaking a language closely related to Russian, would be very different from the experiences of a small indigenous group speaking a very different language at the other end of the continent from Moscow. There are no objective linguistic criteria for what is a distinct language, but Bilaniuk shows us how people naturalize linguistic distinctions into clearly demarcated groups. A standard or official language is never fixed, and its status as such must be continually reasserted and defended against any and all challenges. Speaking like a Ukrainian, or more accurately, being perceived to speak like a Ukrainian, could get one shot in the mid-1930s, when bourgeois nationalism was a capital crime. In the post-Soviet republic, it has become nearly a requirement for public office. The irony that runs all through Bilaniuk's ethnography is that as everywhere in the world, few people in Ukraine speak the standard form, and people who adhered to a purist ideology in their speaking were sometimes rejected as using a language that "was sterile and artificial" (2005:39). *Surzhyk* is a way of speaking that is taken as a mixing of Russian and Ukrainian languages. In everyday contexts it provides the unmarked, everyday forms, a plain and unassuming way of speaking with which people are typically at ease. Bilaniuk explains, however, how *surzhyk* is universally stigmatized as indexing an array of bad things from cognitive deficiency to suspect political loyalties. "The definition of languages is always intertwined with political, economic, and social interests, continually re-created in everyone's words" (Bilaniuk 2005:193). Most often, judgment that an individual or a group (i.e., a village) spoke good Ukrainian was part of a belief that those people were legitimately and authentically Ukrainian. In both Ukraine and Koryakia, a way of speaking indexes ethnic identity, political loyalty, and even moral suitability.

However, if we change the focus from an investigation of groups to an inquiry into what is going on among people in Kamchatka, then the groups disappear and are replaced by a continuum of difference. In any particular instance difference may or may not be used as an index of groups of one kind or another. In answer to my queries about why people practiced a ritual one way while friends in the same village did things another way, I received shrugged shoulders just as often as the standard Soviet understanding of membership in different cultural groups. Native people in Kamchatka have a history of knowing how to speak, or at least knowing how to hear many different ways of speaking. Standardization is clearly counterproductive to current language revival efforts. It is unpopular with the majority of people who use Koryak in everyday life and are most likely to encourage children to take an interest in it. It has likewise proved problematic in sustaining the interest of children in learning the language, once they recognize the differences between the standardized variant they learn in school and the variant spoken by their grandmothers.

Most of the research for this book is based on data from the period 1995–2001. More recent language maintenance activities are shifting to a more community-centered approach but remain crippled by enduring Soviet language ideologies and a lack of funding or concern by those in power. However, the increased availability of computers in Palana and the ever-lowering costs of desktop publishing mean that there is greater hope of producing customized materials for each speech community interested in such programs. The greatest challenge to teaching Koryak remains an ambivalence on the part of those very communities who are shifting from using Koryak in any fashion to primary use of Russian, along with a preference for children to learn not their heritage language—Koryak—but the international language of the modern economy—English—as their second language.[8]

These patterns of language shift are common around the globe (Crystal 2000; Robins and Uhlenbeck 1991; Tsunoda 2005; Walsh 2005). Native Americans, especially in the United States, suffered from boarding schools in ways similar to indigenous Siberians (Adams 1995; Child 1998; Coleman 1993; Prucha 1979; Szasz 1999). The bitter irony is that the Soviets initiated their *internat* system at about the time when most American Indian boarding schools were being shut down or reorganized.

Experience elsewhere shows us that language revival efforts for Koryak could be more effective if they left behind the Soviet logic underpinning much of the post-Soviet activity (e.g., Hinton and Hale 2001; Reyhner 2003). Instead of centralized research and publishing in Palana, it may be better to identify a community with individuals committed to native language transmission among the youngest children. Instead of demanding funding for ambitious publishing programs that never materialize, projects could be organized around volunteer efforts by local grandparents and teachers. Children, teachers, and elders could be consulted about the orthography and changes could be made to suit local preferences. Above all, local people have to be in charge of preserving local languages. A few people in Palana are committed to exactly that, but unfortunately they have not been able to have much effect in changing official policy or mobilizing communities. One should not underestimate the massive resources in time and money needed for such work. It is easy for politicians to say "let them speak their language" but much harder to put in place the necessary infrastructure (economic, political, social, and symbolic support) to enable a shift back to indigenous language use and halt the shift to monolingual practices in the dominant language.

Speaking is an index of knowing culture and traditions more generally. During the course of an extended interview and recording traditional Koryak tales, I asked one respected grandmother if she knew any people who can heal, in an attempt to segue into a discussion of shamanic knowledge and practices. She asked what I meant, and I replied, "With herbs or hands, in the old way." She shook her head negatively, "No, there aren't any any more. All the old, experienced people have died. There are only young people in the village now. They don't know anything. Children don't even know the Koryak language. They can't talk in their own language." This was a common sentiment in Kamchatka. If I was interested in learning about Koryak culture, I needed to talk to people who could speak like Koryaks.

It is important to remember that people can continue to speak like Koryaks using the Russian language. While fewer and fewer storytellers may be adept at performing traditional stories and myths in the Koryak language, that does not necessarily mean a loss of tradition. To be sure, the traditions are changing, but this need not lead to despondency over a loss when we understand that "tradition is not the opposite of change" (Sahlins 2005:51). I look forward to returning to Kamchatka to learn more stories from elders, record them speaking Koryak, and learn better the grammar of a language I find fascinatingly different from anything speakers of European languages know. My future research in traditional stories will also certainly include stories told in Russian as well. Traditions are an ongoing project and part of the lives of young people as much as elders.

Knowing

In Kamchatka it became clear to me after just a short while that local ways of speaking about tradition put elders at the center of knowing culture. According to the prevalent ideology of culture in Kamchatka, elders know tradition the best, whether that be how to speak Koryak, how to dance, perform rituals, make hats, or any other activity that could fall under the rubric "Koryak culture and language" (*koriaksaia kul'tura i iazyk*), as I broadly framed my research interests to local people. I was sent to learn what the elders know and do, and when people related to me their own knowledge of traditions, they often invoked "the grandmothers" or named a particular elder who was important in shaping what they knew and how they did things. Locating traditions with "the elders" suggests an original inseparability of personal *being* from ways of *doing* and *knowing*. Superficially, representations of traditions, particularly through dances (but also sewing, fishing, telling stories, etc.) seem to separate the being from the doing and the knowing. Certainly in the case of Mengo, I heard little discussion of the elders out at fishing camps from whom Gil' learned how to walk and move like a Koryak, and the dancers spoke of their work in terms of executing or improvising a choreography. I have explained how authentic performances are not dependent upon the identity of the performer but instead upon the source of knowledge on which the performance is based.

I should make clear that there is no necessary connection between elders and tradition. To be sure, there is a logic connecting old people to (supposedly) old practices and knowledge. However, Brightman (2006:359) provides the interesting example of Chipewyans, most of whom possibly do not value elders in the way Koryaks seem to do. Recall also the example of the village children peppering me with questions during one Hololo celebration. These children, also, "lived tradition" in a way that middle-aged professionals saw themselves as not living, let alone knowing. In other contexts where the term *tradition* was less salient, it was clear that young people often did know and perform traditions. However, they could not be authorities on traditional knowledge and so were not seen as useful sources for the ethnographer. This is why people in Kamchatka nearly always thought I was goofing off when

I was talking to youth and people my own age. Sometimes I was, but I also learned much about Koryak culture from young people.

Skill in a specific tradition, such as sewing souvenirs in after-school clubs, can be empowering and part of a genuine culture, just as ethnic dance groups present opportunities for the reification and trivialization of tradition while also providing opportunity for genuine connections to elders, traditions, and a potential base for personal empowerment. Schools and after-school groups are not necessarily a trivialization of lived traditions or genuine culture. What I find problematic, and many Kamchatkans see as a loss of culture, is when schoolroom teaching replaces learning through lived experiences with elders. When people in Palana or Petropavlovsk compare the work of the Russian Antonov with that of the Koryak Solodyakov, for example, or the Ukrainian Peskavets's native sewing with a native grandmother's, their race or ethnicity is not discussed; the focus is on the objective traits of the product itself, evaluated for the dual values of faithfulness to an identifiable tradition (i.e., qualities of iconic resemblance in their signification) and formal creativity (i.e., ability to bend old forms into new shapes and to continue in a genuine culture). My point is not to disparage work in schools but to suggest that it could benefit, in terms of filling children's souls, from greater participation by grandparents in after-school sewing clubs and similar activities.

Related discourses surrounding dancing and making suggest that culturites in Kamchatka use a theory of culture much like a standard anthropological notion of culture as a corpus of information (rules, recipes, procedures for a "way of life") that can be transmitted, like a message, from older generations to younger generations, much as a ball is passed from one person to another. This is a model of culture that comes across when talking with folklorists or other professionals working to "preserve traditions" or teach them to children in schools or after-school clubs. It has been dismantled in contemporary anthropology, and I believe it is a misunderstanding of the implicit theory of culture operative in Kamchatka, especially among the kind of people I talked to at the reindeer herd and found in conversation with activists like Nina Milgichil. For example, discussion of Yetneut's choreography (with him and others) often connected particular dances he staged to his experiences and relationships with elders and others performing living traditions at the fishing camp or reindeer herd. The young adults and children I talked to about dancing usually described their dancing as a combination of learning from an elder and emerging from the moment (e.g., the specific drum beat, individual mood, or occasion). Young adults talked to me about their efforts to retain and use knowledge of spoken Koryak in terms of their relationships to their grandparents.

Knowledge is best thought of as a process, as "knowing." Knowledge is inextricably connected to what kind of person one is; you are what you know. I have been arguing that it is even more important to understand how knowledge and the process of knowing are a function of deep, moral relationships. Thus what you know indexes whom you know. I found this idea implicit in Kamchatkan discourse on everyday life and activities. This relational sense of knowledge, person, and value creation fits well with the relational production of meaning grounded in a semiotic approach to symbols. Just as a symbol is meaningful only insofar as it is connected to things and ideas, people's lives are meaningful because they are connected to other people, places, and practices. So long as relationships among Koryaks and other indigenous Kamchatkans continue to support young and old in moral ties and soul-fulfilling ways, the future of Koryak tradition is secure.

Notes

Introduction

1. Population statistics are from the 2002 census. In the 1989 census the population of the KAO was more than forty thousand people. The collapse of the USSR precipitated a rush of settlers out of Siberia back to their home regions, mostly in European Russia and Ukraine. These people were educated professionals or highly skilled tradesmen. Thus Kamchatka, like Siberia generally, suffers from a lack of teachers, doctors, and lawyers as well as skilled mechanics, welders, and builders.

2. The Ushki archeological site in central Kamchatka indicates continuous human habitation in the area for about sixteen thousand years (Dikov 1977, in English as Dikov 2003). Archeologists have used the name Koryak to describe prehistoric cultures in the Okhotsk Sea region going back about a millennium, although this is contentious (see Dikov 2004; Lebedintsev 1990 [in English as Lebedintsev 2000], 2004; Lebedintsev and Orekhov 1999; Orekhov 1999; Semenov 1965; Slobodin 2006; Vasil'evskii 1964, 1969).

3. Nelson Hancock's (2001) research in Mil'kovo was conducted around the same time I was in Kamchatka. He analyzes Kamchadal identity politics, land use, and local discourse of Kamchadal traditions.

4. Tatiana Khelol (Palana Okrug Archive) has been studying the history of closed villages on Kamchatka and the possibility of re-opening some of them as part of a native cultural revival movement. There had been plans to reopen three native villages, but the eco-

nomic catastrophe of the early 1990s wiped out the funds allocated for the project.

5. Just as most Native North Americans have taken Anglicized names for both everyday and official purposes, Native Siberians have Russian names, which follow a pattern of Christian name, patronymic, and surname. Christian name and patronymic are used as polite address. In the past, indigenous Kamchatkans had just one name, and these names were Russianized into surnames by the Soviets. However, many native Kamchatkans living in coastal villages had converted to Orthodoxy and had Russian surnames such as Chechulin, Popov, and Yaganov before the revolution.

6. *Sovkhoz* comes from the terms *sovetskoe khoziaistvo*, "Soviet enterprise." These entities were owned by the national government directly, as opposed to a *kolkhoz* (*kollektivnoe khoziaistvo*) or collective farm, which was supposedly owned by the employees, but the differences experienced by ordinary people in Kamchatka were that state farms tended be larger, integrated systems of amalgamated collective farms. These terms are usually translated as "farms" because they were agricultural enterprises, but in Siberia they were often primarily engaged in fishing, reindeer herding, and other things aside from (or in addition to) raising crops and animals. There is extensive literature on collective farms in Siberia, including Gray (2003, 2005); Humphrey (1998); Konstantinov (2000, 2002); Konstantinov and Vladimirova (2002); Ventsel (2005); Vitebsky (2005).

7. I want to thank especially Laurel Kendall and Ann Wright Parsons of the American Museum of Natural History for their assistance during this visit. See Fitzhugh and Crowell (1988), Kendall et al. (1997) and Jochelson (1908) for photographs and descriptions of Koryak material culture.

8. Reindeer tendons make a soft clicking sound as the animal walks.

9. Dogs are also part of the domestic socio-spiritual world of Koryaks but in a way much different than deer. Sharp (2001) discusses the complex problems of understanding the ambiguous position of dogs in Canadian Dene society and cosmology, which is suggestive of the equally ambivalent position of dogs in northeast Asia.

10. Reindeer herding was commercially viable in the Soviet Union

only with massive subsidies to provision the herders and transport and process the meat. With the end of the USSR, cheap air transport disappeared, and inflation destroyed huge savings accounts amassed by herders. As imported foodstuffs (flour, tea, sugar, apples, etc.) became extremely expensive in the early 1990s, reindeer herders went from being some of the richest men in the village to the poorest. For descriptions and analysis of reindeer herding in Siberia and the Russian North see Anderson (2000), Donahoe (2006), Gray (2004), Gray and Stammler (2002), Habeck (2005), Vitebsky (2005), Vladimirova (2006).

11. Gray (2005) and Kerttula (2000) describe Chukchi based on research in Chukotka, and Kerttula notes a short visit to Achayvayam. Plattet (2005) compares Achayvayam Chukchi with Lesnaya Koryaks.

12. For works in English on Evens see Vitebsky (2005), Gernet (2005); on Evenks see Anderson (2000), Bloch (2004), Ssorin-Chaikov (2003). Ventsel (2005) and Ziker (2002) describe Dolgans in Sakha Republic and Taimyr, respectively, who are similar in many ways to Evenks.

13. The name Paren' is stressed on the second syllable and is thus distinct from the Russian word meaning "youth, guy, fellow." Like nearly all place names in Koryakia, it is a Russianized Koryak word.

14. Jochelson (1928:37) notes good evidence for the presence of Japanese iron items in southern Kamchatka many centuries before Russian contact and for cold-working of iron among Itelmen people (see also Lebedintsev 2000:203–8).

15. This was the first time the census allowed membership in more than one category; see Sokolovskiy (2007).

16. Despite Boas's reputation to the contrary, one can find much grand theorizing in several of his essays and books (1889, 1911, 1928, 1940 [1887], 1974 [1889]). His students picked up a few strands suggested in the work of their teacher and developed them further. For writings I find most useful see Sapir 1921, 1934, 1949 [1924], 1949 [1927], 1949 [1928], 1949 [1932]; Benedict 1934; Mead 1935; Whorf 1956.

17. Boas, Sapir, and Kroeber all present examples of how a culture

may be described and analyzed in terms of a style, and Benedict, Mead, and Sapir present provocative examples of summarizing a culture as a personality or "genius."

18. Anthropologists arguing about culture include Handler (2004), Ingold (2000), Ortner (1999), Sahlins (1999), Wagner (2001), and Silverstein (2004) as well as many others I find less interesting or useful. For the political ramifications of the culture concept, Nadasdy (2003), Feit (1995), Ridington (2001), and Grant (1995) provide a sampling for indigenous Siberians and Native Americans.

19. Sociolinguistics has shown that linguistic variation (most often phonology/accent) is directly linked to social factors such as economic class, social networks (kin, friends, etc.), and personal identity. See Labov (1972), J. Milroy (1992), and L. Milroy (1980) for representative discussions. In Kamchatka linguistic variation is clearly connected to identity claims or loyalties (e.g., Paren' vs. Mikino villagers in Manily or Rekinniki vs. Anapka villagers in Tymlat), but that is not constituted as much of a problem for most speakers of Koryak. People who want to communicate do, even across such wide variations as Karaga Koryak and Chukchi.

20. One could say that without an interpretant (Peirce's term), not only does the dance not have meaning—it does not exist. Thus the question "Does a tree falling in the forest make a noise when there is no one to hear it?" is meaningless.

21. This is a big deal in the Pacific; see the extensive literature on *kastom* (e.g., Hanson 1989; Harrison 1992, 2000; Hendry 2005). Ridington (2002) discusses the so-called pizza test for invalidating aboriginal identity and court claims, and Nadasdy (2003) elaborates on the discursive construction of tradition in court claims.

22. For nuanced analysis of boundaries and borders in a Boasian theory of culture, see Bashkow (2004) and Bunzl (2004).

23. There is a large and quickly growing body of literature on language shift or endangerment and language revival. Williamson et al. (1980) is an early collection on the topic. Fishman (1991) marks a useful baseline on the study of language revival movements. Crystal (2000), Dixon (1997), Edwards (1992), Grenoble and Whaley (1998), Hinton and Hale (2001), Robins and Uhlenbeck (1991), Walsh (2005), and Wurm (1991) are important works addressing

general issues of language shift and maintenance. Bobaljik (1998) analyzes the Itelmen case in Kamchatka.

1. Discovering Koryak Culture through History

1. David Anderson (2000:18ff.) received plenty of unsolicited advice from all kinds of people on where to find Evenkis who know their language and culture. Gray (2005) and Ssorin-Chaikov (2003) were both struck by the degree of ethnographic self-consciousness that the state had instilled in indigenous Siberians, especially among educated natives, who were explicitly enfranchised in state structures in order to lead their people.

2. The caricature of others is implied in mimesis, which Taussig (1993) discusses extensively, and is another reason to prefer Peirce's concept of iconic resemblances, which do not necessarily entail funhouse mirrors in the way mimesis does as an analytic category.

3. Patty Gray (2005) discusses the very similar situation of Chukchis in the Chukotka Autonomous Okrug.

4. I think the best analysis of the invention of Siberian ethnicities is found in Anderson (2000). Bloch (2004) adds insightful comments on issues of indigenous identity and political action in the Evenk Autonomous Okrug. Marjorie Mandelstam Balzer (1999) discusses Khanty culture and ethnic identity as a foundation for making a living and political action in the Khanty-Mansiskiy Autonomous Okrug. Gray (2005) analyzes in detail indigenous political activism in the Chukotka Autonomous Okrug, showing how symbols of Chukchi culture were used as political footballs by activists and administrators alike in an often bitter struggle in the 1990s. That situation was quite different from the political and social context in northern Kamchatka, where indigenous traditions and ethnic identity simply had little traction with anyone in okrug politics.

5. I realize that center-periphery structure is an oversimplification, critiqued even in post-Soviet studies, but it is an accurate reflection of the political worldview of many if not most *Kamchatkans*. My center-periphery model is a characterization of local models; secondary explanations, if you will.

6. Being "simple" in Russian does not carry connotations of stupidity, as it does in English. One important action leading to this

attribute was my habit of drinking tea from cups provided by my hosts. At first I did that out of unreflective politeness, but I came to understand that newcomers and even some ethnographers (Russian and foreign) often came to visit with their own cups. Supposedly this was out of fear of tuberculosis. I did stay with several people who later died of TB, but I have always tested negative upon returning home from Kamchatka, which I attribute to a lifetime diet of fresh fruit and vegetables (thanks, Mom), rare in Kamchatka.

7. Nancy Ries found these laments common among urban Russians in Moscow during *perestroika* in the late 1980s, but they had mostly disappeared by 1994 (1997:162). Although the Muscovite intelligentsia may have shifted their fashions of speaking, Ries's perestroika-era laments were commonplace in Kamchatka throughout the 1990s.

8. Stammler (2005:125–53) describes in detail the history of Soviet collectivization of reindeer herding in Yamal. The remainder of his book covers the post-Soviet period and consequent economic and social changes and continuities in Nenets reindeer-herding practices. Gray (2004) provides an excellent discussion of the changes in Chukchi reindeer herding in the twentieth century from Soviet collectivization to the post-Soviet aftermath, which is more similar to the experiences in Kamchatka than the post-Soviet experience in Yamal. Bilibin's (1932, 1933a, 1933b, 1934) ethnographic work conducted in the midst of collectivization provides fascinating insights into the social organization of herding and the changes as they were being wrought.

9. Gray (2005:87–113) provides a nuanced discussion of the enfranchisement and oppression of indigenous Chukotkans under Soviet rule.

10. This was true until 1997, when Yeltsin decreed that new passports would not include ethnicity (*natsional'nost'*), but it took several years before old identity documents were replaced. In the 2002 census people could indicate multiple ethnic affiliations for the first time. That did not result in a significant change in statistics for ethnic groups in Kamchatka, which are based on which group a person lists first.

11. See Nelson Hancock (2001) for a discussion of Kamchadals in

southern Kamchatka. Margaret Paxson (2005:52–85) describes the long process of in-marrying women becoming *nash* (ours) in a Russian peasant village in a way similar to how in-marrying Russian men become *nash* among Koryaks and other indigenous Kamchatkans.

12. For the Russian original, see Al'kor and Drezen (1935:24–33).

13. Forsyth (1992) provides a general overview of the history of the Russian conquest of Siberia and relations with indigenous Siberians. Slezkine (1994a) examines the topic from a standpoint of intellectual history and focuses more on the Soviet period. The edited volumes by Wood (1991) and Diment and Slezkine (1993) provide samplings of the diversity within Siberia while also providing a sense of major tendencies throughout the region. Kappeler (2001) provides a history of the Russian Empire placing Russian conquest and administration of Siberia in the larger geopolitical context of the Russian state. Hann et al. (2003) include chapters on the contemporary socioeconomic conditions in Siberia and throughout the former Soviet Union. There are several Cold War–era descriptions of Kamchatka and Siberia, which typically focus on geographic and economic factors, as well as some impressions by authors who were able to visit various showcase cities in Siberia, although Kamchatka was closed to foreigners (Kirby 1971; St. George 1970; Taplin 1997). Mowat (1970) is an embarrassing apology for the Soviet regime, showing how effective Potemkin villages can be.

14. All citations are from the Crownhart-Vaughn translation, but I have checked them against the reprint of the original Russian edition (Krasheninnikov 1994), which includes supplementary materials like maps and vocabulary lists not reproduced in the English translation.

15. Steller (2003) contradicts Krasheninnikov and provides terms that make more sense from my point of view. In fairness to Krasheninnikov, his book was published posthumously, although he did finish the complete manuscript.

16. I should remind the reader that this time was before the development of rigorous statistical reasoning, now taken as standard. That, coupled with the monumental task of compiling and processing so many figures by hand, made comprehensive analysis of Jesup

physical data impossible until the application of modern computers (see Jantz 1995; Jantz et al. 1992).

17. See Bogoras (1904–9, 1922, 1925, 1928, 1930) and Shternberg (1906, 1912).

18. Geraci (2001) analyzes the role of Russian Orthodox missionaries in the imperial project in western Siberia. He suggests that Bolshevik programs grew out of lessons learned by Orthodox missionaries in western Siberia. Slezkine (1994a:161ff.) also elaborates the role of Orthodox missionaries in imperial Siberia.

19. The suffix "Tan" is a reference to his childhood name Natan. Vladimir Bogoraz was a pseudonym he assumed as a young man entering revolutionary politics. Despite vituperative Stalinist attacks, Bogoras's work remained popular and influential with scholars and native people alike.

20. See Banks (1996) for a nice discussion of Soviet ethnos theory and a comparison with other theories of ethnicity. Gellner (1988) provides a more general discussion of Soviet anthropology in a sympathetic vein.

21. Comaroff (1991:65) describes how contemporary leaders in Soviet/Russian anthropology, such as Tishkov, Pasauskas, and Yamskov all view ethnicity as natural. At a 2003 conference in St. Petersburg I found that most Russian ethnographers were still working with an implicit theory of ethnos (see Chistov and Tishkov 2003).

22. This was true in the 1990s. Since then, Iokhel'son (1997), Stebnitskii (2000), and Gorbacheva (2004) have been published. All are important books on Koryak culture with perspectives much different from Antropova's (1971). People were only starting to receive and read Iokhel'son in mid-1998. When I asked friends and acquaintances about their impressions of Iokhel'son and Stebnitskii during a short trip in the autumn of 2001, I received only vague replies about the books being interesting. They certainly had not yet entered into the canon, but they may in time. I know that they are used in teacher training at the Palana Peduchilishche, the Teachers' College, now.

23. Although I have not pursued the question in detailed research, conversations with hunters and herders in Kamchatka gave me the impression that indigenous Kamchatkans have a more "path-focused"

understanding of the landscape, similar to that described in Hugh Brody's (1982) *Maps and Dreams*. I do not mean that reindeer herders have or had a vague sense of territory, either now or in the past. The specific areas of access, use, and rights to reindeer-herding territories are complex and shifting and entail negotiations and violence (more common before Pax Sovietica). See Donahoe (2006) for an excellent example from southern Siberia.

24. The Russian word *malochislennii* (literally "numerically small"), which I translate as "minority" in my work, is sometimes translated by scholars as "small," as in the subtitle of Slezkine's (1994a) *Arctic Mirrors: Russia and the Small Peoples of the North*. The criterion "minority" or "small in numbers" is politically important, because it signals that groups like the Sakha, Tyvans, and Buriats number in the hundreds of thousands and face political and economic problems differently than groups like Koryaks and Evens, which number only a few thousand people.

25. Gray (2005) provides the most focused analysis of indigenous politics in Siberia. Køhler and Wessendorf (2002) provide an excellent overview of the development of RAIPON broadly and some details on various regional projects, including those in Kamchatka.

26. See Gray (2005) for the case of Chukotka and how its separation from Magadan Oblast did not entail better support for indigenous rights or amelioration of their problems.

27. Personal communications with friends in Kamchatka and colleague Andrew Gerkey inform me that as of 2009 new housing, schools, and other buildings (mostly built of concrete) destroyed by the earthquake have been replaced. The new buildings are of modern steel and plastic construction and have been received with mixed opinions on their suitability in the wind and cold.

28. This is part of a directed federal policy being consistently implemented by Putin and his team. The first days of 2001 saw speculation that Putin was determined to eliminate the ten autonomous okrugs (most linked with indigenous Siberian peoples) and the Jewish Autonomous Oblast by merging them completely and totally into their neighboring provinces (RFE/RL Newsline, vol. 3, no. 1, January 3, 2001, archived at http://www.rferl.org/content/article/1344476.html).

29. These figures were reported in the electronic listserve news summaryRFE/RL Russia Report, vol. 5, no. 32, October 31, 2005 (archived at http://www.rferl.org/content/article/1344281.html). I realize that Russian elections may not be distinguished by their transparency, but my many conversations with all kinds of people all over northern Kamchatka gave me the consistent impression of extreme ambivalence toward the KAO among the electorate.

30. This continuum of social difference, from newcomer to local, is not so different from the continuum of self (*svoi*) and other (*chuzhoi*) among Russian peasants as analyzed by Margaret Paxson (2005). Paxson explains how in-marrying women from another village only gradually transform from belonging to them (another family, another village) to belonging to us (our family, our village), over the course of becoming a mother, raising children, and demonstrating social loyalties in small and large ways.

2. Genuine and Spurious Culture in Kamchatka

1. Karaga is a Koryak village, but there may well have been an Itelmen woman living there, or the "Kamtschadale" may have been a Russian-Koryak creole person.

2. Some two or three years later Nina Nikolaevna and her husband moved with their youngest son to Palana, although her oldest son remained in Manily with his wife and family.

3. The importance of dancing in ritual practice is mentioned in Stebnitskii (2000) and Gorbacheva (2004). It is analyzed to some extent by Jochelson (1908:65–114) and most fully in Plattet (2005:220–62).

4. The name of the ritual is onomatopoeic, referring to seals calling *olololololo* in the spring, which coincides with the start of the hunting season. People on the Okhotsk shore call the ritual Ololo, while those on the Pacific shore call it Hololo. The ritual complex forms a coherent hunting thanksgiving with many similarities among Nymylan communities, but there are separate subrituals directed to sea mammals versus land mammals, and countless variations apply from village to village. Nymylans in Manily and Paren' apparently do not celebrate an autumn thanksgiving ritual, but individuals told me there was a proper way to "receive" a freshly killed seal or beluga whale.

5. Aleksandra T. Urkachan's research on Ololo and other folklore of her village of Lesnaya was published in her wonderful little book *"Veemlen" (Lesnaia) zemlia moikh predkov* with the financial and editorial assistance of Erich Kasten and the Franckesche Stiftungen in Germany (Urkachan 2002).

6. Gypsy (Tsyganskii) music and dance have a high profile in Russia, as in other parts of eastern and central Europe, and are the most famous non-Slavic folk traditions. Apparently I was moving my shoulders in a rotational pattern back and forth instead of in the more traditional Koryak side-to-side movements.

7. I am indebted to Tim Ingold for the inspiration behind this idea.

8. Levin (1996) provides a fascinating description of a similar process in Soviet and post-Soviet Central Asia, where sacred forms of music were repressed and folklorists recast traditional melodies into ethnic music that supported state ideologies of socialist multiculturalism following the strict organization of *etnos*, whereby each "nation" had its own national tradition.

9. The linguist was Megumi Kurebito of Toyama University, who had coincidentally arrived the day after I did to continue her work documenting and describing Chawchu Koryak (see Kurebito 2000, 2001).

10. While this strategy prevented wind noise from marring the recording, the mosquitoes were thick and even crawled across the camera lens more than once. The Japanese linguist Megumi Kurebito was also eager to watch the group perform, so they had a small group of about four people for an audience in addition to my video camera that afternoon. Most in the village were busy fishing for salmon for winter.

11. See Koester (2002) for an excellent discussion of Itelmen ethnochoreography and its connection to environmental knowledge more generally.

3. Dancing in the Koryak House of Culture

1. I was unfamiliar with the audience clapping in unison to express exceptional applause for a performance until I traveled in Europe, but I have been told it occurs in parts of the United States.

2. The view from Kamchatka is that these are culturally European or Euro-American.

3. Comments in Kamchatka were often couched in terms of "we primitives" (Koryaks, Chukchi, etc.) on the one hand and "you civilized ones" (me, Americans generally, Russians/Europeans, Japanese, etc.) on the other hand. The contexts for such statements usually involved at least one of two common themes: (1) America is the land of all economic wealth and prosperity, while Kamchatka is the land where salaries go unpaid and the electricity is turned off to economize on fuel, or (2) you (me, the American, Europeans generally) have trouble living and getting around in the tundra, while this is "our home." For a more detailed discussion of the latter see King 2002a. Kerttula (2000:22ff., 124ff.) describes how the inland tundra is coded as a Chukchi space while the sea and littoral are understood as Yup'ik space.

4. Photographs and video clips of Mengo performances can be found at http://www.koryaks.net/dance.html, where there is also a description of a special concert in 1998 of Mengo's classic repertoire from the 1970s and 1980s.

5. Yekaterina Gil' and Tatiana Romanova (wife of the current director of Mengo, Mark Niuman) are Even and Itelmen, respectively, and have played a significant role as dancers and artistic leaders in the Kamchatkan dance scene. I do not discuss them in detail because I have little data on their activities, and my interviews with them were limited to several short conversations.

6. This is not to say that rituals are no longer performed and dancing is no longer a part of them. Several villages—Lesnaya and Tymlat, for example—are famous for rituals where dancing continues into the wee hours of the morning. On the other hand, there are also villages like Paren', Manily, and Khayryuzovo, where traditional rituals are no longer carried out and dancing is not as closely associated with ritual celebrations or communicating with animals and spirits.

7. The Koryak Okrug Regional Museum and the okrug library in Palana are limited in their outside funding opportunities because they exist wholly inside the government administration. They would need an independent legal existence to receive funding from the Eurasia Foundation, for example.

8. Nearly unique in the Russian Federation, no governor of the KAO was ever reelected.

9. *Spravki* (singular *spravka*) refers to certificates or signatures that a person needs to collect as part of everyday life in the bureaucratic nightmare that is Russia.

10. I have not investigated Mengo's finances, but I would guess that their foreign tours are mostly sponsored by foreign organizations. They certainly suffered greatly from the same cutbacks that all organizations were experiencing in the 1990s.

11. My use of the term *Eskimo* reflects local usage in both Kamchatka and Alaska.

12. This amounts to fewer than a dozen visitors each year, individuals who learn of the Itelmen festival through personal connections with several Itelmen and German persons living in western Europe.

13. More than other indigenous Kamchatkan people, the Itelmen have incorporated Russian influences to a high degree, including the accordion, into their melodies (see Zhornitskaia 1983:126, 128; 1994:214). But also see Koester (2002) for a discussion of cultural continuities encoded in Itelmen dance and the knowledge contextualizing them. My position is always that it is spurious to attempt a systematic classification of artistic motifs as "Itelmen" versus "Russian."

14. Police concluded after a short investigation that Yetneut's death was suicide.

15. I made several copies of all my video recordings and many of my audio recordings with people all over Kamchatka. In the first instance I duplicated the tape from my camera onto a VHS deck for my hosts and/or the subjects of the video. As we watched the duplication, I received much valuable commentary on what I had videotaped, from further exegesis on the traditions being demonstrated to metacommentary on culture and tradition generally. I also made copies for several colleagues in Palana, including linguists, folklorists, and House of Culturites inspired by Kamchatka folklore in their music and stage productions.

4. The Culture of Schools and Museums

1. The Komsomols were officially the communist youth league and an important step to becoming a member of the Communist Party.

Many people did not progress beyond membership in the Komsomols, however. Some of my colleagues in St. Petersburg belong to a social club that prohibits extending membership to former or present communists. It is a venue for academic men to gather and play chess, drink, and chat about erudite topics. If Komsomol membership is enough to brand one as a "communist," then 99 percent of the Kamchatkan intelligentsia, including some of my dearest friends, would be disqualified.

2. Bloch (2004), Gray (2005:103–15), and Liarskaia (2003, 2004) discuss the relationships among indigenous culture, ethnicity, and the school system in Siberia. Bloch focuses on the Soviet town of Tura, the administrative center of the Evenk Autonomous Okrug and similar in many ways to Palana. Liarskaia discusses how Nenets in Yamal have adapted residential and village schools to accommodate better their own cultural values and needs connected to a life of herding reindeer in the tundra.

3. Before the Soviet Union, indigenous Kamchatkans had one name only. The Soviet program of panoptic enumeration and control of citizens included the Russification of personal names. Beginning in the 1920s and finished before World War II, all people in Kamchatka were given patronymics (often invented) and surnames (typically taken from father's name). See Dedyk (2006) for an excellent description of Koryak personal names.

4. David Koester is completing a monograph on Tatiana Petrovna Lukashkina's life history, which includes much autobiographical material and situates her life in the broader context of being an indigenous Siberian person in the twentieth century. See Gray (2005:103) for the details of native cadres' education in Chukotka, which are very similar to my Kamchatkan material.

5. Soviet and Russian secondary school ends after eleven grades, so an *uchilishche* program includes two years beyond secondary school. Thus it may also be comparable to the associate's degree from American community colleges.

6. The factory's failure cannot be blamed on the director, as nothing except gold mining and fishing has ever been profitable in the KAO.

7. I noted this down as the teacher was talking, and the lack of parallel structure between the Russian and Koryak certainly does not

help the learning of the Koryak terms, which are foreign language words for these girls.

8. Decembrists were participants in a failed coup against the tsar in 1825. They were exiled to central Siberia for life and are credited with bringing European high culture and scholarship to that wild region. I translate the name Narodnaya Volya as People's Will, but Vakhtin (2001b:78) notes that the Russian name is often translated as People's Freedom, and both are correct.

9. Most of these photographs were the work of Dina Brodsky, Waldemar Jochelson's wife. The students' amazement is a testament to the virtue of analog cameras using large-format negatives. Photography at the turn of the twentieth century was cumbersome, involving glass-plate negatives almost the size of a sheet of paper. The benefit, however, is that they produce excellent eight-by-ten-inch prints more than a century later. About a year after I left Palana in 1998, the AMNH presented the Okrug Regional Museum in Palana with several framed Jochelson photographs printed even larger. See Kendall et al. (1997) for a discussion of Jesup-related photography, which provides needed emphasis to the less famous Siberian expeditions. Anderson and Campbell (2009) discuss glass plate photography in the Soviet Polar Census research in the 1920s.

10. The first exhibition, *Crossroads of Continents: Cultures of Siberia and Alaska*, was a groundbreaking project in the 1980s bringing together Soviet and American scholars and museum collections into a fully integrated, jointly curated exhibition on the archeology, history, and cultures of the Bering region (Fitzhugh and Crowell 1988). It toured major cities in North America and Russia with great success. *Crossroads Alaska: Native Culture of Alaska and Siberia* was a smaller exhibit put together to tour smaller towns in Alaska and the Russian Far East in the 1990s (Chaussonnet 1995). I saw the original *Crossroads* catalog in many Kamchatkan homes in 1995 and brought in a few more copies in 1997 (it was easy to find in Seattle's used bookshops). The publication of the Russian edition of the *Crossroads Alaska* catalog, discussed here, was greeted with much excitement in Kamchatka. It is clear that the teacher's use of these books as props and her immediate topic was related to my presence. Indeed, I was invited to attend the class as an additional

prop. However, her message of personal responsibility, love for one's region, and inculcating the value of education in her students was one that she conveyed in many instances and referenced in other conversations with teachers in the lounge. I also heard her say similar things to students later in the year when my presence in the college was more backgrounded.

11. The Chukchi movements south into Alutor areas in the 1920s were undoubtedly due in part to Soviet activities and civil war in the more settled regions of Chukotka near Anadyr and Markovo.

12. However, my Kamchatkan interlocutors may have thought of racism more in terms of what has been reported in larger Russian cities, including Moscow, St. Petersburg, and most notoriously Voronezh—non-Russians with dark skin are being attacked and sometimes beaten or stabbed to death, as in the case of a nine-year-old Tajik girl who was stabbed in a racially motivated attack on her family in St. Petersburg in 2004 (RFE/RL News Digest of Russia, March 23, 2006, archived at http://www.rferl.org).

13. Many grandfathers of primary school–age children are in their fifties and not particularly old or necessarily belonging to the group thought of as elders.

14. Russian marks animals as grammatically animate. It is reasonable and perfectly grammatical for children playing at make-believe to answer the question "who are you?" with "bear" or "fish," etc., as opposed to "people."

15. In Russia children are supposed to be seen and not heard, and it is rude to let children pester adults with their silly questions. I do not pretend to be the first (of any kind) to have visited anywhere in Koryakia. Of course plenty of Americans and other foreigners visit Kamchatka every year, and there probably have been several Americans in that village. However, the vast majority of these visitors do not speak Russian, and I doubt that those children had had a chance to pester an American to their heart's content before.

16. Handler and Gable (1997) present the discursive construction of history as fact and the institutionalization of a collective heritage through the work of Colonial Williamsburg. Merriman (1989) and the contributors to Karp et al. (2007) describe how people understand museums variably as temple, school, and library in their visits, where

museums are sacred places and/or places of learning and/or places where history is stored for the future.

17. The museum continues to suffer from underfunding, but staff retention improved after 2000, and the community continues to value the museum as a teaching resource for children and a gathering place for those interested in both traditional and more contemporary manifestations of "culture."

18. Pirozhenko and Krupina provide an example of *priezzhie* who have made a real home in Kamchatka and integrated with the local community. Krupina volunteered to repair her museum diorama after it was partially damaged in a fire caused by worn-out electrical wiring.

19. People in the former Soviet Union use wool or synthetic rugs following Central Asian practices and hang them on the wall more often than covering the floor with them, for both decoration and warmth.

20. See King (2003) for a fuller discussion of urban-rural differences in opportunities for making a living in Kamchatka.

5. "This Is Not My Language!"

1. See Duranti (1997:69–82) for a comprehensive overview of the history of the concept of speech community from Gumperz's (1965) initial formulation to the modern definition based on communicative interaction. Key publications outlining Dell Hymes's approach summarized in the terms "ways of speaking" and "the ethnography of speaking" include Hymes (1962, 1974, 1989, 1996).

2. See Campbell (2004) for an excellent discussion of what historical linguistics can and cannot tell us about language and history.

3. Fortescue (2005:2–3) notes that Krasheninnikov confused a now extinct variant of Itelmen with Koryak.

4. The genetic affiliation of the languages that make up the northern branch (Chukotian) and those that make up the southern branch (Itelmen or Kamchatkan) has been contentious. There are some skeptics on the connections between the northern and southern branches, due to the paucity of evidence for Itelmen languages and their great difference from Chukotian languages, although Bobaljik (2007) is convinced that Fortescue (2005) has demonstrated the coherence

of Chukotko-Kamchatkan. One problem is that the only remaining variants of Itelmen (Southern and Eastern stopped being spoken before the twentieth century) have experienced heavy borrowing from neighboring dialects of Koryak.

5. Edward Vajda (2008, 2010) makes a convincing case for the genetic relationship of Yeneseic languages like Ket (central Siberia) to Na-Dene languages in North America, as reported in *Science*. This Na-Dene grouping includes a different list of languages than Sapir's early suggestions. Mongolian and Turkic languages are certainly related. Sven Grawunder reports (pers. comm. 2002) that as one moves from one area to the next in Central Asia/southern Siberia, it is impossible to say exactly where languages stop being Turkic and start being Mongolian. These are two ends of a continuum of variation that most likely emerged from a common ancestor language.

6. Recent work highlighting the diversity of Koryak languages includes Mudrak (2000), Kibrik et al. (2000, 2004), M. Kurebito (2001), Nagayama (2003), and Zhukova and T. Kurebito (2004).

7. Stebnickijnak with Ev't'kanak and Qacg'lajv'nak (1932) follows a pattern common to nearly a dozen similar textbooks for indigenous Siberian languages. I have a photocopy of the microfilm edition in my possession.

8. Grant (1995:99) mentions that Stebnitskii was severely criticized for a children's textbook I have not seen. He worked with several Koryak men and included some traditional stories in each book. Apparently some of the textbooks did not have the proper balance of ideological instruction and children's entertainment and was too oriented to a juvenile audience.

9. Reindeer-herding people do eat fly larvae plucked from deer in the spring and describe the larvae as sweet, but I have not tried them myself. Nor have I sampled fermented fish heads prepared in many Nymylan communities. I have tried fermented deer intestines and blood and found it tasty in small quantities. Fermented fish heads smell strongly, and many Koryaks are shy about eating them in front of white people.

10. Dell Hymes (pers. comm.) also heard experience of mouth washing from Indians in Oregon. There are similar stories in an audiovisual presentation of elders' stories of life at the Indian residential

school near Tacoma, Washington, exhibited at the Suquamish Tribal Museum in Washington State (see http://suquamish.org/Museum .aspx).

11. I have five Soviet-era textbooks from the 1980s in my possession, given to me by friends and acquaintances in Kamchatkan villages who thought they were useless for children learning the language in school but that perhaps I would find them useful and/or interesting (Ikavav and Popov 1983, 1989; Ikavav et al. 1990; Ul'ianova 1989; Zhukova et al. 1991). Zhukova (1987) is the textbook used in Koryak language classes in the Teachers' College and best represents the systematic codification of standard Koryak.

12. Vakhtin is pessimistic about the state of Koryak, stating that based on his research, absolutely no children speak it (2001a: 169–70). My observations of reindeer herders suggest that small children are exposed to a lot of Koryak while they are at the herd with their parents, sometimes for months at a time. However, once they start school, their active Koryak language competence is most likely contracting significantly.

13. To be sure, Chukchi variation is not as differentiated as that of Koryak, but differences are noticeable. Fortescue lists three primary dialects of Chukchi that in turn may be divided further into more specific village or regional dialects (2005:x).

14. This is a common feature of post-socialist/communist life. While living in eastern Berlin (1991–93) and in Halle an der Saale (2001–2) I often heard complaints from former GDR people that it was unfair for Westerners, especially West Germans, to dismiss their skills and accomplishments. Statements like "There were many good things to what we had," or "Not everything under communism/ socialism was bad," were often repeated to me by East German engineers, Leningrad artists, Magadan miners, and Kamchatkan reindeer herders as well as Palana language activists working to revive the Koryak language they love.

15. See Tompkins's (1998) excellent book describing the huge effort that she needed to set up such an empowering curriculum in the Canadian North. As a school principal in a small Baffin Island village, she mustered support from the teachers and the community to shift the school to a place that could harmonize Euro-Canadian

learning with Inuit knowledge. She was able to move Inuktitut language from token lessons to the primary language of instruction at lower grades and an important language at all levels. However, she was working in a community where children entered school speaking Inuktitut as their first language, with little or no English.

16. Brian Donahoe (pers. comm.) notes that the situation in Tyva is even more nationalistic than language and cultural revival programs in Sakha.

17. Mutual intelligibility is no simple thing to establish. While many Nymylan speakers complained that they could not understand the standard Koryak on the radio, one Karaga Nymylan speaker told me that she could understand her Chukchi school chum, and the Chukchi girl could understand her Karaga Nymylan. These are two of the most widely variant languages in the northern Chukotian group. Obviously those who bring a hostile attitude toward a language will have lower comprehension.

Conclusion

1. The Canadian newspaper the *Globe and Mail* has been regularly reporting on the horrific rates of infection and death due to tuberculosis among Canadian aboriginals (see Curry 2010).

2. This view is not post-socialist nostalgia for the stagnant 1970s. In Kamchatka at least, the 1970s and 1980s did see unprecedented material wealth among ordinary people.

3. Gorbacheva (2004), based on the author's 1985 dissertation, is the most recent publication in this series.

4. This passage is also discussed by Kuoljok (1985:142–43) and Grant (1995:141–42).

5. Rogister and Vergati (2004) provide an introduction to a special issue of the journal *History and Anthropology* on "tradition revisited." Some of the contributors take a stance more critical to Hobsbawm (1983), and some demonstrate that the whole problem of "invented traditions" is a simplification of practices that are both complex and commonplace.

6. Typologies are, of course, vital to good anthropology, especially where one is interested in morphology (in biology, material studies, or linguistics), but typologies are themselves not explanations (Boas 1974 [1887]).

7. The exchange by Hanson (1991), Levine (1991), and Linnekin (1991) provides a nice discussion of this problem in the context of Maori traditions and the politics of culture. Handler (1993) discusses the pitfalls of engaging in an anthropology of a cultural revival movement with clear political goals.

8. See Morgounova (2010:220ff.) for a similar situation among Siberian Yupik speakers in Chukotka, where English is displacing the teaching of Yupik in local schools.

Glossary

Koryak Words

enelwit: A mixture of rabbit fur and reindeer fat used only as an offering to spirits, usually through burning in a fire.

Hololo: A hunting ritual thanking prey animals (seals, bear, snow sheep) for success the previous year to maintain good relations between hunter and prey. The name is pronounced in Russian either as *Khololo* or *Ololo* depending on the village.

melagetaŋen: Russian, white person.

yayaŋa, *pl.* yayaŋo; *also* **yaraŋa** (Chukchi variant): House, home, used to refer to traditional dome-shaped skin tents. Sometimes called a "yurt" by people unfamiliar with the Koryak term or its more famous Chukchi equivalent "yaraŋa."

Russian Words

The Russian language has three grammatical genders, and adjectives agree in gender and number with the nouns they modify. Masculine is generally indicated with a final consonant (*-ii* or *-yi* on adjectives), feminine with a final *-a*, and neuter with a final *-o* or *-e*. A *-y* or *-i* is added to nouns to make them plural.

intelligent: Educated person, white-collar worker.

internat: Residential school for indigenous Siberian children.

kolkhoz: From *kollektivnoe khoziaistvo*, collective enterprise owned by the workers (as opposed to the state government). Most kolkhozes in Kamchatka were amalgamated into larger sovkhozes by the mid-1960s.

krai: Literally "edge," used to designate large administrative districts with a relatively small overall population density; territory.

kul'tura: Culture.

liudi: People, human beings. Singular is *chelovek,* "person, human being."

mestnyi, *fem.* **mestnaia,** *pl.* **mestnye:** An adjective meaning "local," it usually indicates "native, indigenous" in Kamchatka, especially when referring to people. Particular to Kamchatkan usage, it seems that a white person can never be fully *mestnyi,* even an "old settler" with generations of Kamchatkan residence.

narod, *adj.* **narodnyi:** A people, folk, an ethnic group less "developed" than a nation (*natsiia*) in Soviet culture theory. In everyday speech, *narod* often means "people," as in *gde narod?*—"where is everybody?" As an adjective it can mean "ethnic," but usually it is a socialist term indicating "of the people" and/or low-brow, such as *narodnoe tvorchestvo,* "people's arts, art of the people, folk art."

natsional'nyi, *n.* **natsiia:** National, ethnic. A *natsiia* is a nation of homogeneous and self-conscious ethnicity in Soviet culture theory. This is similar to the British usage of "nation," which typically refers, for example, to England or Scotland and not to the United Kingdom, which would be "the union." In American parlance "ethnic" would be used. In Russian usage, *etnicheskii* can have a more derogatory connotation than *natsional'nyi.*

oblast: Province, administrative district of substantial population and importance.

obychai, *pl.* **obychi:** Custom.

official Koryak: Also called standard Koryak, a variant of Chavchuven Koryak codified by Soviet linguists and educators for teaching in schools; it is often called Palana language or Palana Koryak by Kamchatkan villages, although it is a completely different variant from that which is called Palana Koryak by linguists.

okrug: An administrative district established for a small indigenous group such as Koryak or Chukchi, often translated as "region" or "district" or "area." After World War II the national (later called "autonomous") okrugs were subordinated to neighboring oblasts. In the 1990s all okrugs were recognized as equal constituents of the Russian Federation, but in the early 2000s the federal government began a program of merging okrugs with neighboring oblasts into new territories called "krai."

priezzhii, *pl.* **priezzhie:** newcomer, incomer (literally "those who have arrived").

rod: Clan.

rodnoi: Native, home, consanguineous.

rodnoi iazyk: Native language, mother tongue, heritage language. As is common in Russia, many Koryaks name the Koryak language as rodnoi iazyk even if they barely speak it.

sovkhoz: From *sovetskoe khoziaistvo,* "Soviet enterprise," meaning a large and diversified state farm. In Kamchatka the main activity on such farms was reindeer herding, but they also included agricultural production in dairy, eggs, and other food.

traditsiia, *pl.* **traditsii:** Tradition.

ust'e: River mouth or confluence, prefixed to names of settlements at the mouth of a river.

yasak; *also* **iasak:** Imperial fur tribute levied on each adult man among non-Christian Siberian natives. Yasak was paid to the tsar's personal accounts, while Christians paid taxes to the government. Thus the tsar was not enthusiastic about missionary activity among indigenous people living in fur-trade areas.

yurt: Round Mongolian felt tent. Often used by Russians to refer to the Koryak yayaŋa.

References

Adams, David Wallace. 1995. *Education for Extinction: American Indians and the Boarding School Experience, 1875–1928*. Lawrence: University Press of Kansas.

Al'kor, Ia. P., and A. K. Drezen. 1935. *Kolonial'naia politika tsarizma na Kamchatke i Chukotke v XVIII veke*, vol. 2: *Sbornik arkhivnykh materialov*. Leningrad: Institut narodov Severa.

Anderson, David G. 2000. *Identity and Ecology in Arctic Siberia: The Number One Reindeer Brigade*. Oxford: Oxford University Press.

Anderson, David G., and Craig Campbell. 2009. Picturing Central Siberia: The Digitisation and Analysis of Early Twentieth-Century Central Siberian Photographic Collections. *Sibirica: Interdisciplinary Journal of Siberian Studies* 8(2): 1–42.

Antropova, Valentina V. 1971. *Kul'tura i byt koriakov*. Leningrad: Nauka.

Appadurai, Arjun. 1996. *Modernity at Large: Cultural Dimensions of Globalization*. Minneapolis: University of Minnesota Press.

Atlasov, Vladimir. 1988 [1701]. An Account by the Cossack Piatidesiatnik, Vladimir Atlasov, Concerning His Expedition to Kamchatka in 1697. In *Russian Penetration of the North Pacific Ocean: To Siberia and Russian America. Three Centuries of Russian Eastward Expansion, 1700–1797*, ed. B. Dmytryshyn, E. A. P. Crownhart-Vaughan, and Thomas Vaughan, 3–12. Portland: Oregon Historical Society Press.

Austerlitz, Robert. 1977. The Study of Paleosiberian Languages. In *Roman Jakobson: Echoes of His Scholarship*, ed. D. Armstrong and C. H. v. Schooneveld. Lisse, Netherlands: Peter de Ridder Press.

Balzer, Marjorie Mandelstam. 1999. *The Tenacity of Ethnicity: A Siberian Saga in Global Perspective*. Princeton NJ: Princeton University Press.

Balzer, Marjorie Mandelstam, ed. 1994. *Anthropology and Archeology of Eurasia*. 33(3).

Balzer, Marjorie Mandelstam, and Uliana A. Vinokurova. 1996. Ethnicity or Nationalism? The Sakha Republic (Yakutia). In *Ethnic Conflict in the Post-Soviet World: Case Studies and Analysis*, ed. Leokadia Drobizheva, Rose Gottemoeller, Catherine McCardle Kelleher, and Lee Walker, 157–78. Armonk NE: M. E. Sharpe.

Banks, Marcus. 1996. *Ethnicity: Anthropological Constructions*. London: Routledge.

Bartels, Dennis, and Alice Bartels. 1995. *When the North Was Red: Aboriginal Education in Soviet Siberia*. Montreal: McGill-Queen's University Press.

Bashkow, Ira. 2004. A Neo-Boasian Conception of Cultural Boundaries. *American Anthropologist* 106(3): 443–58.

Barth, Fredrik 1969. Introduction. In *Ethnic Groups and Boundaries: The Social Organization of Culture Difference*, ed. F. Barth, 9–38. London: Allen and Unwin.

Bateson, Gregory. 1936. *Naven: A Survey of the Problems Suggested by a Composite Picture of the Culture of a New Guinea Tribe Drawn from Three Points of View*. Cambridge: Cambridge University Press.

Baudrillard, Jean. 1983. *Simulations*. New York: Semiotext(e).

Benedict, Ruth. 1934. *Patterns of Culture*. Boston: Houghton Mifflin Company.

Benjamin, Walter. 1968. The Work of Art in the Age of Mechanical Reproduction. In *Illuminations: Essays and Reflections*, ed. Hanna Arendt, 217–52. New York: Schocken Books.

Bigenho, Michelle. 2002. *Sounding Indigenous: Authenticity in Bolivian Music Performance*. New York: Palgrave.

Bilaniuk, Laada. 2005. *Contested Tongues: Language Politics and Cultural Correction in Ukraine*. Ithaca: Cornell University Press.

Bilibin, N. N. 1932. Sredi koriakov. *Sovetskii Sever*, 91–97.

———. 1933a. Batratskii trud v kochevom khoziaistve koriakov. *Sovetskii Sever*, 36–46.

———. 1933b. Zhenshchina u koriakov. *Sovetskii Sever*, 92–96.

———. 1934. *Obmen u koriakov*. Leningrad: Izd-vo In-ta narodov Severa.

Bloch, Alexia. 2004. *Red Ties and Residential Schools: Indigenous Siberians in a Post-Soviet State*. Philadelphia: University of Pennsylvania Press.

Boas, Franz. 1897. The Social Organization and the Secret Societies of the Kwakiutl Indians. *Report of the U.S. National Museum for Year ending June 30, 1895*. Washington DC: U.S. National Museum.

———. 1889. On Alternating Sounds. *American Anthropologist* 2(1): 47–53.

———. 1911. Introduction. *Handbook of American Indian Languages*, ed. F. Boas, vol. 1. Bureau of American Ethnology Bulletin 40, 1–76. Washington DC: Government Printing Office.

———. 1928. *Anthropology and Modern Life*. New York: Norton.

———. 1940 [1887]. The Study of Geography. In *Race, Language, and Culture*, 639–47. Chicago: University of Chicago Press.

———. 1974 [1887]. The Principles of Ethnological Classification. In *A Franz Boas Reader: The Shaping of American Anthropology, 1883–1911*, ed. George Stocking, 61–71. Chicago: University of Chicago Press.

———. 1974 [1889]. The Aims of Ethnology. In *A Franz Boas Reader: The Shaping of American Anthropology, 1883–1911*, ed. George Stocking, 67–71. Chicago: University of Chicago Press.

Bobaljik, Jonathan David. 1998. Visions and Realities: Researcher-Activist-Indigenous Collaborations in Indigenous Language Maintenance. In *Bicultural Education in the North: Ways of Preserving and Enhancing Indigenous People's Languages and Traditional Knowledge*, ed. E. Kasten, 13–28. Muenster: Waxmann.

———. 2007. Review of Michael Fortescue, *Comparative Chukotko-Kamchatkan Dictionary*. *Sibirica: Interdisciplinary Journal of Siberian Studies* 6(1): 110–14.

Bogeyaktuk, Anatole, and Charlie Steve. 2004. *Taprarmiuni Kassiyulriit: Stebbins Dance Festival*. Fairbanks: Alaska Native Language Center and University of Alaska Press.

Bogoras, Waldemar (Bogoraz, Vladimir Germanovich). 1904–9. *The Chukchee*. Memoirs of the American Museum of Natural History vol. 11, parts 1–3. Leiden: E. J. Brill.

———. 1922. Chukchee. In *Handbook of American Indian Languages*, ed. Franz Boas. Bureau of American Ethnology Bulletin 40, part 2, 631–903. Washington DC: Government Printing Office.

———. 1925. Ideas of Space and Time in the Conception of Primitive Religion. *American Anthropologist*, n.s., 27(2): 205–66.

———. 1928. The Study of Paleo-Asiatic and Tungus Languages in the USSR for the Last Ten Years (1918–1928). *International Congress of Americanists, 23rd*, New York.

———. 1930. New Data on the Types and Distribution of Reindeer Breeding in Northern Eurasia. In *Proceedings of the 23rd Congress of Americanists*, 403–10.

Bogoraz-Tan, Vladimir G. 1991 [1931]. *Vosem' plemen; Na p'ianoi iarmarke*. Moskva: Gosudarstvennoe izdatel'stvo khudozhestvennoi literatury.

Bourdieu, Pierre. 1984. *Distinction: A Social Critique of the Judgment of Taste*. Trans. R. Nice. Cambridge MA: Harvard University Press.

———. 1991 *Language and Symbolic Power*. Trans. Gino Raymond and Matthew Adamson. Cambridge MA: Harvard University Press.

Briggs, Charles. 1996. The Politics of Discursive Authority in Research on the "Invention of Tradition." *Cultural Anthropology* 11(4): 435–69.

Brightman, Robert A. 1993. *Grateful Prey: Rock Cree Human-Animal Relationships*. Berkeley: University of California Press.

———. 2006. Culture and Culture Theory in Native North America. In *New Perspectives on Native North America: Cultures, Histories and Representations*, ed. S. Kan and P. T. Strong, 351–94. Lincoln: University of Nebraska Press.

Brody, Hugh. 1982. *Maps and Dreams*. New York: Pantheon Books.

Bromley, Yulian V. 1977. *Soviet Ethnography: Main Trends*. Moscow: USSR Academy of Sciences.

Brubaker, Rogers. 1996. *Nationalism Reframed: Nationhood and the National Question in the New Europe*. Cambridge: Cambridge University Press.

Bruner, Edward M. 1993. Lincoln's New Salem as a Contested Site. *Museum Anthropology* 17: 14–25.

———. 1994. Abraham Lincoln as Authentic Reproduction: A Critique of Postmodernism. *American Anthropologist* 96: 397–415.

———. 2005. Through the Looking Glass: Reflections on an Anthropological Life. *Anthropology and Humanism* 30(2): 201–7.

Buckland, Theresa, J. 1999. Introduction. In *Dance in the Field: Theory, Methods and Issues in Dance Ethnography*, ed. T. J. Buckland, 1–30. New York: Palgrave.

Bunzl, Matti. 2004. Boas, Foucault, and the "Native Anthropologist": Notes toward a Neo-Boasian Anthropology. *American Anthropologist* 106(3): 435–42.

Campbell, Lyle. 2004. *Historical Linguistics: An Introduction*. Edinburgh: Edinburgh University Press.

Chaussonnet, Valérie, ed. 1995. *Crossroads Alaska: Native Cultures of Alaska and Siberia*. Washington DC: Smithsonian Institution Press.

Child, Brenda J. 1998. *Boarding School Seasons: American Indian Families 1900–1940*. Lincoln: University of Nebraska Press.

Chinn, Jeff, and Robert Kaiser. 1996. *Russians as the New Minority: Ethnicity and Nationalism in the Soviet Successor States*. Boulder CO: Westview Press.

Chistov, Iu. K., and V. A. Tishkov, eds. 2003. *Rossiiskaia nauka o cheloveke: Vchera, segodnia, zavtra. Materialy mezhdunarodnoi nauchnoi konferentsii, 20–23 marta 2003 g*. Sankt-Peterburg: Muzei antropologii i etnografii im. Petra Velikogo.

Cochrane, Capt. John Dundas. 1825. *Narrative of a Pedestrian Journey through Russia and Siberian Tartary, from the Frontiers of China to the Frozen Sea and Kamchatka*. 2 vols. London: Charles Knight.

Coleman, Michael C. 1993. *American Indian Children at School, 1850–1930*. Jackson: University Press of Mississippi.

Comaroff, John. 1991. Humanity, Ethnicity, Nationality: Conceptual and Comparative Perspectives on the USSR. *Theory and Society* 20: 661–87.

Conklin, Beth A. 1997. Body Paint, Feathers, VCRS: Aesthetics and Authenticity in Amazonian Activism. *American Ethnologist* 24(4): 711–37.

Cooper, Frederick. 1992. Colonizing Time: Work Rhythms and Labor Conflict in Colonial Mombasa. In *Colonialism and Culture*, ed. Nicholas B. Dirks, 209–45. Ann Arbor: University of Michigan Press.

Cowan, Jane K. 1990. *Dance and the Body Politic in Northern Greece*. Princeton NJ: Princeton University Press.

Crowell, Aron L. 2004. Terms of Engagement: The Collaborative Representation of Alutiiq Identity. *Études/Inuit/Studies*, 28(1): 9–35.

Crystal, David. 2000. *Language Death*. New York: Cambridge University Press.

Curry, Bill. 2010. Aboriginals in Canada Face "Third World"-Level Risk of Tuberculosis. *Globe and Mail*, March 11, http://www.theglobeandmail.com/news/national/aboriginals-in-canada-face-third-world-level-risk-of-tuberculosis/article1496790/ (accessed March 14, 2010).

Daly, Ann. 2002. *Critical Gestures: Writings on Dance and Culture*. Middletown CT: Wesleyan University Press.

Dawkins, Richard. 1976. *The Selfish Gene*. Oxford: Oxford University Press.

De Lesseps, Jean Baptiste-Barthelemy. 1790. *Travels in Kamtschatka, during the Years 1781 and 1788*. 2 vols. London: J. Johnson.

Dedyk, Valentina R. 1996. Koriaki. In *Perekrestki kontinentov: Kul'tury korennykh narodov Dal'nego Vostoka i Aliaski*, ed. Valeri Shossonne, 16–17. Washington DC: Smithsonian Institution Press.

———. 2006. Koryak Personal Names. *Sibirica: Interdisciplinary Journal of Siberian Studies* 5(1): 117–40.

Desmond, Jane C., ed. 1997. *Meaning in Motion: New Cultural Studies of Dance*. Durham: Duke University Press.

Dikov, Nikolai Nikolaevich. 1977. Arkheologicheskie pamiatniki

Kamchatki, Chukotki i Verkhnei Kolymy: Aziia na styke s Amerikoi v drevnosti. Moskva: Nauka.

———. 2003. *Archaeological Sites of Kamchatka, Chukotka, and the Upper Kolyma*. Anchorage: U.S. Department of the Interior, National Park Service, Alaska Regional Office, Shared Beringian Heritage Program.

———. 2004. *Early Cultures of Northeastern Asia*. Anchorage: U.S. Department of the Interior, National Park Service, Alaska Regional Office, Shared Beringian Heritage Program.

Dils, Ann, and Ann Cooper Albright, eds. 2001. *Moving History/ Dancing Cultures: A Dance History Reader*. Middletown CT: Wesleyan University Press.

Diment, Galya, and Yuri Slezkine, eds. 1993. *Between Heaven and Hell: The Myth of Siberia in Russian Culture*. New York: St. Martin's Press.

Dittmar, Carl von. 2004 [1856]. Über die Koräken und die ihnen sehr nahe verwandten Tschuktschen. *Mélanges Russes Tirés du Bulletin Historico-philologique*, vol. 3, 1–48. St. Petersburg. Electronic edition ed. M. Dürr, http://www.siberian-studies.org/publications/ sources.html (accessed February 1, 2006).

———. 2004 [1890]. *Reisen und Aufenthalt in Kamtschatka in den Jahren 1851–1855*. Part 1. St. Petersburg. Electronic edition ed. M. Dürr, http://www.siberian-studies.org/publications/sources .html (accessed February 1, 2006).

Dixon, R. M. W. 1997. *The Rise and Fall of Languages*. Cambridge: Cambridge University Press.

Dobell, Peter. 1830. *Travels in Kamtchatka and Siberia; with a Narrative of a Residence in China*. 2 vols. London: Henry Colburn and Richard Bentley.

Doi, Mary Masayo. 2001. *Gesture, Gender, Nation: Dance and Social Change in Uzbekistan*. Westport CT: Bergin and Garvey.

Donahoe, Brian. 2006. Who Owns the Taiga? Inclusive vs. Exclusive Senses of Property among the Tozhu and Tofa of Southern Siberia. *Sibirica: Interdisciplinary Journal of Siberian Studies* 5(1): 87–116.

Dorian, Nancy C. 1999. Linguistic and Ethnographic Fieldwork. In *Handbook of Language and Ethnic Identity*, ed. J. Fishman, 24–41. Oxford: Oxford University Press.

Driver, Harold E., and William C. Massey. 1957. *Comparative Studies of North American Indians*. Philadelphia: American Philosophical Society.

Dunn, Michael. 1999. A Grammar of Chukchi. PhD diss., Australian National University.

———. 2000a. Planning for Failure: The Niche of Standard Chukchi. *Current Issues in Language Planning* 1: 389–99.

———. 2000b. Chukchi Women's Language: A Historical-Comparative Perspective. *Anthropological Linguistics* 42: 305–28.

Duranti, Alessandro. 1997. *Linguistic Anthropology*. Cambridge: Cambridge University Press.

Dyck, Noel, and Eduardo P. Archetti, eds. 2003. *Sport, Dance and Embodied Identities*. Oxford: Berg.

Eco, Umberto 1986. *Travels in Hyperreality: Essays*. San Diego: Harcourt, Brace, Jovanovich.

Edwards, John. 1992. Sociopolitical Aspects of Language Maintenance and Loss: Towards a Typology of Minority Language Situations. In *Maintenance and Loss of Minority Languages*, ed. Willem Fase, Koen Jaspaert, and Sjaak Kroon, 37–54. Amsterdam: J. Benjamins.

Elfimov, Alexei. 1997. The State of the Discipline in Russia: Interviews with Russian Anthropologists. *American Anthropologist* 99(4): 775–85.

Errington, Shelly. 1998. *The Death of Authentic Primitive Art and Other Tales of Progress*. Berkeley: University of California Press.

Fabian, Johannes. 1983. *Time and the Other: How Anthropology Makes Its Object*. New York: Columbia University Press.

Farnell, Brenda. 1999. Moving Bodies, Acting Selves. *Annual Review of Anthropology* 28: 341–73.

Farnell, Brenda, ed. 1995. *Human Action Signs in Cultural Context: The Visible and the Invisible in Movement and Dance*. Metuchen NJ: Scarecrow Press.

Feld, Steven. 1990. Aesthetics and Synesthesia in Kaluli Ceremonial Dance. *UCLA Journal of Dance Ethnology* 14: 1–16.

Fienup-Riordan, Ann. 1990. *Eskimo Essays: Yup'ik Lives and How We See Them*. New Brunswick: Rutgers University Press.

————. 1996. *The Living Tradition of Yup'ik Masks: Agayuliyararput = Our Way of Making Prayer.* Seattle: University of Washington Press.

————. 2000. *Hunting Tradition in a Changing World.* New Brunswick: Rutgers University Press.

Feit, Harvey A. 1995. Colonialism's Northern Cultures: Canadian Institutions and the James Bay Cree. In *On the Land: Confronting the Challenges to Aboriginal Self-Determination in Northern Quebec and Labrador,* ed. Bruce W. Hodgins and Kerri A. Cannon, 105–27. Toronto: Betelgeuse Books.

Fishman, Joshua A. 1991. *Reversing Language Shift: Theoretical and Empirical Foundations of Assistance to Threatened Languages.* Philadelphia: Multilingual Matters.

Fitzhugh, William W., and Aron Crowell, eds. 1988. *Crossroads of Continents: Cultures of Siberia and Alaska.* Washington DC: Smithsonian Institution Press.

Folgelson, Raymond D. 1974. On the Varieties of Indian history: Sequoyah and Traveller Bird. *Journal of Ethnic Studies* 2(1): 105–12.

Forsyth, James. 1992. *A History of the Peoples of Siberia: Russia's North Asian Colony, 1581–1990.* Cambridge: Cambridge University Press.

Fortescue, Michael D. 1998. *Language Relations across the Bering Strait: Reappraising the Archaeological and Linguistic Evidence.* London: Cassell.

————. 2005. *Comparative Chukotko-Kamchatkan Dictionary.* Trends in Linguistics Documentation 23. Berlin: Mouton de Gruyter.

Freed, Stanley A., Ruth S. Freed, and Laila Williamson. 1988. The American Museum's Jesup North Pacific Expedition. In *Crossroads of the Continents,* ed. William W. Fitzhugh and Aron Crowell, 97–103. Washington DC: Smithsonian Institution Press.

Gable, Eric, and Richard Handler. 1996. After Authenticity at an American Heritage Site. *American Anthropologist* 98: 568–78.

Gapanovich, I. I. 1932. *Kamchatskie koriaki: Sovremennoe polozhenie plemeni i znachenie ego olennego khoziaistva.* Tientsin, China: A. J. Serebrennikoff and Company.

Geertz, Clifford. 1973. *The Interpretation of Cultures.* New York: Basic Books.

Geraci, Robert P. 2001. *Window on the East: National and Imperial Identities in Late Tsarist Russia*. Ithaca: Cornell University Press.

Gell, Alfred. 1998. *Art and Agency: An Anthropological Theory*. Oxford: Clarendon Press.

Gellner, Ernest. 1988. *State and Society in Soviet Thought*. Oxford: Blackwell.

Gernet, Katharina. 2005. The Effects of Free Market Economy on Reindeer Herding in the Bystrinskyi National District, Central Kamchatka. *Journal of Small Business and Entrepreneurship* 18(2):201–6.

Girard, René. 1978. *"To Double Business Bound": Essays on Literature, Mimesis, and Anthropology*. Baltimore: Johns Hopkins University Press.

Gleason, Gregory. 1990a. Leninist Nationality Policy: Its Source and Style. In *Soviet Nationality Policies: Ruling Ethnic Groups in the USSR*, ed. Henry R. Huttenbach, 9–23. London: Mansell.

———. 1990b. *Federalism and Nationalism: The Struggle for Republican Rights in the USSR*. Boulder CO: Westview Press.

Goldenweiser, Alexander A. 1917. The Autonomy of the Social. *American Anthropologist* 19(3): 447–49.

Golovnev, Andrei V., and Gail Osherenko. 1999. *Siberian Survival: The Nenets and Their Story*. Ithaca: Cornell University Press.

Gorbacheva, Valentina V. 2004. *Obriady i prazniki koriakov*. Sankt-Peterburg: Nauka.

Graff, Ellen. 1997. *Stepping Left: Dance and Politics in New York City, 1928–1942*. Durham: Duke University Press.

Grant, Bruce. 1995. *In the Soviet House of Culture: A Century of Perestroikas*. Princeton NJ: Princeton University Press.

Gray, Patty. 2003. Volga Farmers and Arctic Herders: Common (Post)Socialist Experiences in Rural Russia. In *The Postsocialist Agrarian Question: Property Relations and the Rural Condition*, ed. Chris Hann and the Property Relations Group, 293–320. Münster: Lit Verlag.

———. 2004. Chukotka Reindeer Husbandry in the Twentieth Century: In the Image of the Soviet Economy. In *Cultivating Arctic Landscapes: Knowing and Managing Animals in the Circumpolar*

North, ed. David G. Anderson and Mark Nuttal, 136–53. Oxford: Berghahn Books.

———. 2005. *The Predicament of Chukotka's Indigenous Movement: Post-Soviet Activism in the Russian Far North.* Cambridge: Cambridge University Press.

Gray, Patty A., and Florian Stammler. 2002. Siberia Caught between Collapse and Continuity. *Max Planck Research: Science Magazine of the Max Planck Society* 3: 54–61.

Grenoble, Lenore A. 2003. *Language Policy in the Soviet Union.* Dordrecht: Kluwer Academic Publishers.

Grenoble, Lenore A., and Lindsay J. Whaley, eds. 1998. *Endangered Languages: Language Loss and Community Response.* Cambridge: Cambridge University Press.

Gumperz, John J. 1965. The Speech Community. *Encyclopedia of the Social Sciences* 9(3): 382–86.

Gumperz, John J., and Jan-Petter Blom. 1972. Social Meaning in Linguistic Structures: Code Switching in Northern Norway. In *Directions in Sociolinguistics*, ed. J. J. Gumperz and D. Hymes, 407–34. New York: Holt, Rinehart, and Winston.

Gurvich, Ilia Samoilovich. 1987. Etnoiazykovye protsessy. In *Etnicheskoe razvitie narodnostei Severa v sovetskii period*, ed. I. S. Gurvich, 136–51. Moskva: Nauka.

Gurvich, Ilia Samoilovich, and Kuz'ma Grigor'evich Kuzakov. 1960. *Koriakskii natsional'nyi okrug: Ocherki geografii, istorii, etnografii, ekonomiki.* Moskva: Izd-vo Akademii nauk SSSR.

Habeck, Joachim Otto. 2005. *What It Means to Be a Herdsman: The Practice and Image of Reindeer Husbandry among the Komi of Northern Russia.* Münster: Lit Verlag.

Hancock, Nelson. 2001. Ethnicity and State Measures: Social and Political Constructions of Kamchadal Identity, 1700–2000. PhD diss., Columbia University.

Handler, Richard. 1986. Authenticity. *Anthropology Today* 2(1): 2–4.

———. 1988. *Nationalism and the Politics of Culture in Quebec.* Madison: University of Wisconsin Press.

———. 1993. Fieldwork in Quebec, Scholarly Reviews, and Anthropological Dialogues. In *When They Read What We Write: The*

Politics of Ethnography, ed. C. B. Brettell, 67–74. Westport CT: Bergin and Garvey.

———. 2003. Cultural Property and Culture Theory. *Journal of Social Archaeology* 3(3): 353–65.

———. 2004. Afterword: Mysteries of Culture. *American Anthropologist* 106(3): 488–94.

Handler, Richard, and Eric Gable. 1997. *The New History in an Old Museum: Creating the Past at Colonial Williamsburg.* Durham: Duke University Press.

Handler, Richard, and Jocelyn Linnekin. 1984. Tradition, Genuine or Spurious. *Journal of American Folklore* 97: 273–90.

Hanks, William F. 1996. *Language and Communicative Practices.* Boulder CO: Westview Press.

Hann, Chris, and the "Property Relations" Group. 2003. *The Postsocialist Agrarian Question.* Münster: Lit Verlag.

Hanson, Allan. 1989. The Making of the Maori: Culture Invention and Its Logic. *American Anthropologist* 91(4): 890–902.

———. 1991. Reply to Langdon, Levine, and Linnekin. *American Anthropologist* 93(2): 449–50.

Harris, David. 1996. *A Society of Signs?* London: Routledge.

Harrison, Simon. 1992. Ritual as Intellectual Property. *Man* 27(2): 225–44.

———. 2000. From Prestige Goods to Legacies: Property and the Objectification of Culture in Melanesia. *Comparative Studies in Society and History* 42: 662–79.

Hazard, John N. 1990. Codification of Soviet Nationality Policies. In *Soviet Nationality Policies: Ruling Ethnic Groups in the USSR,* ed. Henry R. Huttenbach, 47–61. London: Mansell.

Hendry, Joy. 2005. *Reclaiming Culture: Indigenous People and Self-Representation.* Basingstoke: Palgrave Macmillan.

Hewitt, Andrew. 2004. *Social Choreography: Ideology as Performance in Dance and Everyday Movement.* Durham: Duke University Press.

Heyes, Scott. 2002. Protecting the Authenticity and Integrity of Inuksuit within the Arctic Milieu. *Études/Inuit/Studies* 26: 133–56.

Hinton, Leanne, and Kenneth L. Hale, eds. 2001. *The Green Book of Language Revitalization in Practice.* San Diego: Academic Press.

Hirsch, Francine. 1997. The Soviet Union as a Work-in-Progress: Ethnographers and the Category Nationality in the 1926, 1937, and 1939 Censuses. *Slavic Review* 56: 251–78.

———. 2005. *Empire of Nations: Ethnographic Knowledge and the Making of the Soviet Union*. Ithaca: Cornell University Press.

Hobsbawm, Eric. 1983. Introduction: Inventing Traditions. In *The Invention of Tradition*, ed. E. Hobsbawm and T. Ranger, 1–14. Cambridge: Cambridge University Press.

Hobsbawm, Eric, and Terence Ranger, eds. 1983. *The Invention of Tradition*. Cambridge: Cambridge University Press.

Howard, James Henri. 1981. *Shawnee! The Ceremonialism of a Native Indian Tribe and Its Cultural Background*. Athens: Ohio University Press.

Hughes-Freeland, Felicia. 2008. *Embodied Communities: Dance Traditions and Change in Java*. Oxford: Berghahn Books.

Humphrey, Caroline. 1994. Remembering an "Enemy": The Bogd Khaan in Twentieth-Century Mongolia. In *Memory, History, and Opposition under State Socialism*, ed. R. S. Watson, 21–44. Santa Fe: School of American Research Press.

———. 1998. *Marx Went Away—but Karl Stayed Behind*. Ann Arbor: University of Michigan Press.

Hymes, Dell H. 1962. The Ethnography of Speaking. In *Anthropology and Human Behavior*, ed. T. Gladwin and W. C. Sturtevant, 13–53. Washington DC: Anthropology Society of Washington.

———. 1968. Linguistic Problems in Defining the Concept of "Tribe." *Essays on the Problem of Tribe*, ed. June Helm, 23–48. Seattle: University of Washington Press and American Ethnological Society.

———. 1974. *Foundations in Sociolinguistics: An Ethnographic Approach*. Philadelphia: University of Pennsylvania Press.

———. 1989 [1974]. Ways of Speaking. In *Explorations in the Ethnography of Speaking*, ed. R. Bauman and J. Sherzer, 433–51. Cambridge: Cambridge University Press.

———. 1996. *Ethnography, Linguistics, Narrative Inequality: Toward an Understanding of Voice*. London: Taylor and Francis.

Iailetkan, A. I. 1980. *Fakul'tativnyi kurs po koriakskomu iazyku dlia 7–8 klassov*. Moskva: Rotaprint, Ministerstva Prosveshcheniia RSFSR.

Ikavav, Marina F., and Mikhail I. Popov. 1983. *Koriakskii iazyk: Uchebnik i kniga dlia chteniia v pervom klasse*. Leningrad: Prosveshchenie.

———. 1989. *Koriakskii iazyk: Uchebnik i kniga dlia chteniia dla vtorogo klassa*. Leningrad: Prosveshchenie.

Ikavav, Marina F., Mikhail I. Popov, and Irina S. Agin'. 1990. *Koriakskii iazyk: Uchebnik i kniga dlia chteniia dlia tret'ego klassa*. Leningrad: Prosveshchenie.

Ikuta, Hiroko. 2007. Iñupiat Pride: *Kivgiq* (Messenger Feast) on the Alaskan North Slope. *Études/Inuit/Studies* 31(1–2): 343–64.

———. 2010. Sociality of Dance: Eskimo Dance among Yupiget on St. Lawrence Island and Iñupiat in Barrow, Alaska. PhD diss., Department of Anthropology, University of Aberdeen.

Ingold, Tim. 2000. *The Perception of the Environment: Essays on Livelihood, Dwelling, and Skill*. London: Routledge.

Ingold, Tim, and Elizabeth Hallam. 2007. Creativity and Cultural Improvisation: An Introduction. In *Creativity and Cultural Improvisation*, ed. E. Hallam and T. Ingold. Oxford: Berg.

Ingold, Tim, and Terhi Kurtilla. 2000. Perceiving the Environment in Finnish Lapland. *Body and Society* 6(3–4): 183–96.

Iokhel'son, Vladimir I. 1997. *Koriaki: Material'naia kul'tura i sotsial'naia organizatsiia*. Sankt-Peterburg: Nauka.

Jakobson, Roman. 1942. The Paleosiberian Languages. *American Anthropologist*, n.s., 44: 602–20.

Jakobson, Roman, Gerta Hüttl-Worth, and John Fred Beebe. 1957. *Paleosiberian Peoples and Languages: A Bibliographical Guide*. New Haven: HRAF Press.

Jantz, Richard L. 1995. Franz Boas and Native American Biological Variability. *Human Biology* 67(3): 345–53.

Jantz, Richard L., D. R. Hunt, A. B. Falsetti, and P. J. Key. 1992. Variation among North Amerindians: Analysis of Boas's Anthropometric Data. *Human Biology* 64(3): 435–61.

Jochelson, Waldemar. 1908. *The Koryak*. Memoirs of the American Museum of Natural History vol. 10, parts 1–2: The Jesup North Pacific Expedition. Leiden: E. J. Brill.

———. 1928. *Archaeological Investigations in Kamchatka*. Washington DC: Carnegie Institution of Washington.

Jolly, Margaret. 1992. Spectres of Inauthenticity. *Contemporary Pacific* 4:49–72.

Kaeppler, Adrienne Lois, Judy Van Zile, and Elizabeth Tatar. 1993. *Hula Pahu: Hawaiian Drum Dances*. Honolulu: Bishop Museum Press.

Kagedan, Allan. 1990. Territorial Units as Nationality Policy. In *Soviet Nationality Policies: Ruling Ethnic Groups in the USSR*, ed. Henry R. Huttenbach, 163–76. London: Mansell.

Kan, Sergei. 2001. The "Russian Bastian" and Boas: Why Shternberg's "The Social Organization of the Gilyak" Never Appeared among the Jesup Expedition Publications. In *Gateways: Exploring the Legacy of the Jesup North Pacific Expedition, 1897–1902*, ed. I. Krupnik and W. W. Fitzhugh, 217–56. Washington DC: Smithsonian Institution Press.

Kaneff, Deema, and Alexander D. King. 2004. Owning Culture. *Focaal, European Journal of Anthropology* 44: 3–19.

Kappeler, Andreas. 2001. *The Russian Empire: A Multiethnic History*, trans. A. Clayton. Harlow, England: Pearson.

Karklins, Rasma. 1986. *Ethnic Relations in the USSR: The Perspective from Below*. Boston: Allen and Unwin.

———. 1994. *Ethnopolitics and the Transition to Democracy: The Collapse of the USSR and Latvia*. Baltimore: Johns Hopkins University Press.

Karp, Ivan, Corinne Kratz, Lynn Szwaja, and Tomás Ybarra-Frausto, eds. 2007. *Museum Frictions: Public Cultures/Global Transformations*. Durham: Duke University Press.

Kasten, Erich. 2004. Ways of Owning and Sharing Cultural Property. In *Properties of Culture—Culture as Property: Pathways to Reform in Post-Soviet Siberia*, ed. E. Kasten, 9–32. Berlin: Dietrich Reimer Verlag.

———. 2005. The Dynamics of Identity Management. In *Rebuilding Identities: Pathways to Reform in Post-Soviet Siberia*, ed. E. Kasten, 237–60. Berlin: Dietrich Reimer Verlag.

Keane, Webb. 1997. *Signs of Recognition: Powers and Hazards of Representation in an Indonesian Society*. Berkeley: University of California Press.

Kekketyn, Khechai [Ketsai], and Sergei N. Stebnitskii. 1938. *Kal-*

eiyln'yen: N'yekhevkin chyvinyt. Leningrad: Gosudarstvennoe uchebno-pedagogicheskoe izdatel'stvo Narkomprosa RSFSR.

Kendall, Laurel, Barbara Mathé, and Thomas Ross Miller. 1997. *Drawing Shadows to Stone: The Photography of the Jesup North Pacific Expedition, 1897–1902.* Seattle: University of Washington Press.

Kennan, George. 1986 [1870]. *Tent Life in Siberia.* Layton: Gibbs M. Smith.

Kerttula, Anna M. 2000. *Antler on the Sea: The Yup'ik and Chukchi of the Russian Far East.* Ithaca: Cornell University Press.

Khazanova, Vigdariia. 2000. *Klubnaia zhizn' i arkhitektura kluba 1917–1941.* Moskva: Izdatel'stvo Zhiraf.

Kibrik, Aleksandr E. 1991. The Problem of Endangered Languages in the USSR, trans. A. Eulenberg. In *Endangered Languages,* ed. R. H. Robins and E. M. Uhlenbeck, 257–73. Oxford: Berg.

Kibrik, A. E., S. V. Kodzasov, and I. A. Murav'eva. 2000. *Iazyk i fol'klor aliutortsev.* Moskva: IMLI RAN Nasledie.

———. 2004. *Language and Folklore of the Alutor People.* Trans. A. E. Kibrik, I. A. Muravyova, M. Megumi Kurebito, Y. Nagayama, ed. M. Kurebito. Endangered Languages of the Pacific Rim, vol. A2-042. Suita, Japan: Osaka Gakuin University.

Kinase, Takashi. 2002. Difference, Representation, Positionality: An Examination of the Politics of Contemporary Ainu Images. In *Self- and Other-Images of Hunter-Gatherers: Papers Presented at the Eighth International Conference on Hunting and Gathering Societies (CHAGS 8), National Museum of Ethnology, Osaka, October 1998,* ed. Henry Stewart, Alan Barnard, and Keiichi Omura, 171–81. Osaka, Japan: National Museum of Ethnology.

Kincaid, Christina. 2003. Translating the House of Culture: Reuse in a Post-Soviet Context. Masters of Architecture thesis, University of California, Berkeley.

King, Alexander D. 1999. Soul Suckers: Vampiric Shamans in Northern Kamchatka, Russia. *Anthropology of Consciousness* 10(4): 74–85.

———. 2002a. Reindeer Herders' Culturescapes in the Koryak Autonomous Okrug. In *People and the Land: Pathways to Reform in Post-Soviet Siberia,* ed. E. Kasten, 63–80. Berlin: Dietrich Reimer Verlag.

———. 2002b. "Without Deer There Is No Culture, Nothing." *Anthropology and Humanism* 27(2): 133–64.

———. 2003. Social Security in Kamchatka: Rural and Urban Comparisons. In *The Postsocialist Agrarian Question*, ed. Chris Hann and the "Property Relations" Group, 391–418. Münster: Lit Verlag.

———. 2005. The Brief History of Writing Koryak. Presentation at the Annual Meetings of the American Anthropological Association, November 30–December 4. Washington DC.

———. 2011. Palana's House of Koryak Culture. In *Reconstructing the House of Culture: Community, Self and the Makings of Culture in Russian and Beyond*, ed. O. Habeck and B. Donahoe. Oxford: Berghahn Books.

Kirby, E. Stuart. 1971. *The Soviet Far East*. London: Macmillan.

Kisliuk, Michelle Robin. 1998. *Seize the Dance! Baaka Musical Life and the Ethnography of Performance*. New York: Oxford University Press.

Klokov, Konstantin B. 2000. Nenets Reindeer Herders on the Lower Yenisei River: Traditional Economy under Current Conditions and Responses to Economic Change. *Polar Research* 19: 39–47.

Koester, David. 2002. When the Fat Raven Sings: Mimesis and Environmental Alterity in Kamchatka's Environmentalist Age. In *People and the Land: Pathways to Reform in Post-Soviet Siberia*, ed. E. Kasten, 45–62. Berlin: Dietrich Reimer Verlag.

———. 2005. Global Movements and Local Historical Events: Itelmens of Kamchatka Appeal to the United Nations. *American Ethnologist* 32(4): 642–59.

Køhler, Thomas, and Kathrin Wessendorf, eds. 2002. *Towards a New Millenium: Ten Years of the Indigenous Movement in Russia*. Copenhagen: IWGIA.

Konstantinov, Yulian. 2000. Pre-Soviet Pasts of Reindeer-Herding Collectivities: Ethnographies of Transition in Murmansk Region. *Acta Borealia* 17(2): 49–64.

———. 2002. Soviet and Post-Soviet Reindeer-Herding Collectives: Transitional Slogans in Murmansk Region. In *People and the Land: Pathways to Reform in Post-Soviet Siberia*, ed. E. Kasten, 171–86. Berlin: Dietrich Reimer Verlag.

———. 2005. *Reindeer-herders: Field-Notes from the Kola Peninsula (1994–95)*. Dissertations and Documents in Cultural Anthropology. Uppsala: Uppsala Universitet.

Konstantinov, Yulian, and Vladislava Vladimirova. 2002. Ambiguous Transition: Agrarian Reforms, Management, and Coping Practices in Murmansk Region Reindeer Herding. Max Planck Institute for Social Anthropology Working Papers 35.

Korsakov, G. M. 1940. *Samouchitel' nymylanskogo (koriakskogo) iazyka*. Leningrad: Gosudarstvennoe uchebno-pedagogicheskoe izdatel'stvo Narkomprosa RSFSR.

———. 1952. Brief Remarks on the Structure of the Nymylan (Koryak) Language and Its Dialects. Trans. John Richard Krueger. Bound mimeo. Alexandria VA.

Korsakov, G. M., and Sergei Nikolaevich Stebnitskii. 1939. *Nymylansko (koriaksko)-russkii slovar'*. Moskva: Gos. izd-vo inostr. i nats. slovarei.

Kosygin, Vladimir V. (Koianto), ed. 1993. *Podvizhniki vozrozhdeniia i razvitiia kul'tury narodov Kamchatki*. Petropavlovsk-Kamchatskii: RIO KOT.

Kozlov, V. I. 1988. *The Peoples of the Soviet Union*. Bloomington: Indiana University Press.

Krasheninnikov, Stepan Petrovich. 1755. *Opisanie zemli Kamchatki*. Sankt-Peterburg: Imperatorskaia akademiia nauk.

———. 1972. *Explorations of Kamchatka, North Pacific Scimitar: Report of a Journey Made to Explore Eastern Siberia in 1735–1741, by Order of the Russian Imperial Government*. Trans. E. A. P. Crownhart-Vaughn. Portland: Oregon Historical Society.

———. 1994. *Opisanie zemli kamchatki : V dvukh tomakh*. Petropavlovsk-Kamchatskii: Kamshat.

Krauss, Michael E. 1997. The Indigenous Languages of the North: A Report on Their Present State. In *Northern Minority Languages: Problems of Survival*, ed. Hiroshi Shoji and Juha Janhunen, 1–34. Senri Ethological Studies 44. Osaka, Japan: National Museum of Ethnology.

Kravchenko, Valerii. 1995. *Mengo*. Petropavlovsk-Kamchatskii: RIO KOT.

Kreinovich, E. A., ed. 1934. *Iazyki i pis'mennost' paleoaziatskikh* narodov. Iazyki i pis'mennost' narodov Severa, vol. 3. Moskva: Gosudarstvennoe uchebno-pedagogicheskoe izdatel'stvo.

Krupnik, Igor I. 1995. Koryak. In *Crossroads Alaska: Native Culture of Alaska and Siberia*, ed. V. Chaussonnet, 28–29. Washington DC: Arctic Studies Center, National Museum of Natural History, Smithsonian Institution.

———. 2005. "When Our Words Are Put to Paper": Heritage Documentation and Reversing Knowledge Shift in the Bering Strait Region. *Études/Inuit/Studies* 29(1–2): 67–90.

Kuoljok, Kerstin Eidlitz. 1985. *The Revolution in the North: Soviet Ethnography and Nationality Policy*. Stockholm: Uppsala.

Kurebito, Megumi. 2000. Argument-Modifying Type of Diminutive/ Augmentative Suffixes in Koryak. In *Languages of the North Pacific Rim*, ed. Osahito Miyaoka, vol. 5, 139–57.

Kurebito, Megumi, ed. 2001. *Comparative Basic Vocabulary of the Chukchee-Kamchatkan Language Family: 1*. Endangered Languages of the Pacific Rim, vol. A2-011. Suita, Japan: Osaka Gakuin University.

Kushanov, A. I., ed. 1993. *Istoriia i kul'tura koriakov*. Sankt-Peterburg: Nauka.

Labov, William. 1966. *The Social Stratification of English in New York City*. Washington DC: Center for Applied Linguistics.

———. 1972. *Language in the Inner City*. Philadelphia: University of Philadelphia Press.

Lebedev, V. V., and Iu. B. Simchenko. 1983. *Achaivaiamskaia vesna*. Moskva: Mysl'.

Lebedintsev, A. I. 1990. *Drevnie primorskie kul'tury Severo-Zapadnogo Priokhotia*. Leningrad: Nauka.

———. 2000. *Early Maritime Cultures of Northwestern Priokhot'e*. Anchorage: U.S. Department of the Interior, National Park Service, Alaska Regional Office, Shared Beringian Heritage Program.

———. 2004. *Materialy po istorii Severa Dal'nego Vostoka*. Magadan: SVKNII DVO RAN.

Lebedintsev, A. I., and A. A. Orekhov, eds. 1999. *Istoriia, arkheologiia i etnografiia Severo-Vostoka Rossii*. Magadan: Severo-Vostochnyi Kompleksnyi nauchno-issledovatel'skii institut (Rossiiskaia akademiia nauk).

Lee, Penny. 1996. *The Whorf Theory Complex: A Critical Reconstruction*. Amsterdam: J. Benjamins.

Levin, Theodore Craig. 1996. *The Hundred Thousand Fools of God: Musical Travels in Central Asia (and Queens, New York)*. Bloomington: Indiana University Press.

Levin, Maksim Grigorevich, and L. P. Potapov, eds. 1964. *The Peoples of Siberia*. Chicago: University of Chicago Press.

Levine, H. B. 1991. Comment on Hanson's "The Making of the Maori." *American Anthropologist* 93(2): 444–46.

Liarskaia, Elena V. 2003. Severnye internaty i transformatsiia traditsionnoi kul'tury (na primere nentsev Iamala). PhD diss., European University in St. Petersburg.

———. 2004. Northern Residential Schools in Contemporary Yamal Nenets Culture. *Sibirica: Journal of Siberian Studies* 4(1): 74–87.

Linnekin, Jocelyn. 1991. Cultural Invention and the Dilemma of Authenticity. *American Anthropologist* 93(2): 446–49.

Lowie, Robert H. 1935. *The Crow Indians*. New York: Holt, Rinehart and Winston.

MacCannell, Dean. 1999. *The Tourist: A New Theory of the Leisure Class*. Berkeley: University of California Press.

Margaritov, V. 1899. Kamchatka i ee obitateli. *Zametki priamurskogo otedela IRGO*, 5, vyp. 1.

Martin, Randy. 1998. *Critical Moves: Dance Studies in Theory and Politics*. Durham: Duke University Press.

Martin, Terry. 2001. *The Affirmative Action Empire Nations and Nationalism in the Soviet Union, 1923–1939*. Ithaca: Cornell University Press.

Mathur, Nita. 2002. *Cultural Rhythms in Emotions, Narratives and Dance*. New Delhi: Munshiram Manoharlal Publishers.

Mauss, Marcel. 1990. *The Gift: The Form and Reason for Exchange in Archaic Societies*. Trans. W. D. Halls. New York: W. W. Norton.

McDonald, Maryon. 1989. *We Are Not French! Language, Culture, and Identity in Brittany*. London: Routledge.

McElroy, Ann. 2008. *Nunavut Generations: Change and Continuity in Canadian Inuit Communities*. Long Grove IL: Waveland Press.

McNeil, William H. 1996. *Keeping Together in Time: Dance and Drill in Human History*. Cambridge MA: Harvard University Press.

Mead, Margaret. 1935. *Sex and Temperament in Three Primitive Societies*. New York: W. Morrow and Company.

Mel'chuk, I. A. 1973. *Model' spriazheniia v aliutorskom iazyke*. 2 vols., Predvaritel'nye publikatsi problemnoi gruppy po eksperimental'noi i prikladnoi lingvistike. vyp. 45, 46. Moscow: Institut russkogo iazyka AN SSSR.

Mel'chuk, I. A. and E. N. Savvina, 1978. Towards a Formal Model of Alutor Surface Structure: Predicative and Completive Constructions. *Linguistics*, Special Issue: 5–39.

Melvin, Neil J. 2003. *Soviet Power and the Countryside: Policy Innovation and Institutional Decay*. Basingstoke, England: Palgrave.

Merriman, Nick. 1989. Museum Visiting as a Cultural Phenomenon. In *The New Museology*, ed. P. Vergo, 149–71. London: Reaktion Books.

Metcalf, Peter. 2002. *They Lie, We Lie: Getting on with Anthropology*. London: Routledge.

Milroy, James. 1992. *Linguistic Variation and Change: On the Historical Sociolinguistics of English*. Oxford: Basil Blackwell.

Milroy, Lesley. 1980. *Language and Social Networks*. Oxford: Basil Blackwell.

Morgounova, Daria. 2010. Dynamics of Talk in Two Arctic Villages: Minorities' Resistance to Dominance in the Russian Federation and the United States. PhD diss., University of Copenhagen.

Morphy, Howard. 1995. Aboriginal Art in a Global Context. In *Worlds Apart: Modernity through the Prism of the Local*, ed. D. Miller, 211–39. London: Routledge.

Mowat, Farley. 1970. *The Siberians*. Boston: Little, Brown.

Mudrak, O. A. 2000. *Etimologicheskii slovar' chukotsko-kamchatskikh iazykov*. Moskva: Iazyki russkoi kul'tury.

Musina, Roza N. 1996. Contemporary Ethnosocial and Ethnopolitical Processes in Tatarstan. In *Ethnic Conflict in the Post-Soviet World: Case Studies and Analysis*, ed. Leokadia Drobizheva, Rose Gottemoeller, Catherine McCardle Kelleher, and Lee Walker, 195–208. Armonk NY: M. E. Sharpe.

Nadasdy, Paul. 2003. *Hunters and Bureaucrats: Power, Knowledge, and Aboriginal-State Relations in the Southwest Yukon.* Vancouver: University of British Columbia Press.

Nagayama, Yukari. 2003. *Grammatical Outline of Alutor.* Endangered Languages of the Pacific Rim, vol. A2-038. Suita, Japan: Osaka Gakuin University.

Nelson, Edward. 1983 [1899]. *The Eskimo about Bering Strait.* Washington DC: Smithsonian Institution Press.

Ness, Sally Ann. 1992. *Body, Movement, and Culture: Kinesthetic and Visual Symbolism in a Philippine Community.* Philadelphia: University of Pennsylvania Press.

Orlova, E. P. 1999. *Itel'meny: Istoriko-etnograficheskii ocherk.* Sankt-Peterburg: Nauka.

Orekhov, Aleksandr A. 1999. *An Early Culture of the Northwest Bering Sea.* Anchorage: U.S. Department of the Interior, National Park Service, Alaska Regional Office, Shared Beringian Heritage Program.

Ortner, Sherry. 1999. *The Fate of "Culture": Geertz and Beyond.* Berkeley: University of California Press.

Pakhomov, Yevgeny. 1994. Special Issue: Passport to Koryak Land. *Passport to the New World.* November–December: 27–47.

Parmentier, Richard J. 1994. *Signs in Society: Studies in Semiotic Anthropology.* Bloomington: Indiana University Press.

Paxson, Margaret. 2005. *Solovyovo: The Story of Memory in a Russian village.* Bloomington: Indiana University Press.

Pegg, Carol. 2001. *Mongolian Music, Dance, and Oral Narrative.* Seattle: University of Washington Press.

Peirce, Charles S. 1992. *The Essential Peirce: Selected Philosophical Writings,* vol. 1: 1867–1893. Ed. N. Houser, C. J. W. Kloesel, and Peirce Edition Project. Bloomington: Indiana University Press.

———. 1998. *The Essential Peirce: Selected Philosophical Writings,* vol. 2: 1893–1913. Ed. Peirce Edition Project. Bloomington: Indiana University Press.

Penney, David W. 2004. *North American Indian Art.* London: Thames and Hudson.

Pika, Aleksandr, ed. 1999. *Neotraditionalism in the Russian North: Indigenous Peoples and the Legacy of Perestroika.* Seattle: University of Washington Press.

Plattet, Patrick. 2005. Le double jeu de la chance: Imitation et substitution dans les rituels chamaniques contemporains de deux populations rurales du Nord-Kamtchatka (Fédération de Russie, Extrême-orient sibérien)—les chasseurs maritimes de Lesnaia et les éleveurs de rennes d'Atchaïvaiam. PhD diss., Université de Neuchatel, Switzerland.

Price, Sally. 1989. *Primitive Art in Civilized Places*. Chicago: University of Chicago Press.

Prucha, Francis Paul. 1979. *The Churches and the Indian Schools, 1888–1912*. Lincoln: University of Nebraska Press.

Rafael, Vicente L. 1992. Confession, Conversion, and Reciprocity in early Tagalog Colonial Society. In *Colonialism and Culture*, ed. Nicholas B. Dirks, 64–88. Ann Arbor: University of Michigan Press.

Rasputin, Valentin. 1996. *Siberia, Siberia*. Evanston IL: Northwestern University Press.

Rethmann, Petra. 1995. Soviet Body Politics. *Anthropology of East Europe Review* 13(2): 45–49.

———. 2001. *Tundra Passages: History and Gender in the Russian Far East*. University Park: Pennsylvania State University Press.

Reyhner, Jon Allan, Octaviana Trujillo, Roberto Luis Carrasco, and Louise Lockard, eds. 2003. *Nurturing Native Languages*. Flagstaff: Northern Arizona University.

Reyhner, Jon Allan, and Jeanne M. Oyawin Eder. 2004. *American Indian Education: A History*. Norman: University of Oklahoma Press.

Ridington, Robin. 1990. *Little Bit Know Something: Stories in a Language of Anthropology*. Iowa City: University of Iowa Press.

———. 1991. On the Language of Benjamin Lee Whorf. In *Anthropological Poetics*, ed. I. Brady, 241–66. Savage MD: Rowman and Littlefield.

———. 2001. Voice, Narrative and Dialogue: The Persistence of Hunter-Gatherer Discourse in North America. In *Identity and Gender in Hunting and Gathering Societies: Papers Presented at the Eighth International Conference on Hunting and Gathering Societies (Chags 8), National Museum of Ethnology, October 1998*, ed. T. Yamada and I. Keen, 117–130. Osaka, Japan: National Museum of Ethnology.

————. 2002. When You Sing It Now, Just Like New: Re-Creation in Native American Narrative Tradition. In *Self- and Other-Images of Hunter-Gatherers: Papers Presented at the Eighth International Conference on Hunting and Gathering Societies (CHAGS 8), National Museum of Ethnology, Osaka, October 1998*, ed. H. Stewart, A. Barnard, and K. Omura, 113–31. Osaka, Japan: National Museum of Ethnology.

Ries, Nancy. 1997. *Russian Talk-Culture and Conversation during Perstroika*. Ithaca: Cornell University Press.

Robins, R. H., and E. M. Uhlenbeck, eds. 1991. *Endangered Languages*. Oxford: Berg.

Rogister, John, and Anne Vergati. 2004. Introduction: Tradition Revisited. *History and Anthropology* 15(3): 201–5.

Royce, Anya Peterson. 2002. *The Anthropology of Dance*. Princeton NJ: Princeton Book Company.

————. 2004. *Anthropology of the Performing Arts: Artistry, Virtuosity, and Interpretation in a Cross-Cultural Perspective*. Walnut Creek CA: AltaMira Press.

Rywkin, Michael. 1990. Searching for Soviet Nationalities Policy. In *Soviet Nationality Policies: Ruling Ethnic Groups in the USSR*, ed. Henry R. Huttenbach, 62–72. London: Mansell.

Sahlins, Marshall. 1999. Two or Three Things That I Know about Culture. *Journal of the Royal Anthropological Institute*, n.s., 5: 399–421.

————. 2005. On the Anthropology of Modernity: Or, Some Triumphs of Culture over Despondency Theory. In *Culture and Sustainable Development in the Pacific*, ed. A. Hooper, 44–61. Canberra: Australian National University E Press.

Sapir, Edward. 1917. Do We Need a "Superorganic"? *American Anthropologist*, n.s., 19(3): 441–47.

————. 1921. *Language: An Introduction to the Study of Speech*. New York: Harcourt Brace Jovanovich.

————. 1931. Custom. In *Encyclopedia of the Social Sciences*, vol. 4, 658–62. New York: Macmillan.

————. 1933. Language. In *Encyclopaedia of the Social Sciences*, vol. 9, 155–69. New York: Macmillan.

————. 1934. Symbolism. In *Encyclopaedia of the Social Sciences*, vol. 14, 492–95. New York: Macmillan.

———. 1949 [1924]. Culture, Genuine and Spurious. In *Selected Writings of Edward Sapir in Language, Culture and Personality*, ed. D. G. Mandelbaum, 308–31. Berkeley: University of California Press.

———. 1949 [1927]. The Unconscious Patterning of Behavior in Society. In *Selected Writings of Edward Sapir in Language, Culture and Personality*, ed. D. G. Mandelbaum, 546–59. Berkeley: University of California Press.

———. 1949 [1928]. The Status of Linguistics as a Science. In *Selected Writings of Edward Sapir in Language, Culture and Personality*, ed. D. G. Mandelbaum, 160–66. Berkeley: University of California Press.

———. 1949 [1932]. Cultural Anthropology and Psychiatry. In *Selected Writings of Edward Sapir in Language, Culture and Personality*, ed. D. G. Mandelbaum, 509–21. Berkeley: University of California Press.

———. 1949 [1933]. The Psychological Reality of Phonemes. In *Selected Writings of Edward Sapir in Language, Culture and Personality*, ed. D. G. Mandelbaum, 46–60. Berkeley: University of California Press.

Sauer, Martin. 1802. *An Account of a Geographical and Astronomical Expedition to the Northern Parts of Russia Performed by Joseph Billings in the Years 1785 to 1796*. London.

Schieffelin, Edward L. 1976. *The Sorrow of the Lonely and the Burning of the Dancers*. New York: St. Martin's Press.

Schindler, Debra. 1991. Theory, Policy, and the *Narody Severa*. *Anthropological Quarterly* 64(2): 68–79.

Semenov, A. V. 1965. The Ancient Culture of the Koryak National District. *Arctic Anthropology* 3: 107–15.

Sergeev, M. A. 1955. *Nekapitalisticheskii put' rasvitiia nadodov Severa*. Moskva: Isdatel'stvo akademii nauk SSSR.

Sharp, Henry S. 2001. *Loon: Memory, Meaning, and Reality in a Northern Dene Community*. Lincoln: University of Nebraska Press.

Shimkin, Demitri B. 1990. Siberian Ethnography: Historical Sketch and Evaluation. *Arctic Anthropology* 27(1): 36–51.

Shnirelman, Victor. 2001. Ethnicity in the Making: The Tlingits of

South-East Alaska on the Eve of the 21st Century. In *Identity and Gender in Hunting and Gathering Societies: Papers Presented at the Eight International Conference on Hunting and Gathering Societies (CHAGS 8), National Museum of Ethnology, October 1998,* ed. T. Yamada and I. Keen, 53–65. Osaka, Japan: National Museum of Ethnology.

Shossonne, Valeri, ed. 1996. *Perekrestki kontinentov: Kul'tury korennykh narodov Dal'nego Vostoka i Aliaski.* Ed. I. Krupnik, trans. P. A. Aleinikova. Washington DC: Smithsonian Institution Press.

Shternberg, Lev. 1906. The Inau Cult of the Ainu. In *Boas Anniversary Volume: Anthropology Papers Written in Honor of Franz Boas . . . Presented to Him on the Twenty-fifth Anniversary of His Doctorate,* ed. Berthold Laufer, 425–37. New York: G. E. Stechert.

———. 1912. The Turano-Ganowanian System and the Nations of North-East Asia. In *International Congress of Americanists, Proceedings of the 18th Session, London, 1912,* 319–33. London: Harrison and Sons.

Sil'nitskii, A. P. 1897. *Poezdka v kamchatku i na reku Anadyr'.* Khabarovsk.

———. 1902. *Poezdka v severnye okrugi Primorskoi oblasti.* Khabarovsk.

Silverstein, Michael. 2004. "Cultural" Concepts and the Language-Culture Nexus. *Current Anthropology* 45(5): 621–52.

———. 2005. The Poetics of Politics: "Theirs" and "Ours." *Journal of Anthropological Research* 61(1): 1–24.

———. 2006. Old Wine, New Ethnographic Lexicography. *Annual Review of Anthropology* 35: 481–96.

Slezkine, Yuri. 1994a. *Arctic Mirrors: Russia and the Small Peoples of the North.* Ithaca: Cornell University Press.

———. 1994b. The USSR as a Communal Apartment, or How a Socialist State Promoted Ethic Particularism. *Slavic Review* 53(2): 414–52.

Slobodin, Sergei B. 2006. The Paleolithic of Western Beringia: A Summary of Research. In *Archaeology in Northeast Asia,* ed. D. E. Dumond and R. L. Bland, 9–23. University of Oregon An-

thropological Papers no. 65. Anchorage: U.S. Department of the
Interior, National Park Service, Alaska Regional Office, Shared
Beringian Heritage Program.

Smith, Graham, ed. 1996. *The Nationalities Question in the Post
Soviet State*. London: Longman.

Sokolovskiy, Sergei V. 2007. Identity Politics and Indigeneity Construction in the Russian Census of 2002. *Sibirica: Interdisciplinary
Journal of Siberian Studies* 6(1): 59–94.

Spencer, Paul, ed. 1985. *Society and the Dance: The Social Anthropology of Process and Performance*. Cambridge: Cambridge
University Press.

Ssorin-Chaikov, Nikolai V. 2003. *The Social Life of the State in
Subarctic Siberia*. Stanford: Stanford University Press.

St. George, George. 1970. *Siberia: The New Frontier*. London: Hod-
der and Stoughton.

Stammler, Florian. 2005. *Reindeer Nomads Meet the Market: Culture,
Property and Globalisation at the "End of the Land."* Münster:
Lit Verlag.

Starr, S. Frederick. 1997. The Fate of Empire in Post-Tsarist Russia
and in the Post-Soviet Era. In *The End of Empire? The Transformation of the USSR in Comparative Perspective*, ed. K. Dawisha
and B. Parrott, 243–60. Armonk NY: M. E. Sharpe.

Stebnitskii, Sergei N. 1930. Koriakskie deti. *Sovetskii sever* 4: 39–47.
Moskva.

———. 1931. *U koriakov na Kamchatke*. Moskva: Izdatel'stvo
Krest'ianskaia gazeta.

———. 1932. *Shkola na tundre*. Moskva: OGIZ Molodaia gvardiia.

———. 1934. Nymylanskii (koriakskii) iazyk. In *Iazyki i pis'mennost'
paleoaziatskikh narodov*, ed. E. A. Kreinovich, Iazyki i pis'mennost'
narodov Severa vol. 3, 47–84. Moskva: Gosudarstvennoe uchebno-
pedagogicheskoe izdatel'stvo.

———. 1937. Osnovnye foneticheskie razlichiia dialektov nymylanskogo (koriakskogo) iazyka. In *Pamiati V. G. Bogoroza (1865–
1936): Sbornik statei*, ed. I. I. Meshchaninov, 285–307. Moskva:
Izdatel'stvo akademii nauk SSSR.

———. 1938a. Avtobiografii nymylanov. *Sovetskaia etnografiia* 1.

———. 1938b. Nymylany-aliutortsy. (K voprosu o proiskhozhdenii
olenevodstva u iuzhnykh koriakov). *Sovetskaia etnografiia* 1.

———. 2000. *Ocherki etnografii koriakov*. St. Petersburg: Nauka.

Stebnickijnak with Ev't'kanak and Qacg'lajv'nak. 1932. *Jissa-Kalikal: Kalikal Jagjusavn'kin N'm'l'ac'ajan*. Leningrad: Uchpedgiz. [Photocopy in author's possession.]

Steller, Georg Vil'gel'm [Wilhelm]. 1999. *Opisanie zemli Kamchatki*. Trans. G. G. Genkel' and A. Gorlimnyi. Petropavlovsk-Kamchatskii: Kamchatskii Pechatnyi Dvor.

———. 2003. *Steller's History of Kamchatka: Collected Information Concerning the History of Kamchatka, Its Peoples, Their Manners, Names, Lifestyle, and Various Customary Practices*. Trans. M. Engel and K. Willmore. Fairbanks: University of Alaska Press.

Stocking, George W. 1968. *Race, Culture, and Evolution: Essays in the History of Anthropology*. New York: Free Press.

———. 1992. *The Ethnographer's Magic and Other Essays in the History of Anthropology*. Madison: University of Wisconsin Press.

Sutton, Richard Anderson. 2002. *Calling Back the Spirit: Music, Dance, and Cultural Politics in Lowland South Sulawesi*. Oxford: Oxford University Press.

Swift, Mary Grace. 1968. *The Art of the Dance in the USSR*. Notre Dame: University of Notre Dame Press.

Szasz, Margaret Connell. 1999. *Education and the American Indian: The Road to Self-Determination since 1928*. Albuquerque: University of New Mexico Press.

Taksami, Chuner M. 1967. *Nivkhi: Sovremennoe khoziaistvo, kul'tura i byt*. Leningrad: Nauka.

Taplin, Mark. 1997. *Open Lands: Travels through Russia's Once Forbidden Places*. South Royalton vt: Steerforth Press.

Taussig, Michael. 1993. *Mimesis and Alterity*. New York: Routledge.

Taylor, Charles. 1992. *The Ethics of Authenticity*. Cambridge MA: Harvard University Press.

Thomas, Helen. 1995. *Dance, Modernity and Culture: Explorations in the Sociology of Dance*. London: Routledge.

Thomason, Sarah G. 2001. *Language Contact*. Edinburgh: Edinburgh University Press

Tishkov, Valery A. 1992. The Crisis in Soviet Ethnography. *Current Anthropology* 33(4): 371–94.

——. 2003. *Rekviem po etnosu: Issledovaniia po sotsial'no-kul'turnoi antropologii.* Moskva: Nauka.

Tompkins, Joanne. 1998. *Teaching in a Cold and Windy Place: Change in an Inuit School.* Toronto: University of Toronto Press.

Toren, Christina. 1988. Making the Present, Revealing the Past: The Mutability and Continuity of Tradition as Process. *Man,* n.s., 23(3): 696–717.

Trevor-Roper, Hugh. 1983. The Invention of Tradition: The Highland Tradition of Scotland. In *The Invention of Tradition,* ed. Eric Hobsbawm and Terence Ranger, 15–42. Cambridge: Cambridge University Press.

Trilling, Lionel. 1974. *Sincerity and Authenticity.* Oxford: Oxford University Press.

Tsunoda, Tasaku. 2005. *Language Endangerment and Language Revitalization.* Berlin: Mouton de Gruyter.

Ul'ianova, A. I. 1989. *Detskie i shkol'nye gody Il'icha* [Childhood and school years of Ilich]. Trans. A. E. Kainyna from Russian to Koryak. Leningrad: Prosveshchenie.

Urban, Greg. 2001. *Metaculture: How Culture Moves through the World.* Minneapolis: University of Minnesota Press.

Urkachan, Aleksandra T. 2002. *"Veemlen" (Lesnaia) zemlia moikh predkov.* Petropavlovsk-Kamchatskiy: Kamshat.

Vajda, Edward. 2008. Verbs across the Bering Strait. *Science* 319 (March 21, 2008): 1595.

——. 2010. A Siberian Link with Na-Dene Languages. *Archeological Papers of the University of Alaska,* n.s., 5(1–2): 33–99.

Vakhtin, Nikolai B. 1994. Native Peoples of the Russian Far North. In *Polar Peoples: Self-Determination and Development,* ed. M. R. Group, 29–80. London: Manchester Free Press.

——. 1998. Copper Island Aleut: A Case of Language "Resurrection." In *Endangered Languages: Language Loss and Community Response,* ed. L. A. Grenoble and L. J. Whaley, 317–27. Cambridge: Cambridge University Press.

——. 2001a. *Iazyki narodov Severa v xx veke: Ocherki iazykovogo sdviga.* Sankt-Peterburg: Dmitrii Bulanin.

——. 2001b. Franz Boas and the Shaping of the Jesup Expedition Siberian Research, 1895–1900. In *Gateways: Exploring the*

Legacy of the Jesup North Pacific Expedition, 1897–1902, ed. I. I. Krupnik and W. W. Fitzhugh, 71–92. Washington DC: Smithsonian Institution Press.

———. 2005. Two Approaches to Reversing Language Shift and the Soviet Publication Program for Indigenous Minorities. *Études/ Inuit/Studies* 29(1–2): 131–47.

Vakhtin, Nikolai, Evgenii Golovko, and Peter Shvaittser. 2004. *Russkie starozhily Sibiri: Sotsial'nye i simvolicheskie aspekty samosoznaniia.* Moskva: Novoe izd-vo.

Vasil'evskii, Ruslan Sergeevich. 1964. Ancient Koryak Culture. *American Antiquity* 30: 19–24.

———. 1969. The Origin of the Ancient Koryak Culture on the Northern Okhotsk Coast. *Arctic Anthropology* 6: 150–63.

Vdovin, I. S. 1973. *Ocherki etnicheskoi istorii koriakov.* Leningrad: Nauka.

Ventsel, Aimar. 2005. *Reindeer, Rodina and Reciprocity: Kinship and Property Relations in a Siberian Village.* Münster: Lit Verlag.

Vitebsky, Piers. 2005. *Reindeer People: Living with Animals and Spirits in Siberia.* Boston: Houghton Mifflin.

Vitebsky, Piers, and Sally Wolfe. 2001. The Separation of the Sexes among Siberian Reindeer Herders. In *Sacred Custodians of the Earth? Women, Spirituality and the Environment*, ed. A. M. Low and S. Tremayne, 81–95. New York: Berghahn Books.

Vladimirova, Vladislava. 2006. *Just Labor: Labor Ethic in a Post-Soviet Reindeer Herding Community.* Uppsala: Uppsala University.

Vysokovskii, Aleksandr. 1995. Stillborn Environments: The New Soviet Town of the 1960s and Urban Life in Russia Today. Kennan Institute Occasional Papers 261. Washington DC.

Wagner, Roy. 1974. Are There Social Groups in the New Guinea Highlands? In *Frontiers of Anthropology: An Introduction to Anthropological Thinking*, ed. M. J. Leaf, 95–122. New York: Van Nostrand.

———. 1981. *The Invention of Culture.* Chicago: University of Chicago Press.

———. 1986. *Symbols That Stand for Themselves.* Chicago: University of Chicago Press.

————. 2001. *An Anthropology of the Subject: Holographic Worldview in New Guinea and Its Meaning and Significance for the World of Anthropology*. Berkeley: University of California Press.

Walsh, Michael. 2005. Will Indigenous Languages Survive? *Annual Review of Anthropology* 34: 293–315.

Whorf, Benjamin Lee. 1956. *Language, Thought, and Reality: Selected Writings of Benjamin Lee Whorf*. Cambridge: MIT Press.

Willerslev, Rane. 2007. *Soul Hunters: Hunting, Animism, and Personhood among the Siberian Yukaghirs*. Berkeley: University of California Press.

Williams, Drid. 2004. *Anthropology and the Dance: Ten Lectures*. 2nd ed. Chicago: University of Illinois Press.

Williams, Maria. 1996. Alaska Native Music and Dance: The Spirit of Survival. PhD diss., University of California, Los Angeles.

Williamson, Robert Clifford, John A. Van Eerde, and Joshua A. Fishman, eds. 1980. *Language Maintenance and Language Shift*. The Hague: Mouton.

Wood, Alan, ed. 1991. *The History of Siberia: From Russian Conquest to Revolution*. London: Routledge.

Wright, Susan. 1998. The Politicization of "Culture." *Anthropology Today* 14(1): 7–15.

Wulff, Helena. 2007. *Dancing at the Crossroads: Memory and Mobility in Ireland*. Oxford: Berghahn Books.

Wurm, Stephen A. 1991. Language Death and Disappearance: Causes and Circumstances. In *Endangered Languages*, ed. R. H. Robins and E. M. Uhlenbeck, 1–18. Oxford: Berg.

Yamada, Takako. 2001. Gender and Cultural Revitalization Movements among the Ainu. In *Identity and Gender in Hunting and Gathering Societies: Papers Presented at the Eighth International Conference on Hunting and Gathering Societies (CHAGS 8), National Museum of Ethnology, October 1998*, ed. T. Yamada and I. Keen, 237–57. Osaka, Japan: National Museum of Ethnology.

Zhornitskaia, Mariia Ia. 1983. *Narodnoe khoreograficheskoe iskusstvo korennogo naseleniia Severa-Vostoka Sibiri*. Moscow: Nauka.

————. 1994. Traditional Choreographic Art of Northeastern Siberia. In *Anthropology of the North Pacific Rim*, ed. William W. Fitzhugh and Valérie Chaussonnet, 205–16. Washington DC: Smithsonian Institution Press.

Ziker, John P. 2002. *Peoples of the Tundra: Northern Siberians in the Post-Communist Transition*. Prospect Heights IL: Waveland.

Zhukova, Alevtina N. 1967. *Russko-koriakskii slovar'*. Moscow: Sovetskaia entsiklopediia.

———. 1968a. Koriakskii iazyk. In *Iazyki narodov SSSR*, vol. 5: *Mongol'skie, tunguso-man'chzhurskie i paleoaziatskie iazyki*, ed. V. V. Vinogradov, 271–93. Leningrad: Nauka.

———. 1968b. Aliutorskii iazyk. In *Iazyki narodov SSSR*, vol. 5: *Mongol'skie, tunguso-man'chzhurskie i paleoaziatskie iazyki*, ed. V. V. Vinogradov, 294–309. Leningrad: Nauka.

———. 1972. *Grammatika koriakskogo iazyka: Fonetika, morfologiia*. Leningrad.

———. 1980. *Iazyk palanskikh koriakov*. Leningrad: Nauka.

———. 1987. *Koriakskii iazyk: Uchebnik dlia uchashchikhsia pedagogicheskikh uchilishch*. Leningrad: Prosveshchenie.

———. 2001. The Basic Principles of the Koryak Writing. In *Languages of the North Pacific Rim*, ed. O. Miyaoka and F. Endo, 59–64. Suita, Japan: Osaka Gakuin University.

Zhukova, A. N., M. F. Ikavav, and I. S. Agin'. 1991. *Bukvar' dlia pervogo klassa koriakskikh shkol*. Leningrad: Prosveshchenie.

Zhukova, Alevtina, and Tokusu Kurebito. 2004. *A Basic Topical Dictionary of the Koryak-Chukchi Languages*. Tokyo: Research Institute for Languages and Cultures of Asia and Africa, Tokyo University of Foreign Studies.

Index

Page numbers in bold type refer to entries in the glossary.

Index | 323

Mauss, Marcel, 100–101
meaning, theory of, 20–25, 30–31,
    34, 109–10, 135, 142–43, 154,
    206, 212, 234, 246, 249–50, 262
Mengo: history of, 117–21, 123–24,
    130; performances, 14, 111–12,
    127–29, 146, 247, 250; reception
    in Palana, 111–12, 121–22, 125,
    127–28, 247–48; reception in
    villages, 100, 126–27, 140–41
Middle Pakhachi: Chukchi identity
    among people of, 15–16, 28–29,
    61; cultural conservatism in, 1–2,
    9, 85; language in, 28–29, 30–31,
    195, 197, 221, 223–27; and
    reindeer herding, 10–14, 15–16,
    49–50, 186–87, 235–37, 241
Mikino, 6, 204, 266n19
Milgichil, Nina, 88, 95–103, 150,
    204, 262
Milgichil, Vasili, 88, 101, 204
Mil'kovo, 3, 263n3
missionaries, 88, 96, 98–99, 101
mobility, 14, 15, 65–66, 76, 94, 122–
    23, 147. See also transport
modernity, 37–38, 46, 104, 161–62,
    212, 217, 222, 224–26, 231–32,
    254
Moroshechnoe, 4. See also closed
    villages
Moscow, 47, 48–51, 77–78, 117–18,
    122–23, 134, 143, 208, 214, 219,
    268n7
Muchigin Yayai, 104–7
museums, 149, 181, 189; in schools,
    168, 182. See also Koryak Okrug
    Regional Museum
music, 19, 82, 95, 106–8, 112, 130,
    131–32, 247; and shamanism,
    89–91, 96, 99

narod, 78, 114–15, 116, 198, 286;
    in Kamchatkan discourse, 13, 56,
    125, 176

narodnost', 73
narratives, 96, 153, 156–58, 216,
    259
nationalism, 26, 27, 46–47, 50–51,
    56, 164, 173, 176, 185–86,
    208–9, 225–26, 230, 243, 252–53,
    255–56
Native Americans: compared to
    Native Kamchatkans, 6, 36–37,
    66, 86–87, 143–44, 161, 175,
    235, 238–39, 249–53, 260, 264n5,
    282n1; ethnic politics, 164, 173,
    252, 238–39; in schools, 158,
    216–17, 224, 257–58
nature. See under discourse
newcomers, 9, 54–55, 59–60, 81,
    93, 120, 164–65, 184, 188–90,
    250–51, 267n6, 279n18
newspapers, 31–32, 50, 195, 220,
    242
Niuman, Mark, 121–24, 127, 144–
    45, 274n5
nomadism. See mobility; primitives
Nymylan: culture, 88–93; ethnicity,
    75, 131, 247–48, 93; geographic
    distribution of, 6; language, 29–31,
    169–70, 200–201, 204, 227–30,
    232, 266n16, 282n17

Olyutorskiy Rayon, 6, 9, 16, 49,
    79–90, 171
Orientalism, 42, 211–12
Orthodox church. See Russian
    Orthodox Church
Ossora, 3, 5, 6, 16, 77, 90, 108,
    181–82, 184, 185, 187

Palana: as administrative center, 6,
    48–50, 87–88, 114, 219; social
    life in, 7–8, 30, 119, 127–28, 130,
    139–41, 151–52, 188, 191–92
Palana Regional Museum. See
    Koryak Okrug Regional Museum

Sapir, Edward, 24, 27, 32, 36–38, 83, 100, 142, 176–77, 202–3, 235, 244–45, 248, 250–51

Saussure, 23

schools: assimilation in, 51–52, 67, 151, 154, 207, 209, 215–16, 233; classroom observations, 170–71, 229; *internat* system, 96, 148, 158–60, 180–81, 208, 257–58, 285; introductions, 153–55, 156–58; language revitalization in, 31–32, 170, 194, 196, 221–26, 228–32, 257; and reification of culture, 22, 39, 169–72, 179, 261; secondary, 8; Soviet-era, 68, 148, 157, 192, 209–16; students running away from, 158; teachers and cultural revival in, 96–98, 103, 104–8, 147, 169–72, 177–80. *See also* higher education; Palana Teachers' College; textbooks

semiotics: theory, 20, 22–24, 34, 249–50, 255; icon, 25–26, 84, 93, 109–10, 125–26, 134, 137, 194; index, 25, 30, 34, 83, 93, 110, 124, 137, 154, 212, 223–24, 256–59, 262; indexical icon, 26, 34, 86, 93, 126, 135–36, 146, 251, 255

Severin, Valentin, 189, 190

shamans, 83, 97–100, 258–59; repression of, 69, 104, 209, 210–11

Shternberg, Lev, 63, 66–67, 69

Silverstein, Michael, 24, 25–26, 251, 254–55

singing. *See* music

Slava, 11, 13, 24, 186–87, 236

Smithsonian Institution, xiv–xv

Sopochnoe, 4. *See also* closed villages

souvenir factory, 164, 166–67, 169–70, 172–73

sovkhoz, 287. *See also* state farms

spirits: and dance, 96–97, 104, 119;

interactions with, 1–2, 88–89, 97, 274n6

Stalinism: ideology of, xi, 69, 70, 148, 151, 209–15; and repression, 63–64, 69, 98, 104, 151–52, 270n19

standardization: language, 31–32

state farms, 7–8

Stebnitskii, Sergei, 67, 69, 75, 152–53, 207, 209–15, 239, 241, 270n22, 280n8

Steller, Georg, 57–58, 198–99, 269n15

storytelling, 95–96, 105–6, 155, 183, 259. *See also* narratives

St. Petersburg, 9, 47, 49, 57–58, 149–51, 163, 220, 275n1

Taksami, Chuner, 149, 184, 239–41

teachers: as educated elite, 14, 35, 68, 148–49; and native traditions, 35, 39; in social life

Teachers' College. *See* Palana Teachers' College

television, 2. *See also* newspapers

textbooks: currently used, 208, 221–22, 226, 229–30, 257; Soviet, 209–15

Tilichiki, 17, 49, 79–80, 184–86, 236

tradition: in daily life, 17, 22, 70–71, 140, 168–69, 186–87, 215, 236–37, 260; invention of, 32–33, 38–39, 141–43, 244–45, 253–54, 282n5; in Kamchatkan discourse, 1, 18–19, 33, 85–86, 95–103, 105–6, 114–16, 129, 134–37, 151, 165–66, 172, 180, 229, 238–39, 249–50; theory of, 26–27, 32–33, 37–39, 83, 109–10, 142–44, 158–59, 192–93, 224, 234–36, 242–45, 248–49, 259–62. *See also* modernity

Breinigsville, PA USA
05 April 2011
259132BV00005B/1/P